The Fall of the West

The Story behind Covid, the Levelling-Down of the West and the Shift of Power to the East with the Rise of China

A Warning to the Western World

T0243992

JOHN HUNT PUBLISHING

First published by O-Books, 2022
O-Books is an imprint of John Hunt Publishing Ltd., 3 East St., Alresford,
Hampshire SO24 9EE, UK
office@jhpbooks.com
www.johnhuntpublishing.com
www.o-books.com

For distributor details and how to order please visit the 'Ordering' section on our website.

Text copyright: Nicholas Hagger 2020

ISBN: 978 1 78904 949 7
978 1 78904 950 3 (ebook)
Library of Congress Control Number: 2021950053

Biblical quotations are taken from the Authorized Version of the Bible (the King James Bible), the rights in which are vested in the Crown, and are reproduced by permission of the Crown's Patentee, Cambridge University Press.

A CIP catalogue record for this book is available from the British Library.

Design: Stuart Davies

UK: Printed and bound by CPI Group (UK) Ltd, Croydon, CR0 4YY
Printed in North America by CPI GPS partners

We operate a distinctive and ethical publishing philosophy in all areas
of our business, from our global network of authors to production and
worldwide distribution.

The Fall of the West

The Story behind Covid, the Levelling-Down
of the West and the Shift of Power to the East
with the Rise of China

A Warning to the Western World

Nicholas Hagger

BOOKS

Winchester, UK
Washington, USA

Also by Nicholas Hagger

The Fire and the Stones
Selected Poems
The Universe and the Light
A White Radiance
A Mystic Way
Awakening to the Light
A Spade Fresh with Mud
The Warlords
Overlord
A Smell of Leaves and Summer
The Tragedy of Prince Tudor
The One and the Many
Wheeling Bats and a Harvest Moon
The Warm Glow of the Monastery Courtyard
The Syndicate
The Secret History of the West
The Light of Civilization
Classical Odes
Overlord, one-volume edition
Collected Poems 1958–2005
Collected Verse Plays
Collected Stories
The Secret Founding of America
The Last Tourist in Iran
The Rise and Fall of Civilizations
The New Philosophy of Universalism
The Libyan Revolution
Armageddon
The World Government
The Secret American Dream
A New Philosophy of Literature
A View of Epping Forest
My Double Life 1: This Dark Wood
My Double Life 2: A Rainbow over the Hills
Selected Stories: Follies and Vices of the Modern Elizabethan Age
Selected Poems: Quest for the One
The Dream of Europa
The First Dazzling Chill of Winter
Life Cycle and Other New Poems 2006–2016
The Secret American Destiny

Peace for our Time
World State
World Constitution
King Charles the Wise
Visions of England
Fools' Paradise
Selected Letters
The Coronation of King Charles
Collected Prefaces
A Baroque Vision
The Essentials of Universalism
Fools' Gold
The Promised Land
The Building of the Great Pyramid

"The man of letters as such, is not concerned with the political or economic map of Europe; but he should be very much concerned with its cultural map.... The man of letters... should be able to take a longer view than either the politician or the local patriot.... The cultural health of Europe, including the cultural health of its component parts, is incompatible with extreme forms of both nationalism and internationalism.... The responsibility of the man of letters at the present time... should be vigilantly watching the conduct of politicians and economists, for the purpose of criticizing and warning, when the decisions and actions of the politicians and economists are likely to have cultural consequences. Of these consequences the man of letters should qualify himself to judge. Of the possible cultural consequences of their activities, politicians and economists are usually oblivious; the man of letters is better qualified to foresee them, and to perceive their seriousness."

T.S. Eliot,
The Man of Letters and the Future of Europe, 1944

"Reflect, (of a mirror) show an image of; reproduce to the eye or mind; meditate on.
Reflection, a reflected image; an idea arising in the mind."

Concise Oxford Dictionary

"Reflect, transitive, of mirrors or other polished surfaces: to give back or exhibit an image of (a person or thing); to mirror; intransitive, to bestow attention or regard upon a person or thing, to turn one's thoughts (back on), to fix the mind or attention on or upon the subject; to ponder, meditate on.
Reflection. The action of a mirror or other polished surface in exhibiting or reproducing the image of an object; the action of turning (back) or fixing the thoughts on some subject; meditation, deep or serious consideration."

Shorter Oxford English Dictionary

"As I stared at the mural's centre
In this Cathedral-tomb,
The Archangel became a Shadow
With a sword and wings outstretched,
And I saw in the second icon
The future of the West,

From the Atlantic to the Urals:
Into the People's Square,
From the Cathedral gates,
File in the morning rush-hour
An *élite* of self-made Saints
Each still on the last hour's quest.
They reach the central banner
In the forum of statues and graves,
The great mazed mandala
Under which the supplicants wait;
Decades of contemplation
Show in their white-haired peace
As, trusting to perfect feelings,
They value each equal they greet;
Until, whispering on silence,
They glide to the Leaders' Hall,
Their hearts, with a World-Lord's wholeness,
At the centre of life, of all,
Their hearts where all past and future meet."

Nicholas Hagger, 'Archangel', lines 276–300

"Professor Irie, who was in charge of me, asked me [in 1966] if I would teach a course on the decline of the West to the [Japanese] postgraduates.

I said, 'What if I think that the West is not declining?'

He said, 'Oh, but we would still like a course of lectures entitled "The Decline of the West".'

I promised I would begin this in the second semester in the following February, and began assembling material on Gibbon, Spengler and Toynbee for this course."

Nicholas Hagger,
My Double Life 1: This Dark Wood, p.211

"We now sense – even if we do not explicitly formulate it – that the dominance of the West as a political civilisation and economic entity may really be dying. If it is, that is the end not only of the post-war settlement, but also of a phenomenon which has existed since the 18th century. Without that dominance, most of us have no alternative view of the world, so we are confused. China, however, does have an alternative view. It thinks it has proved the West's decadence, almost surpassed its economic dominance and developed a political system of what we call totalitarianism.... We plan 2050 as the year of net zero. China has chosen the same year as its target for global military superiority.... If the West actually achieves net zero by that date – which China has no intention of attempting itself – we will be unable to resist Chinese military might."

Charles Moore, The Daily Telegraph, 6 November 2021, p.22

"The Fall of the West was a mental attitude!"

Nicholas Hagger, 'The Fall of the West', line 144, 1976,
in Collected Poems

The front cover shows a map of the world with the 140 countries (in blue) that have signed co-operation documents relating to China's Belt-and-Road Initiative of infrastructure projects and now border the West's east and south; and (inset left) the Laboratory at the University of North Carolina, where NIAID-sponsored gain-of-function research took place in 2002 (see pp.85–86) and (inset right) SARS-CoV-2.

Acknowledgements

I am grateful to David Lorimer for sending me a flow of articles on SARS-CoV-2 during the early days of lockdown and onwards, and for putting me in touch with Brian Snellgrove, who kindly made available his 11,500 privately organised websites on current affairs. I am also grateful to John Hunt for his keen personal interest in *The Syndicate*. This book was written between 25 June and 27 July 2021 (in 33 days) during rising Covid cases, and then amended from 3 August until 2 September and from 24 September until 1 November. I am grateful to my excellent PA Ingrid Kirk for transcribing my work remotely, assisting me with my research and enabling me to finish the book so quickly. I could not have done it without her.

CONTENTS

CONTENTS

showing section headings and structure

Preface: American Gain-of-Function Research and Covid-19:
The Syndicate, the Rise of China and the Fall of the West

1. The Story of the Syndicate's New World Order So Far,
   and Population-Capping

2 The Syndicate's Authoritarian Levelling of the West and the East through Pipelines and Integration

Preface

American Gain-of-Function Research and Covid-19: The Syndicate, the Rise of China and the Fall of the West

Trilogy on the West
The Fall of the West is the third work in my trilogy on the West. The first, *The Syndicate* (2004), presented the dynastic *élite* commercial families whose trillions have gone into looting the world's resources and who sought to create a New World Order, a self-interested world government, throughout the 20th century. The second work, *The Secret History of the West* (2005), examined the Syndicate's roots in Freemasonry and revolutions since 1453 (the beginning of the Renaissance), including the Masonic American, French and Russian revolutions.

The genesis of The Fall of the West
I had always envisaged a third work, but was busy writing other books and bided my time. Covid-19 set me wondering whether it was a natural virus, a lab leak or a deliberate release. In May 2020, during lockdown, David Lorimer sent me Joseph Mercola's interview with Francis Boyle, who drafted the Biological Weapons Anti-Terrorism Act of 1989, in which he saw Covid-19 as a potential bio-weapon. My reply on 11 May 2020 included the following:

> It was in a newspaper over the weekend (Saturday's *Daily Telegraph*, report by Nick Allen) that the event in the Institute of Virology, Wuhan, took place between 6 and 11 October, and was followed by roadblocks round the Institute from 14 to 16 October (confirmed on lab mobile data). This may corroborate the escape of a benign bat coronavirus with three modifications added by Chinese researchers (to make it more airborne, attach itself to receptors in lungs and paralyse the immune system), Boyle's bio-weapon. It could have been released by someone working with... the joint US-Chinese co-funded project to study animal-to-human transmission (which has worked on a different floor of the Institute of Virology since 2016). If you come across a document that mentions a deliberate leak between 6 and 11 October at the Institute of Virology as distinct from a leak via a wet market elsewhere in Wuhan, I would be very interested to see it.

I was aware of the three modifications during human engineering of viruses at a very early stage. Lorimer said he had reread *The Syndicate* and was rereading *The Secret History of the West,* and he wondered if the virus was from the same stable as 9/11 (in which I showed that the Syndicate, particularly Dick Cheney, was heavily involved). He urged me to complete the trilogy.

I wrote to Lorimer on 6 June 2020 outlining a three-step approach to establishing the facts, and setting out my methodology:

> There is a spectrum of views on the virus. The conventional wisdom is that all viruses have come from animals, and that the transfer of this one to humans began in a wet market. MI5 and the Government (Johnson and Hancock) say there is no evidence that the virus was man-made. Having read the British-Norwegian Report (Dalgleish-Sorensen), Dearlove is breaking ranks to some extent, saying the report sees the virus as a chimera, composed of more than one virus, and this could be man-made. All a bit speculative, but the ex-Head of MI6 is raising the possibility of the Chinese paying reparations. Further along the spectrum is Mercola, who has a degree in biology but is a seller of alternative medicine – and knows more about Wuhan than most biologists. Also Boyle, more a lawyer who says the virus is a pathogen, in effect a bio-weapon; and Leitenberg, another biological weapons expert.
>
> No one (apart from the two of us) has wondered aloud whether the escape was deliberate, and from the same stable as 9/11, and there's still no evidence of this. Arguably in a position to know are NIAID (Fauci) and their co-partner in the Wuhan project NIH (Collins), but they may not be in the know. What we still want to know is what really happened in Wuhan around 6 October 2019. They shut down their project on 26 April [2020], and they're silent. Perhaps they agreed funding and are removed from day-to-day Wuhan and just don't know – although their project was modifying the virus, turning it into a virus composed of more than one virus.
>
> What we need is for Mercola to interview a Wuhan researcher who can give an eyewitness account of what happened in Wuhan in October, and put it in his next newsletter. After such an interview the researcher would be unable to continue living in China, which has been arresting and silencing those who have spoken out – so there are at least three or four such people he could interview if they are willing to be interviewed. The eyewitness could say what the project was doing – splitting bat genes to discover more about diseases? Collins' funding may have been to try to get to the aetiology of diseases by requesting experiments on their genes (nobly if riskily motivated). Mercola needs to find an eyewitness despite China's stifling of news about an event in

October and forcing whistle-blowers to retract. China has clearly been covering up.

I have a feeling of having been through this before. I visited China with the writer Frank Tuohy in March 1966 and, despite Mao's stifling of news about it, discovered the Cultural Revolution at Peking University (as described in *My Double Life 1: This Dark Wood*). Having spoken to an eyewitness student I was able to get access to the University's Vice-President and interrogate him for more than an hour. No one believed us, not the China-watchers, not even the British Legation in Peking, whose Chargé d'affaires [Donald Hopson] had us to lunch with all staff sitting round the lunch-table to listen. Then in August 1966 news broke and the little red book was being waved everywhere (and I got £50 from *Encounter* for the world scoop of the Cultural Revolution). The issue this time is: was what happened in October deliberate?

The first step is to find the equivalent of my student and interrogate the equivalent of the Vice-President, perhaps the Acting Heads of the two labs in Wuhan, the Wuhan Institute of Virology and the Wuhan Center for Disease Control and Prevention, and find out on the ground what actually happened. (I'd do this myself if someone commissioned me to cover the story, made the arrangements with the Chinese and paid my fares.) The next step is to get a list of all who worked on the project and identify how many were Americans and how many were Chinese. If only to eliminate a deliberate releasing we must ask Cicero's question – to whose advantage might it have been? When you look at the indebtedness of every government after lockdown and the need of all governments to borrow from central banks, one commercial set-up stands out among all others, and they also control the Bilderberg Group....

But we're getting ahead of ourselves. First there has to be eyewitness evidence of the virus's being man-made. Then there has to be eyewitness evidence of an escape, which may be accidental. Finally, there must be scrutiny of the escape to eliminate whether it was deliberate. At that stage it may be found to be deliberate, but this conclusion can't be reached until then. Ahead is a three-step process.

Both these letters are in my *Selected Letters*.

After June 2020 I was sent a few more of Mercola's interviews with experts, and while investigating the origin of coronavirus in accordance with the principles and three-step process set out in my second letter I drew on some of his interviews. Links can be found in the Notes, References and Sources. In July 2021, after I had assembled these, President Biden, concerned at the spread of the Delta variant of Covid-19 among the unvaccinated, attacked social media platforms as conduits that spread misinformation about the Covid-19 vaccines, and named a dozen writers in this connection, including Mercola, who responded by removing all his work (15,000 articles) from his website, and all his new work after it had been shown for 48 hours. I have assumed that eventually the links will be restored in the interests of free speech and will be accessible, and so have retained the links that I used. I should make it clear that I am not an 'anti-vaxxer' like Mercola – I have had two doses of the Pfizer vaccine against Covid, and a booster, and these stood me in good stead when I tested positive for Covid on 19–20 November 2021 and had it very mildly, and I have encouraged my family and acquaintances to have their jabs – and that in this work I am looking objectively at the evidence for how the pandemic began, and am not trying to dissuade anyone from being vaccinated.

I was fully prepared to find that China was responsible for the outbreak of Covid-19, and I had a sense of *déjà vu*, having encountered Chinese lying when I discovered the Chinese Cultural Revolution in 1966, as we have just seen (on p.xix).

Lockdowns intensified my work on other books. Then on 10 February 2021 I recorded in my diary:

> David Lorimer wrote saying he is going through *The Syndicate* to find out what's going on, that pp.265–266 are prophetic, and he's now going through *The Secret History of the West*. My next work should be called *The Future of the West*, how Rothschilds and Rockefellers are doing things to it and how it should be a good Promised Land/New World Order.

That night I was fed the title of the new work in my sleep, as has happened with most of my works. I wrote in my diary for 11 February 2021:

> Woke and lay still and the actual title of my next work was fed to me by the Muses: *The Fall of the West*. My poem [titled 'The Fall of the West'] (May 1976...) saw the fall of the West as a mental attitude, so it has two meanings – actual or a mental attitude. I am back to 1963 when I went to Japan to study the East and go to China, nearly 60 years later.... The book is about the undermining of the West by secret societies and revolutions (*The Secret History of the West*) and [by] the Syndicate (*The Syndicate*), which supported Communism, [that] leads to the fall of the West – from empire to levelled-down member of a... world government.... The fall of the West – compare Gibbon. To discover whether this was a possibility [was] the reason I went to the East. Two world wars brought

about the fall of the West, bankrupted the West and left it tottering, along with right-wing policies, Trump's encouragement of the invasion of Congress.... The fall of the West – into a World State.

The title that came to me in sleep echoed the title of my 1976 poem 'The Fall of the West'. This confronted international terrorism, which was attempting to secure the fall of the West in the 1970s. It urged resistance to terrorism and claimed that the fall of the West could be averted by the right "mental attitude".

The title also drew on the title of a course of lectures I was asked to give in 1966, when I was a Professor in Japan. I was asked to teach a year's course to eight postgraduate students to be titled 'The Decline of the West'. I based my lectures on Gibbon, Spengler and Toynbee, and my poems during 1966–1967 were full of images of the decline of the West, especially 'The Silence', 'Archangel' and 'Old Man in a Circle'. In the 1960s I became the poet of the decline of the West. During my teaching of world history to the postgraduates, and also (for three years) to Emperor Hirohito's second son Prince Hitachi (whose State visit to the UK in 1965 I helped to arrange), I came up with a fourth way of seeing civilisations, which I researched for 25 years and brought out as *The Fire and the Stones* (in part later revised as *The Rise and Fall of Civilizations*).

The Syndicate
In the course of charting 25 civilisations going through 61 similar stages, a project that predicted the end of Communism and a coming United States of Europe, I stumbled across the activities of what I came to call the Syndicate in their groups such as the Bilderberg Group and the Club of Rome, within the North-American and European civilisations.

The Syndicate are a number of mega-rich dynastic families, most notably the Rothschild and Rockefeller families.

The Rothschilds rose in the 18th century and acquired the Bank of England after the Battle of Waterloo in 1815 in the 19th century; the US Federal Reserve System and the Russian central bank in the early 20th century; and the Chinese central bank in 1982. They were the richest banking family in the world through much of the 19th and 20th centuries, and are believed to control the central banks of 187 of the 193 UN nation-states.[1]

Rockefellers were their protégés. They borrowed from the Rothschilds to install America's railroad system and rose to equal heights. They funded the Russian Revolution and all the Soviet five-year plans after 1925 – Stalin sold a half-interest in Russian oil including oil in Baku to the Rockefellers in return for funding for his five-year plans – and also funded China. They were behind the UN, which opened on their land, and in the 1940s they paid most of the UN's staff.

Both Rothschilds and Rockefellers – the foremost families in the Syndicate – were behind the 1954 Treaty of Rome, and what is now the European Union, which they saw as a stepping-stone to their world government. The two families share power in the Bilderberg Group's annual meetings, and from 1927 funded the 'Rothschild'-affiliated Council on Foreign Relations and were involved with the Club of Rome.

Having arrived at a fourth way of understanding history in Japan, I see the history of civilisations in terms of stages. I questioned whether the Syndicate could arrest the flow of history with a world government. I saw a world government as stage 46 of a number of living civilisations brought together by the younger North-American civilisation. I heard Fukuyama, author of *The End of History and the Last Man*, speak. His view of endless liberal democracy following the fall of the Berlin Wall was at variance with my view of history as going through stages. As I saw it, the Syndicate could bring together a number of living civilisations in the West and East and create a world government for *a while*, but this would come to an end and the flow of civilisations' stages would continue.

The Syndicate and The Fall of the West
In *The Fall of the West* I bring into the 21st century the story of the ultra-rich Syndicate's attempt to create a world government to suit their vast commercial interests: their continuation of their levelling-down of the West through wars and revolutions, and their levelling-up of the East, using their control of central banks and foundations to fund a network of oil and natural-gas pipelines and to encourage China's expanding trade. I assess the evidence for the origins of Covid-19 and see the West as being harder hit by Covid than China, whose rise alarms some in the American administration and factions in the Syndicate. I look in some detail at the future of the West.

When I had finished *The Fall of the West* Lorimer sent me a video of a documentary by Tim Gielen, *Monopoly: Who Owns the World*, on the financial monopoly of key Syndicate corporations, which endorses my finding in *The Syndicate*, the first book in my trilogy, and confirms some of the evidence I present in *The Fall of the West*. *Monopoly* (https:www.stopworldcontrol.com/monopoly) independently supplements and complements the background to *The Fall of the West*.

During the writing of my trilogy I have changed my attitude

towards the Syndicate. In *The Syndicate* I was opposed to the Syndicate. It wanted a New World Order based on wealth and greed, the self-interested values of Lucifer, whereas I wanted a New World Order based on values that would benefit humankind, like Christ's. I saw the stages of civilisations triumphing over their attempt to unify the world.

But as I wrote *The World Government* (2010) I underwent a change. I was on the side of a world government that had enough international authority to solve the world's problems and benefit humankind, and I reinforced the positive New World Order in *World State* and *World Constitution* (both 2018). It was not the world government that was wrong, but the people running it for their own profit, without caring about (at the time of writing) the 7.91 billion world citizens.[2]

I saw that most of the living civilisations were already in a federal stage, and that the North-American civilisation (which includes the US) was the youngest civilisation with the energy to turn the other civilisations into a positive World State; and I became very interested in the process of getting a World State to happen. I wanted the outcome, the end, to be a democratic World State; but I saw that the means, the process by which it reached its end, could be semi-authoritarian if it could lead to a democratic World State later on.

I produced an Outline for *The Fall of the West*, but I had to cope with other books. I had to finish *The Promised Land, Fools' Gold*, and then *The Building of the Great Pyramid*, and cope with the proofreading of *The Essentials of Universalism*. I was not able to start *The Fall of the West* until 25 June 2021. This was a good time to start reviewing the evidence as there was now a considerable body of opinion that SARS-CoV-2 was man-made and not natural.

Wuhan and Covid-19
The origins of the event that happened at Wuhan in the autumn of 2019 have been endlessly analysed without the evidence producing a conclusive result. Was Covid-19 a natural transmission from an animal, a leak from the laboratory of the Wuhan Institute of Virology or Wuhan Center for Disease Control (CDC), or a deliberate release by China, which would set back the Chinese economy, or by a faction within America-the Syndicate? Biden asked the CIA and intelligence community to investigate the origins of Covid-19, and the report to him was inconclusive (see pp.157–160).

I have arrived at my own conclusion by studying the evidence. As we shall see, gain-of-function work on bat coronavirus was happening in the US, funded at the University of North Carolina by NIAID (part of the NIH, Director, Dr Fauci) in 1999, and in 2002 US patent number

7279327 was taken out for the three main modified features of SARS-CoV-2, Covid-19. The US Centers for Disease Control and Prevention (CDC) tried to file a patent for the entire gene sequence of the SARS coronavirus in 2003. In 2009 and 2010 American policy towards China became more hostile, which resulted in China expanding in the South China Sea and surrounding US bases in 2012 and 2013. In 2013 Ralph Baric of the University of North Carolina sent a humanised mouse to Shi Zhengli of the Wuhan Institute of Virology. In 2014 the Obama administration placed a moratorium on gain-of-function research, and the American NIH took its work to China. NIH used EcoHealth Alliance (whose president was the British Peter Daszak) as an intermediary in the funding, and gave Daszak $3.4 million to fund gain-of-function research to last five years, some of which Daszak gave to the Wuhan Institute of Virology. Daszak had links to the US military Establishment, and from 2013 to 2020 EcoHealth Alliance received $103 million from the US Pentagon and State Department, who were evidently extremely interested in the military aspects of coronavirus as a bio-weapon. The moratorium was lifted in 2017.

The Syndicate were referred to by Eisenhower as "the military-industrial complex", and in the NIH (Director, Francis Collins), NIAID (Director, Dr Fauci), the University of North Carolina, EcoHealth Alliance and the Wuhan Institute of Virology there was a commercial complex making money from finding cures for diseases, and a military complex quietly applying its gain-of-function work to develop a military bio-weapon.

I am satisfied that SARS-CoV-2, Covid-19, is an engineered man-made bio-weapon, and its development began in the US more than 20 years ago, and is known to America and a faction within the Syndicate, whose funding took the medical project to China. I see the focus on China by the CIA-and-intelligence-community report as a blaming exercise. If the release of Covid-19 was deliberate it was likely to have been released by a faction in the American Syndicate, and as I show in my evidence, likely to have been released at the Military World Games which took place in Wuhan on 18 October 2019, when many athletes fell ill with Covid-like symptoms.

My experience of Chinese lying about the Cultural Revolution in 1966
As I have already said, I have been fully prepared to accept that China was responsible for the outbreak of Covid-19. I experienced Chinese lying at first hand on 16 March 1966, when I visited the University of Peking [Beijing] expecting to see 9,600 students and found there were only a dozen. A professor told me they were away on "socialist re-

education". One of the dozen told me they were exempted from being sent to work under peasants as they had health certificates, implying that working in the countryside was compulsory. I was assured that all the students were on the campus, and in the face of persistent lying from my guide and others I insisted on speaking with the University's Vice-President, which happened on 19 March. It then became clear they had all been sent out to work under peasants as part of a purge on the bourgeoisie which came to be known as the Cultural Revolution.

Frank Tuohy, the British novelist and short-story writer who had invited me to accompany him to China to help him write newspaper articles, and I were invited to a working lunch in the British Legation with the Chargé d'affaires, Donald (later Sir Donald) Hopson, and all their staff. I gave an account of what I had found and was told that the Legation had no idea that such a purge had begun. We had scooped the world, although we were not believed until the Cultural Revolution broke in August 1966, when Red Guards waved Mao's *Little Red Book* and arrested and brought to trial and executed many landlords and "enemies of the regime". (I visited a Chinese commune in March 1966, and a group of Chinese showed me the pigsty where they had imprisoned the landlord, and there was consternation when I shook his hand to show that he was a human being and should not be treated like a pig.) We were then credited with having discovered the Cultural Revolution. (See *Encounter*, December 1966, 'From a China Diary'.)[3]

Having experienced at first hand much Chinese evasion and downright lying and untrustworthiness between March and August 1966 (see my work *My Double Life 1: This Dark Wood*, pp.505–516 for full details), I have been alert to Chinese evasiveness about Wuhan now, particularly to China's sending Major-General Chen Wei to take charge of the lab at the Wuhan Institute of Virology in January 2020 (see pp.69, 74), suggesting a link between EcoHealth Alliance (Daszak) and the Chinese military. But the evidence for the provenance of Covid-19 is so overwhelmingly American-Syndicate and medical-commercial that I have no hesitation in seeing the origin of Covid-19 as being American rather than Chinese (and the CIA-and-intelligence-community Report of August 2021 as a cover-up).

The Syndicate's authoritarian New World Order: The Great Reset
The Syndicate are working for a centralised world government, as we have seen, one that will stabilise the world's population at 8 billion by 2030. (At the time of writing it is 7.91 billion and rising at about 57 million a year.) Various projects and reports have led up to this: *The Kissinger Report* (1974) and *The Global 2000 Report* (1980–1981),

both of which had strong links to 'Rockefellers'; the UN's Agenda 21 (1992); the 'Rockefellers'' report in conjunction with the Global Business Network *Scenarios for the Future of Technology and International Development* (2010), which has four scenarios, one of which is Lock Step, how to cope with a global pandemic, which looks like a dress rehearsal for Covid-19; the UN's Agenda 2030 (2015); and Event 201 (2019), funded by the Bill and Melinda Gates Foundation, the Johns Hopkins Center for Health Security and the World Economic Forum, which again presents a scenario for a pandemic until 2025 that looks like a dress rehearsal for Covid-19, and a new virus from 2025 to 2028 it calls 'SPARS'. Event 201 has strong 'Rockefeller' and Syndicate links as Gates is related to Nelson Rockefeller.

Now that Covid-19 has happened there is a new Syndicate structure, a rebranding of Nelson Rockefeller's New World Order: The Great Reset. This is a new, centralised and more authoritarian governance that is preparing for a world government, globalisation and the surveillance of populations through digital technologies (including the internet and CCTV). It unites the physical, biological and digital to develop AI (artificial intelligence) and brings in a green revolution against oil and natural gas. There will be a central bank digital currency (CBDC, which will be controlled by central banks, i.e. 'Rothschilds'). All this will be a 'Fourth Industrial Revolution', to quote the title of its – and the World Economic Forum's – founder, Klaus Schwab, who was a friend of David Rockefeller and Zbigniew Brzezinski, both Syndicate stalwarts. On 13 June 2019 Schwab and António Guterres (Secretary-General of the UN) signed a deal to combine the Great Reset with the 17 Sustainable Goals of the UN's Agenda 2030, which (although it is not mentioned) will include population sustainability.

There is great interest in the Great Reset's links to the World Bank – which in a document has stated the end of Covid-19 as 2025 – and to Deagel.com, the US's most secret intelligence service. As you will see, Deagel.com forecasts a drop of 0.5 billion in the world population of 2025 and a 50 to 80 per-cent drop in the populations of North America (the US and Canada) and Europe (the UK, Germany, France and Italy). The US's population is set to drop from a forecast of 326 million to just under 99.2 million, a drop of more than 227 million, and the UK's from 65.6 million to 14.6 million, a drop of 51 million. The Great Reset seems to involve the collapse of the Western world's financial system, effectively the fall of the West, and the migration of its population as if from a nuclear-laid-waste or perhaps a biologically-contaminated landscape. Now Covid-19 is in our air it seems that we are living in a new Biological Age, when a virus can be released at any time.

The rise of China

China's rise has been stunning. Its Belt-and-Road Initiative of initially-Chinese-funded infrastructure projects has spread to 140 countries (see map on the front cover) and nearly surrounds the West. The US has troops in 140 countries and 800 military bases in 70 countries, but following its departure from Afghanistan and withdrawal of combat troops from Iraq it seems weak and the momentum seems to have passed to China. Power seems to have shifted from West to East, in accordance with the Syndicate's policy for over 100 years, to level down the West and level up the East so they can both exist within a world government.

China is authoritarian. It has persecuted the Tibetans and now the Uyghurs in Xinjiang and has clamped down on democratic freedom in Hong Kong, contrary to the agreement made with the UK in 1997. It has a plan to invade Taiwan, and is building up to 145 missile silos. China and America have been in a Cold War since 2009–2010 (from the US's perspective) and 2012–2013 (from China's perspective), and bio-warfare between them may already have begun.

The two New World Orders and the fall of the West

There are two New World Orders and world governments: the Syndicate's authoritarian world government, which will be run for the benefit of a few dynastic mega-rich families; and the democratic, presidential, partly-federal world government I set out in my works *The World Government* (2010), *World State* and *World Constitution* (both 2018), a world government with enough federal authority to abolish war, enforce disarmament, combat famine, disease and poverty and solve the world's financial, environmental and virological problems.

The Syndicate has made progress towards the authoritarian New World Order. It has covered the world with a network of pipelines and helped fund China to trade with as many countries as the US has troops in to achieve a kind of balance. The Great Reset, if it works, will bring both sides together into a state that resembles Communist China rather than America, with no ownership of property and everything rented, so all humankind is equal.

The key problem in this post-Covid time of bio-weapons is to keep the peace, prevent the fall of the West forecast by Deagel.com, and lead the West into survival, from which it can still democratise and free the world. How this is done is the key question, which I answer at the end of this work.

Now we are perhaps living in a Biological Age with viruses being treated as bio-weapons to block rivals' economies, the sudden fall of the West is a possibility that cannot be ruled out. It is extremely important that the West should survive, and it will require nimble, dexterous diplomacy to achieve such a survival and avert its collapse in a pragmatic way. If the West is to fall, it should fall into a democratic partly-federal World State of the kind I have set out, but how to get there from where we are now, after Covid-19, is the question.

In the footsteps of Moses and Raleigh
I have said (in my work *The Promised Land*) that I feel like Moses on Mount Nebo, able to see the Promised Land beneath him at around the age of 80 but knowing he will not personally enter it. Like Moses I am pointing the way for the next generation so Westerners in their prime will be able to enjoy milk and honey rather than the devastation of an uninhabitable West whose financial system has collapsed.

I also feel I am in the footsteps of a polymath with whom I have much in common, Sir Walter Raleigh, who was the first Metaphysical poet, wrote *The History of the World* (from the creation to 146BC) during his 13-year confinement in the Bloody Tower while awaiting execution, and had Syndicate-like commercial interests overseas and in America, including sponsoring the first English colony in America on Roanoke Island (now in North Carolina). I have continued his Metaphysical poetic tradition, written my history of the world (*The Fire and the Stones*, in part revised as *The Rise and Fall of Civilizations*) and have had commercial interests overseas and in America. Raleigh was beheaded for independent-mindedness that was regarded as disobedient and treasonous (for attacking a Spanish fort in South America against James I's command), and while awaiting execution in the Bloody Tower, where he occupied two rooms, he scratched a self-portrait of his own laurelled head on a wall, found recently beneath a layer of paint. As I write I can see my own severed head on the front cover of my *Collected Prefaces*.

I am aware that in this work I am continuing Raleigh's independent-mindedness – and truth-telling. It would be easier to blame China than to have given the picture of events I have presented on my jigsaw of evidence. But the truth is sacrosanct, even if it is inconvenient. In an earlier time my findings might have led to my incarceration in the Bloody Tower to await the executioner's axe – and the end of my thinking about the West. The West has stood for freedom of speech, unlike the present authoritarian China, and that is why it is of paramount importance that its democratic principles should survive.

13–15 August, 24–25 September, 23 November 2021

The Gillings School of Global Public Health at the University of North Carolina, Chapel Hill (above), and (below) the Wuhan Institute of Virology with the location of its National Biosafety Level (BSL) P4 laboratory on left, arrowed

1

The Story of the Syndicate's New World Order So Far, and Population-Capping

The fall of the West as levelling down

'The Fall of the West.' The idea brings to mind the sacking of Rome; the Visigoths led by Alaric swarming into Rome, which was led by the weak and vacillating Emperor Honorius, and sacking the city for three days in 410AD.

Alaric's Goths were Christian, and treated Rome's holiest places

with great respect.[1] They nominated the basilicas of St Peter and St Paul as places of sanctuary, and escorted holy ladies there before methodically ransacking their houses. They had entered Rome by the Salarian Gate and for three days raped and pillaged the city's wealth including the houses of rich senators, burnt the area round the Salarian Gate and the old Senate building and carried off huge treasures and the sister of the Western Roman Emperor. They left along the Appian Way, leaving behind them comparisons with the sack of Troy.

The sack of Rome by Alaric the Visigoth in 410AD

The Roman world was shaken to its foundations. Rome had not been sacked for more than 700 years; all thought it was safe from invasion. It had been looted and burned. It was no longer *Roma Aeterna*: Rome, the Eternal City. The pagans blamed the Christians; whatever gods had looked after Rome for 700 years had deserted Rome now. Augustine, bishop of Hippo, met Roman refugees and defended the Christians in the work he began in 410AD, *The City of God*.

'The Fall of the West' conjures a painting (inspired by Gibbon's *The Decline and Fall of the Roman Empire* and disconcertingly showing Vandals in Muslim garb) of Genseric the Vandal sacking Rome again in 455AD. Vandal horsemen rear up in a street between temples, women huddle together and cower, some are carried away, men entreat on hands and knees, implore or lie dead.

1

The sack of Rome by Genseric the Vandal in 455AD: Genseric's Invasion of Rome, by Karl Pavlovich Bryullov (1799–1852), painted between 1833 and 1836, State Tretyakov Gallery, Moscow, Russia

The attacks on America on 9/11 in 2001 gave the West a similar shock to the one the Romans experienced in 410AD, and the events involving the pandemic in 2019–2020 gave the West another shock, like the sacking of Rome in 455AD. The West no longer seemed impregnable. The West is a combination of the European and North-American civilisations' industrialised democracies, and there may be echoes of the sacking of Rome in the occupation of the US Capitol following the last days of Trump's Presidency in November 2020. As the election results were due to be certified in the building on 6 January 2021, the Capitol was invaded and nearly sacked for the first time since 1814, when British soldiers burned the building.

The sacking of Rome in 410AD, and again in 455AD, did not result in the fall of the Western Roman Empire, which was a process that began in 395 and ended with the deposing of the last Western Roman Emperor in 476, and the Eastern Roman Empire continued in Constantinople (Byzantium renamed after Constantine I, the first Byzantine Emperor). Like the fall of the Roman Empire, and the fall of the British Empire, the fall of the West is not a sudden event but a long-drawn-out process.

The fall of the West is in fact the result of a long-levelling-down of the Western nation-states from their past imperial supremacy through wars, revolutions and anti-colonial movements, nationalistic populism and now a pandemic.

The British Empire and the Pax Britannica
The British Empire has gone through two stages. The first British Empire was in America from 1607 to 1783. The second British Empire was amassed as a consequence of the Industrial Revolution in Britain between 1760 and 1840 and its industrialisation of the world by the export of innovatory manufacturing machines during the 18th and 19th centuries. In 1900 Britain ruled over a greater population and land area than any other power. The *Pax Britannica* lasted from 1815 to 1914, from the end of the Napoleonic Wars to the First World War, and fulfilled the same function as the *Pax Romana* from 27BC to 180AD. Like Rome, Britain was the strongest country militarily and economically, and a benign global hegemon, and the *Pax* was a cover for the assembling of the British Empire and for British imperialism.

The decline of the British and European empires, and the rise of the US
But maintaining imperial rule and defending the Empire involved massive public expenditure that delayed social reform. Britain's decline began between 1880 and 1914. (This coincided with the decline in British Christianity caused by the churches' abandoning of the Inner Light, which was so prevalent in the Metaphysical poets of the 17th century.) During these years Britain became vulnerable both militarily and economically.

The First World War weakened both Britain and Germany, and after the US's entry into the war in 1917 it became clear that Britain's naval predominance would never be restored. From 1917 to 1970 there were repeated attempts to modernise British industrial structure and to change the nature of the State, and modernisation took place as the British hegemony was transferred following colonial unrest and independence movements, especially after the Suez débâcle in 1956. There was further decline from the 1960s as the left-wing and right-wing narratives collided, and there was a faltering economic performance.[2]

This same pattern applied to all the European empires: as well as the British Empire, the French, German, Dutch, Belgian, Austro-Hungarian, Italian, Spanish and Portuguese empires. All the Western empires suffered levelling-down following the First and Second World Wars, revolutions and independence movements.

After the Second World War the US led the West, and the *Pax*

Americana began in earnest with the Marshall Plan of 1945. It increasingly replaced the *Pax Britannica*, and the US took over the British global role and presided over the fall of the Berlin Wall and the end of Communism.

The Syndicate

In fact, as I showed in *The Syndicate* (2004), the levelling-down through wars and independence movements was more than circumstantial. There has been a long process of deliberate undermining that has seen the West decline from its imperial greatness and international superiority and superpowerdom to parity with the rising East, so it is ready to be absorbed into the New World Order of what I have called the Syndicate.

In *The Syndicate* I described the network of *élite* families which at the beginning of the 21st century was poised to form a world government, having promoted levelling-down throughout the 20th century. As I showed, it was a self-interested project of billionaire, mega-rich families bent on looting the world's resources for their own ends, and not for the benefit of humankind.

I referred to the families collectively as 'the Syndicate'. *The Concise Oxford Dictionary*'s definition of a 'syndicate' is "a combination of individuals or commercial firms to promote some common interest", and this combination of influential families had a common interest.[3]

The dynastic families of the Syndicate in the early 20th century were the Rothschild, Rockefeller, Schiff, Warburg, Morgan, Harriman and Milner families. To these have been added over the years the Astor, Bundy, Bush, Collins, du Pont, Eaton, Freeman, Kennedy, Li, Onassis, Reynolds, Russell and Van Duyn families.

At this point I want to echo what I wrote in *The Syndicate*[4] as every word applies to this work:

> It is now difficult to distinguish between the individuals and their commercial firms, conglomerates of companies or corporations which shared the common interest of the Syndicate. By placing inverted commas round family names ('Rothschilds', 'Rockefellers') I seek to make clear that I am not referring to particular individuals but to a particular emphasis of a commercial pattern. When I have used, and from now on when I use, the terms 'Rothschilds' or 'Rothschildite', and 'Rockefellers' or 'Rockefellerite', I am defining an emphasis, a shade within the ethos and outlook on life of the Syndicate rather than the influence of a specific individual; in the case of the 'Rothschilds', a commercial drive associated with their 19th-century financial dominance

4

and imperialism, and in the case of the 'Rockefellers', a commercial drive associated with their 20th-century acquisition of oil and shaping of international events through revolutions. 'Rothschildian' is a descriptive adjective meaning 'belonging to' the commercial enterprise of 'Rothschilds', as in 'Rothschildian oil interests'. 'Rockefellerite' can similarly mean 'belonging to' the commercial enterprise of 'Rockefellers'. A 'Rockefellerite' means a follower of the 'Rockefeller' faction within the Syndicate and its policies; a 'Rothschildite' means a follower of the 'Rothschild' faction within the Syndicate and its policies. 'Rockefellerite' and 'Rothschildite' mean 'pertaining to the faction and policies' of 'Rockefellers'/'Rothschilds'. (Compare 'Thatcherite', which can indicate a member of the Thatcher faction or a follower of a Thatcher policy; or even an economic or commercial direction.)

In the rest of this book I am not making any imputation against the specific behaviour of any individual, family, company or corporation among the Syndicate families and their institutionalised fortunes. Rather, I am presenting the achievements of the Syndicate families as part of a pattern.

I believe some of the corporate leaders and bankers among the *élite* families had a noble, altruistic vision of a unified world without war, disease or famine: of a Utopia, a Paradise. Revolutions and ideas of new world orders frequently begin with a noble aim of banishing inequality, hunger, disease and war. However, if this noble ideal was to be imposed by stealth without the consent of the people of the US, Europe and other countries of the world, then it was fundamentally undemocratic and wrong in principle, no matter how well-intentioned.

Others had an ignoble, exploitative, self-interested, capitalist vision which was to maximise their billions, turn them into more billions. To increase their profits, they desired sympathetic world leaders whose political policies would assist their commercial interests and would be happy to install puppet presidents and prime ministers who would implement their commercial policies. They would use the political situation for their own commercial ends, and were not averse to assisting both sides in a conflict if it suited them.

Each of the branches of the Syndicate have their own blend of idealism, practicality and ambition. But the different branches of the Syndicate, particularly the two factions of the Rothschilds and Rockefellers, are not really in conflict. It's more like the number-one supplier of, say, washing powder, with competing brands of its own product on the shelf. We think we have a choice, but it's offered to us by the same company. We don't realise how powerful and how connected it is because it operates in secret.

The rise of the 'Rothschilds' and 'Rockefellers'
In *The Syndicate* I told of the Rothschilds' rise to control the world's banking system, having bought the Bank of England in 1815 for a knock-down price;[5] how they now control 187 of the 193 central banks of UN member states,[6] many of which are officially described as 'state-owned' or 'government-owned', all (including, recently, Afghanistan and Iraq) except the central banks of Sudan, Cuba, Libya, China, Iran and North Korea; and how they were worth $500 billion in 1940 (more than $20 trillion at today's values);[7] and how they may have $1 trillion today, and may even have $100 trillion.[8]

I told how the 'Rothschilds'' protégés 'Rockefellers' funded the building of American railroads and were worth $5 billion in 1937, $200 billion at today's values.[9] Some claim that 'Rockefellers' have $400 billion at today's values, and that they have since overtaken 'Rothschilds'.[10]

The Syndicate's links with the EU, Stalin and Russian oil, nuclear weapons and oil pipelines
In *The Syndicate* I told how the Rothschilds were behind the English monarchy – when I worked for MI6 I was told in 1972 that the Rothschild family control MI6 and that I was ultimately working for the Rothschilds[11] – and how, together with the American Council on Foreign Relations, they were behind the Treaty of Rome which led to the European Union. And I told how 'Rockefellers' were behind Stalin, and from 1926 financed his five-year plans, the first one through Schiff's Kuhn, Loeb and Co., who now acted for 'Rockefellers'[12] – in return for a half-interest in Russian oil (including Baku's oil), which they bought in 1925.

I told how the Syndicate made loans to fund the development of nuclear weapons by both sides during the Cold War, and sold arms to both sides during Eisenhower's presidency: 'Rockefellers' were financing the Soviet Union's purchase of missiles (with some input from 'Rothschilds'), 'Rothschilds' the American purchase of missiles (with some input from 'Rockefellers'). During the Cold War the Syndicate made a fortune out of servicing the Soviet and US stockpiling of nuclear weapons. Many of the 69,401 nuclear weapons in the world in 1985 (reduced to 13,080 nuclear weapons at the start of 2021) were bought with money borrowed from the two dynastic *élites*.[13]

I also told how the Syndicate covered the earth with oil pipelines, including a pipeline in Afghanistan that needed to be defended from the Taliban.

The Olympians: The Committee of 300, the "military-industrial complex"
It can be argued that there has always been a Syndicate, that even when Khufu was building the Great Pyramid there was a self-interested *élite* bent on profiting from the project at the expense of those who dragged the massive blocks of stone into place.

There is a view that the roots of the Syndicate are in a powerful group the British aristocracy founded in 1727, known as the Olympians. Its 300 members had been carefully chosen to organise politics, commerce, banking, the media and the military, and run the world. The group has been called the Committee of 300.[14] It is said that Queen Victoria overhauled the Committee so that it could speak through institutions such as the Royal Institute of International Affairs, and that Queen Elizabeth II is a prominent member – some say the Committee of 300 is under her control.[15] This group is also known as the Hidden Hand or Unseen Hand.[16] All agree the Rothschild family have been extremely prominent in the group.

Nowadays the 300 include leaders in the military and industry, including insurance, banking, real estate, entertainment and high technology.[17] Heads of foreign governments have referred to them as "The Magicians", and Stalin referred to them as "The Dark Horses". Eisenhower referred to them with understatement as "the military-industrial complex".[18] He was referring to the military, and the defence industry that produces its weapons, and the corporations that carry out the US's wishes, all of which (he thought) have too much power. This appellation is still used in articles today.

The Bilderberg Group
The Olympians may be the context from which the Syndicate grew and from which the Bilderberg Group was founded. The 'Rothschilds' and 'Rockefellers' share power in the Bilderberg Group,[19] which meets every year and seems to be ahead of coming wars and revolutions. Some 120–150 influential people take part in the Bilderberg Group's annual meetings, drawn from industry, finance, academia, the media and politics.

The Bilderberg Group has met every year since 1954 to foster dialogue between Europe and North America to prevent a Third World War, and to bolster free-market Western capitalism around the globe. In 1954 the participants called the Group "the Alliance". Unable to learn its name, journalists dubbed the participants the "Bilderbergers" as they first met at the Hotel de Bilderberg in Oosterbeek, Holland, in May 1954. The meeting was hosted by Prince Bernhard of the Netherlands (Queen Juliana's husband). He was a major shareholder in Royal Dutch Shell, the Rothschild-dominated oil company.

First meeting of the Bilderberg Group, 1954 (left), hosted by Prince Bernhard (right)

The Bilderberg Group's governing council included representatives of N.M. Rothschild, Schröder Bank, the *New York Times*, the Royal Institute for International Affairs (RIIA), the CIA and Henry Kissinger.[20] It is reputed to have been created by Alastair Buchan, the son of the British author John Buchan, with input from the historian Arnold Toynbee, and its members were handpicked by Baron Edmond de Rothschild and Laurance Rockefeller, and comprised 100 of the world's *élite*, many drawn from the Council on Foreign Relations, the English-Speaking Union, the Pilgrims Society and the Round Table. Both Edmond and Guy de Rothschild were prominent Bilderbergers, and David Rockefeller was an active member for the 'Rockefellers'.[21]

The meetings are secret, and there is an exclusion zone of half a mile round the hotel where they take place, and helicopters hover in the sky to enforce this. Nothing is published regarding the meetings, which are based on the Chatham House Rule that anyone who comes to a meeting is free to use information received but is not allowed to reveal the identity of speakers or participants. The idea is to encourage candid debate while preserving privacy. The Chatham House Rule was named after the headquarters of the Royal Institute of International Affairs, which is based in Chatham House, and the Rule originated in 1927.

At the 1993 meeting David Rockefeller thanked newspaper editors for being discreet for nearly four decades, for without the lack of publicity "it would have been impossible to develop our project (or plan) for the world". He said: "The supranational sovereignty of an intellectual *élite* is surely preferable to the self-determination of nations practised in past centuries."[22]

Despite the secrecy a few persistent journalists have been able to obtain access to the guest lists and agenda, and these have trickled out in the *American Free Press* and in books such as Daniel Estulin's *The True Story of the Bilderberg Group* and *Jim Tucker's Bilderberg Diary*.

On 9 December 1998 I encountered the Secretary of the Bilderberg Group, Martin Taylor, at a dinner at Grosvenor House and persuaded him to ring me. I did not know that evening that he had just resigned as Barclays' Chief Executive over his Bank's agreement to contribute to a fund to bail out Russia. I wanted to establish what the Bilderberg Group was working towards. I said: "As I understand it, there will be a United States of the World with an earth dollar or an earth single currency, and the United States of Europe is a stepping-stone to it with a single currency." He said, "That's right." I asked what time-scale. He said, "20 years," i.e. 2018. That was the Bilderberg Group's plan in 1998. He told me he had attended the Bilderberg Group three times.[23]

The Syndicate's links with Freemasonry
I also investigated the links of the dynastic families that make up the Syndicate to secret organisations associated with Freemasonry and Luciferianism.

In *The Secret History of the West* (2005), the second volume of my trilogy on the Syndicate, I told how Rothschilds had funded Adam Weishaupt from 1770 to 1776, and how on 1 May 1776 he founded the Order of the Illuminati for Rothschilds' Sionist English Freemasonry (see p.10), which had been begun by Francis Bacon and drew on the Priory of Sion. Weishaupt became a Freemason in 1777, and he merged his Sionist Illuminati and the Templar Grand Orient in 1778.[24] The Illuminati had links with Luciferianism. Lucifer, Satan, was a rebel who had a revolutionary attitude to Heaven and wanted to challenge God for the leadership of the universe. He and his followers lauded the seven deadly sins, especially greed, and this resonated with Mayer Amschel Rothschild, the founder of the Rothschild dynasty's banking business.

In *The Secret History of the West* I looked at the background to the rise of the Syndicate. Its roots were in the Freemasonic revolutions such as the French revolution, and I charted all the revolutions since 1453, the date of the beginning of the Renaissance that led to the Reformation and the fracturing of Catholic unity and of the supremacy of Catholic Rome. I investigated the links between Freemasonic sects and revolutions: Templarism and the American revolution; the Sionist-Illuminatised Templar Grand Orient and the French revolution; and the Templar Grand Orient and Lenin's Communist Russian revolution.

The Syndicate, which succeeded these Freemasonic revolutions, was heavily involved in the Grand Orient, which was behind the French and Russian revolutions and is currently behind the New World Order revolution in Europe, as I showed in *The Syndicate*. The head of Grand Orient Freemasonry at the time of the inauguration of the European Union (the United States of Europe) at Maastricht on 31 December 1992 was President François Mitterrand, then the most powerful 33rd-degree Freemason in Europe. It was he who unveiled the glass pyramid of 673 windows outside the Louvre. The pyramid is an Illuminati symbol adopted by Adam Weishaupt in 1776. It is found on the American Great Seal and dollar bill above the tag *Novus Ordo Seclorum* ('New Secular Order' or 'New Order of the Ages').[25]

The Syndicate and Nelson Rockefeller's New World Order
The Sionist 'Rothschilds' and Templar 'Rockefellers' united Sionism and Templarism within the Bilderberg Group, and since 1954 the US and Europe have combined as the West to conduct the Cold War, tear down the Berlin Wall and Communism, and create the European Union, as *The Syndicate* tells. The 'Rothschilds' and 'Rockefellers' also managed the West's decline as they made loans to both sides of the Cold War so both sides could develop nuclear weapons and live in a peace based on stalemate, for the first side to use nuclear weapons faced immediate retaliation and extinction. Nuclear weapons could therefore not be used.

The Syndicate have attempted to create new conditions within globalism that can lead to a world government – an authoritarian world government or New World Order under which all oil pipelines, natural resources and the environment would be under the control of the alliance of Syndicate families, who would operate with some secrecy.

As *The Syndicate* says,[26] the term 'New World Order' was first used in the modern media by New York Governor Nelson Rockefeller, who was quoted in *AP* (26 July 1968) as saying that "as President he would work towards international creation of a 'new world order'". He had already called for world federalism in his book *The Future of Federalism* (1962), claiming that current events compellingly demanded a "new world order" as the old order was crumbling. "There will evolve the bases for a federal structure of the free world."

In 1967 Richard Nixon echoed this call for a New World Order, and in 1990 Bush Sr said that "a New World Order can emerge" that could "shape the future for generations to come". It is important to grasp that the first mention of a New World Order was by a Rockefeller in 1962, and that in 1967 Nixon was echoing Rockefeller's call.

The New World Order would be authoritarian, and there would be no global democracy. In the interests of sustainability and making the available food go round, the 'Rockefellers' and the Syndicate plan that their New World Order should depopulate the world by aggressive family planning, and by allowing wars, diseases and famines to contribute to their goal of population reduction.

The Club of Rome and global population control

Population reduction and the New World Order began with Nelson Rockefeller and is a 'Rockefellerite' idea. It was developed by the Club of Rome, which inspired the creation of the World Economic Forum. The Club of Rome was founded in 1968 during a private meeting between Italian industrialist Aurelia Peccei and Scottish chemist Alexander King at a Rockefeller family residence in Bellagio, Italy. In 1972 it brought out *The Limits to Growth*, which warned that the earth was overpopulated and that population growth would reach the earth's limit within a century. Critics associated its population reduction with Nazi eugenics.

In 1973 the Club of Rome published a report that was a model for global governance and split the world into ten interconnected political and economic regions.[27]

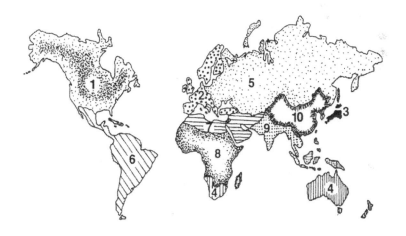

10 zones in the Club of Rome's world government

This report was a revised plan for a world government outlined by the 'Rockefellerite' Club of Rome. It split the world into ten political/economic regions or zones that would unite the entire world under one government. These were originally called "Kingdoms" to reflect the ten kingdoms within Atlantis in Plato's account in *Critias*. The word "Kingdoms" was omitted when the plan was published in a book, *Mankind at the Turning Point*, which argued that the world's problems could only be solved "in a global context". These zones are:

1. North America
2. Western Europe
3. Japan
4. The rest of the developed market economies (Israel, Australia, Tasmania, New Zealand, Oceania, South Africa)
5. Eastern Europe including the free Soviet Union
6. Latin America
7. North Africa and the Middle East
8. Main Africa
9. South and South-Eastern Asia including India
10. "Centrally-planned Asia", meaning Communist Asia (Mongolia, North Korea, North Vietnam, and China)

In *The First Global Revolution* (1991) the Club of Rome argued that its policy of limiting population growth would gain support if there could be a common enemy: "pollution, the threat of global warming, water shortages, famine and the like would fit the bill." In other words, the Green Movement and climate change would limit population growth.

On a personal note, I encountered Alexander King at a meeting at the Royal Overseas League in 1998, and was taken to a room where a smallish, elderly bespectacled man in a collar and tie and blazer stood alone with a glass of whisky in his hand. He led me to an area where we were by ourselves, and I had a few minutes alone with him before he spoke to a room full of people. I showed him a map I had with me of the ten regions,[28] and asked him if there is going to be a New World Order. Later I chatted to him and he said, "I've been to some of the Bilderberg meetings, you know. They might just be able to bring about a world government. I don't want America ruling the world, it's not practical."[29] The Club of Rome began the population-reduction movement, and the Green Movement, in the 20th and 21st centuries.

The Kissinger Report *(1974) and global population control*
The beginning of the US government population-control program can be dated to 10 December 1974. On that date the US National Security Council completed its top-secret *National Security Study Memorandum* or *NSSM 200*,[30] also known as *The Kissinger Report* as Kissinger, an adviser to 'Rockefellers', was Secretary of State at the time. Its subject

was 'Implications of Worldwide Population Growth for US Security and Overseas Interests' and was the result of collaboration between the CIA, the US Agency for International Development (USAID) and the Departments of State, Defense and Agriculture. The document was declassified in 1990, and is regarded as the foundation on which US government population control has been constructed, and can still be found on the USAID website.[31] I did not have access to this document when I was writing *The Syndicate*.

The US and UN made decisions to withhold aid from Algeria, Ecuador, Kenya, Yemen, Zambia and St Lucia. The Report's primary purpose was to maintain access to the mineral resources of less-developed countries (LDCs). It concentrated on the fastest-growing developing countries. The Report dwells on the legalisation of abortion, financial incentives for countries to increase their abortion, sterilisation and contraception-use rates, mandatory population control, and coercion such as withholding disaster and food aid unless an LDC implements population-control programs. The Report specifically declared that the US must cover up its population-control activities to avoid charges of imperialism, and must induce the UN to follow these population-control activities.

The Report has encouraged abuses. For example, for many years the US funded the United Nations Population Fund (UNFPA), which in turn donated more than $100 million to China's population-control program, and a $12-million computer complex to monitor the population-control program and train thousands of Chinese population-control officials – in April 2017 Trump ended the US's funding of the UNFPA. More children were aborted under China's one-child policy than the entire population of the United States. Other countries threatened with the withholding of food are Peru and India (to sterilise women) and Uganda (to roll back HIV infection).

The Report sets out the detailed strategy by which the US government aggressively promotes population control in developing nations to have better access to their natural resources: avoiding LDCs' government action, labour conflicts, sabotage and civil disturbances caused by population pressure, by keeping the population low; keeping down the number of the young, who are more likely to challenge imperialism; getting LDC leaders to commit to population control, so bypassing their people; designing programs with financial incentives for LDCs to increase their abortion, sterilisation and contraception-use rates, including paying women to have abortions; indoctrinating children; sex education; using coercion such as withholding disaster and food aid unless a targeted LDC implements population-control programs.

In the 1960s the world's population was increasing at 2 per cent per year, whereas now it is increasing at less than 1 per cent per year due to existing population-control programs. The Report predicted the population of the world would stabilise at 10 to 13 billion. Some demographers predicted it would balloon to 22 billion. It is now estimated that by 2100 world population will be 11 billion. Since then, as we are about to see, the 'Rockefellerite' *Global 2000 Report* envisages stabilising the world's population at 8 billion.

All this, overseen by Kissinger, an adviser to the 'Rockefellers', was top-secret US government policy from 1954 and coloured *The Global 2000 Report*, written by a Rockefeller staff member and linked to the phrase "useless eaters" in LDCs, in 1980–1981 (see below). The inference can be drawn that these methods have been operating behind the scenes of the US government since *The Global 2000 Report*, which has been accepted by every President since 1980, and are still in force now, when the goal is of capping a sustainable world population at 8 billion to prevent world shortages of food. There is no escaping that these covert population-control policies and 'imperialistic' attitudes towards LDCs' natural resources may be behind the covert US policy towards China we will soon consider (see p.76), which assists the goals of population control and accessing LDCs' natural resources.

The 'Rockefellers' and the West's policy of depopulation
The Global 2000 Report to the President of the US (1980) was written by Gerald O. Barney, then a staff member of the Rockefeller Brothers Fund (RBF) in the field of environmental studies. The RBF is distinct from the Rockefeller Foundation. It was founded in 1940 as a philanthropic vehicle for the five third-generation Rockefeller brothers – John, Nelson, Laurance, Winthrop and David – and received $58 million from John D. Rockefeller Jr in 1951. The RBF "advances social change that contributes to a more just, sustainable and peaceful world".[32] *The Global 2000 Report* was therefore a 'Rockefellers'' project.

The Global 2000 Report is in three volumes. Volume 1 summarises the Report's findings. The Report was shaped by a directive from President Carter on 23 May 1977: "I am directing the Council on Environmental Quality and the Department of State, working in co-operation with... other appropriate agencies, to make a one-year study of probable changes in the world's population, natural resources and environment through the end of the century. This study will serve as the foundation of our longer-term planning." In other words, the Report was to become the US administration's policy. The Preface to

The three volumes of *The Global 2000 Report* (1980–1981)

Volume 2, *Global Future, Time to Act: Report to the President on Global Resources, Environment and Population*, was signed by Gus Speth, Chairman, Council on Environmental Policy, and Edmund Muskie, Secretary of State, who stated: "This report is only the beginning of a process the United States and other countries across the globe must engage in over the next few years."[33]

Stabilising the world's population at 8 billion by family planning
In Volume 1 the Report predicts that the world's population would rise from 4 billion in 1975 to 6.35 billion in 2000, and 10 billion by 2030.[34] The Report lowered the figure of 6.35 billion to 6.18 billion as 170 million were expected to die of disease and famine by 2000.[35] In fact, the world's population reached 6 billion on 5 August 1999, just before 2000, suggesting that 350 million may have died of disease and famine, not 170,000 – or that family planning was more successful than forecast.

The Global 2000 Report, Volume 1, also says: "If the fertility and mortality rates projected for 2000 were to continue unchanged into the twenty-first century, the world's population would reach 10 billion by 2030. This same rate of growth would produce a population of nearly 30 billion before the end of the twenty-first century."[36] One of the main findings is: "Ninety per cent of this growth will occur in the poorest countries."[37] Sustainability in relation to climate change and green policies therefore includes preventing the world's population from rising to nearly 30 billion, which would be unsustainable because there would not be enough available food.

Global Future, Time to Act (Volume 2, January 1981, six months later) says:

Family planning services are currently believed to be available to approximately a third of poor couples in developing nations, and used by one quarter. Demographers have concluded that if availability and usage in the developing world could be doubled by the end of the decade, world population in the year 2000 would be half a billion lower than the global median projected of 6.3 billion. Even more striking, this effort could also mean that global population would eventually stabilise at 8 billion, versus the 12.2 billion that would result if higher fertility rates continued over a longer period of time. The difference of 4.2 billion is almost equal to the *total* current [i.e. 1981] world population.[38]

The higher fertility rates were to be combated through a program of family planning, sterilisation, contraception and abortion. *Global Future* goes on to advocate "biomedical research" to improve contraception and lists in the recommendations that "a study undertaken by NIH (National Institutes of Health), other appropriate government agencies, private foundations and industry should determine the feasibility and the need for a new government or quasi-government organisation that could co-ordinate and fund research necessary for research and development of new contraception", and "that an additional study should be taken by NIH in co-operation with FBA, the Patent Office, the Department of Justice and industry to propose steps which might be taken to increase incentives for the pharmaceutical industry to develop raw contraceptive methods".[39]

The NIH, for which Dr Fauci was a physician and which has worked with him since he became Director of the NIAID (National Institute of Allergy and Infectious Diseases) in 1984, is at the forefront of *Global Future*'s 'Rockefellerite' thinking in 1981 on biomedical research for population reduction. In coming pages we will need to remember the links between *The Global 2000 Report* plan and: the Rockefeller Foundation as a precursor of the World Health Organization (WHO); Bill Gates, a relative of the Rockefellers (see pp.38 and 41, the seventh cousin three times removed of Nelson Rockefeller, the 41st Vice-President of the United States who first used the term 'the New World Order'); and the Gates Foundation's collaborations with the NIH and NIAID.

Culling the world's "useless eaters" by 2 billion by 2030
As the world's population was just below 6 billion in 2000, stabilising it at around 8 billion and the prediction for 2030 that the population will be 10 billion meant that the world's population had to be reduced by 2 billion by 2030, so that the population is then 8 billion, not 10 billion.

In *The Syndicate* I wrote:

> *The Global 2000 Report* and *Global Future* have guided the economic and foreign policies of the US since 1980 and have been accepted by every President since then. If these Reports are policy rather than statements of likelihood, it follows that to achieve the targets of *The Global 2000 Report* and *Global Future* the world population has to be reduced by 2 billion.... If the world-government-in-waiting is operating a system of quotas and culls, and if... it is a question of wiping out 2 billion... "useless eaters" [a phrase in the Reports][40] to make policy work – ... then we can expect the population targets to be achieved by nuclear war.[41]

Population reduction by pandemic: culling 1 billion by 2037 and another 1 billion by 2057

However, there is another way. War by virus can be as deadly as war by nuclear weapons, and a viral attack does not result in immediate visible retaliation and extinction. The continuation of the high fertility rates means, to quote John Coleman, an ex-intelligence officer:

> At least 4 billion "useless eaters"[42] shall be eliminated by the year 2050 by means of limited wars, organised epidemics of fatal rapid-acting diseases and starvation. Energy, food and water shall be kept at subsistence levels for the non-*élite*, starting with the White populations of Western Europe and North America, and then spreading to other races. The population of Canada, Western Europe and the United States will be decimated more rapidly than on other continents, until the world's population reaches a manageable level of 1 billion.[43]

The official projections for world population have changed since 1980. In October 2021 Worldometer gave the world population as 7.91 billion, and (on the present rate of growth) forecast that it will be 8 billion in 2023, as forecast by the UN – in 2026, according to the US Census Bureau – and 9 billion in 2037, 10 billion in 2057. By 2037 one billion have to be prevented or to die (not 2 billion by 2030 as Coleman forecast), and by 2057 another 1 billion (not another 2 billion as Coleman forecast). According to the UN forecast, the world population was set to exceed the sustainable limit of 8 billion by 2023, and what a coincidence, Covid came along.

According to Coleman the aim is to get the world's population down to 1 billion. In 1804 the world's population was 1 billion. In 1900 it was 1.6 billion. In 1939, when I was born, the world's population was around 2 billion. And as 2 billion are to be prevented or to die by 2057, the cull will amount to the entire total of humankind when I was born.

As the UK's Prime Minister Boris Johnson wrote in *The Daily Telegraph* on 25 October 2007: "The world's population is now 6.7 billion, roughly double what it was when I was born. If I live to be in my mid-eighties, then it will have trebled in my lifetime.... I simply cannot understand why no one discusses this impending calamity, and why no world statesmen have the guts to treat the issue with the seriousness it deserves.... We seem to have given up on population control." On a personal note, I sent Johnson a copy of *The Syndicate* in 2004, and he was therefore presumably aware of *The Global 2000 Report* when he wrote this.

In 2021, the world's population was 7.91 billion, and as I have just said, 1 billion needs to be prevented (by following international family-planning policies) or wiped out in the 2020s to give 8 billion and not 9 billion in 2037. Even though his figure of 4 billion has to be adjusted to 2 billion by the 2050s, has Coleman put his finger on the principle of the US policy of preventing or eliminating 2 billion by 2057 by means of "limited wars, organised epidemics of fatal rapid-acting diseases and starvation"?

The productive world citizens in both the West and the East will be vaccinated against Covid-19. Millions of "useless eaters" can be expected to die. We are living in a time when there is a population reduction of the unvaccinated by pandemic.

Is Covid natural or has it been engineered to cap the world's population at 8 billion in the interests of humankind?
This book examines whether Covid-19 (short for corona virus disease 2019, co-vi-d-19) is the result of animal-to-human transmission or of an accidental release, or whether the US or China or the Syndicate have engineered Covid in the 'best' interests of humankind to deliver depopulation that will standardise the world's population at a sustainable 8 billion; and whether the US or China or the Syndicate have organised a pandemic of a fatal rapid-acting disease to achieve this standardising in the 'best' interests of humankind.

Has Covid been engineered as a bio-weapon to be used against either the US or China, or both, and precipitate the fall of the West or China?
It also examines whether the US has used Covid as a bio-weapon to prevent China from becoming the number-one superpower and precipitating the fall of the West. Or whether China has used Covid as a bio-weapon to destroy the superpowerdom of the US and the

Western economy and prevent the US from precipitating the fall of China. Or whether the Syndicate has used Covid as a bio-weapon to level down both the US and China to precipitate its self-interested world government.

The question: Has the Syndicate engineered Covid to cap the world's population at 8 billion and bring in its self-interested world government – and precipitate the fall of the West and China?
The question is, have the Syndicate (including 'Rockefellers' and 'Rothschilds') used the pandemic to cap the world population at 8 billion and to bring in their world government that includes a levelled-down West and China?

As in *The Syndicate*,[44] I will set out the case for the prosecution and the case for the defence, and you, the reader, will be the jury and give your verdict. I will lay evidence before you, and you will decide.

At this point, members of the jury, regarding the Syndicate's policy of population-capping to limit humankind at 8 billion, I rest my case.

2

The Syndicate's Authoritarian Levelling of the West and the East through Pipelines and Integration

But first we need to see what the Syndicate have been doing between 2000 and 2021, and who was acting for the Syndicate during these two decades.

The Syndicate, 9/11 and the Trans-Afghan pipelines
The most notorious event since 2000 was 9/11, the attack on the World Trade Center's Twin Towers on 11 September 2001 which saw three buildings fall: WTC1 and WTC2, and WTC7.

I covered the attacks in *The Syndicate* (ch.9), in *The Secret American Dream* (ch.8) and more fully in *Armageddon* (bk.1), my second epic poem, which was about the War on Terror in 26,000 lines of blank verse. In *Armageddon* I dwelt on the details of the attack: how Osama bin Laden, operating from a cave in Afghanistan and with links to Saudi Arabia, sent hijackers to pilot four planes; how Vice-President Dick Cheney was tipped off by Israel that they were coming and shut down American air space and the US defence system for 'air exercises' so the hijacked planes encountered no resistance; how the attacks were monitored from WTC7, which housed CIA officers on the top floor; how WTC1 and WTC2 were brought down by controlled explosions after the planes hit the Twin Towers; and how WTC7, which was not hit by any aircraft, collapsed due to deliberate use of nano-thermite to obliterate evidence.[1]

A third plane on course for the White House, which was obscured by trees, changed course and crashed into the Pentagon; and a fourth plane crashed on its way to the Capitol's Rotunda. All the targets were symbols of American industrial, commercial, military and political power.

The attacks were genuine attacks by Arab terrorists even though bin Laden was from a family worth $7 billion and had inherited $300 million from his father's estate, according to sources,[2] and even though his brother had been a business partner of President George W. Bush (Bush Jr), and had helped drive the Russians from Afghanistan as a CIA asset between 1979 and 1989, when he founded al-Qaeda.

Bin Laden had acquired nuclear-suitcase bombs which he planned to explode in ten American cities. At the end of *Armageddon* (and also the end of *The Secret American Dream*) I listed bin Laden's 69 historical attempts to acquire weapons of mass destruction and unleash Armageddon in the US – his 69 attempts to buy nuclear weapons.[3] Knowing some of this, Cheney allowed the attacks on American buildings, including the Pentagon, to happen so that (as happened after Pearl Harbor) public opinion would swing behind an invasion of Afghanistan to end bin Laden's nuclear threat and the beginning of a War on Terror, which later extended to Iraq.

Bush was unaware of what Cheney was doing, and was, "for his own safety," got up into the air during the attacks on the Twin Towers. It is safe to say that Cheney was working with the Syndicate and those who planned to attack Afghanistan, their motive being to implement the Trans-Afghan Pipelines (TAP). The Syndicate had oil and gas interests in Afghanistan.[4] Cheney had served as Chairman and Chief Executive of Halliburton Company, the world's largest oil field services company, and co-ran energy-related companies.

The Syndicate's Trans-Afghan oil and gas pipelines
For decades a 762-mile-long *gas* pipeline had been planned to run from the Turkmen Dauletabad fields through Afghanistan to Multan in Pakistan, and on to India (TAPI). There were rumours that the Taliban were created in 1994 by the CIA and Pakistan's ISI (Inter-Services Intelligence Agency) to guard pipelines that would carry oil and gas from ex-Soviet republics across Afghanistan to Pakistan.

From May 1987 to August 1998 Unocal, the spearhead for 'Rockefellers'' Standard-Oil interests, tried to secure an *oil* pipeline deal with the Taliban, Turkmenistan and Pakistan that would run from Turkmenistan's Chardzhou oil refinery to Afghanistan, Pakistan and India, and in February 2001 Bush Jr began to negotiate with the Taliban to get the oil pipeline project resumed. Unocal now planned to build a 1,030-mile-long oil pipeline from Turkmenistan to Pakistan's Arabian coast. The 'Rockefellerite' Unocal's top adviser during the negotiations with the Taliban was Hamid Karzai, who was later installed by the Bush administration as Afghanistan's new ruler.

It looked as if the war in Afghanistan was primarily fought to build the 'Rockefellerite' Trans-Afghan gas pipeline (Turkmenistan [Dauletabad]–Afghanistan–Pakistan[Multan]–India) and the Trans-Afghan oil pipeline (Turkmenistan[Chardzhou]–Afghanistan–Pakistan–India, planned to be constructed by General Electric in conjunction with Bechtel), and to create a secure environment for these two pipelines. Both Iran and Turkey attempted to get alternative pipelines in place, but at the time of writing the *gas* pipeline is going ahead. Work started in Turkmenistan in December 2015, in the Afghan sector in February 2018 and in the Pakistan sector in September 2018.

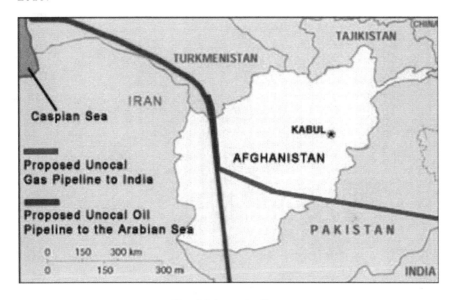

The Afghan pipelines

It is expected that this gas pipeline will start to operate in 2021. In February 2021 the Taliban guaranteed the safety of this gas pipeline, paving the way for a US withdrawal from Afghanistan by 11 September 2021, and also the withdrawal of all US combat troops from Iraq.

The Trans-Afghan *oil* pipeline has been backed by the US government, but Western companies have preferred a 'Rockefellerite' oil pipeline through the Caspian Sea to Azerbaijan, Georgia and the Black Sea that avoids Afghanistan (see p.25).

Iraqi oil

The 2003 Second Iraq War now looks like the Syndicate's oil war.[5] Donald Rumsfeld, Defense Secretary, told the 2002 Bilderberg Group Meeting at Chantilly, Virginia, that an invasion of Iraq would not take place until 2003. And it was not on the agenda. Cheney, Rumsfeld and Wolfowitz were all linked to 'Rothschildite' Israel, as was the UK Prime Minister Tony Blair (who was later rewarded for his support for the Iraq War with a job with the 'Rothschildite' J.P. Morgan). 'Rothschilds' were appalled at Bush's American-supremacist stance of pre-emptive military action, which cut across their plans for a New World Order, and the 'Rockefellers' were also appalled.

The PNAC (Project for the New American Century) groups within the Bush administration wanted to be less dependent on Saudi oil by drawing on Iraqi oil. The $50-million contract for putting out the wellhead oil fires after the invasion was given to a subsidiary of Halliburton, the oil company of which Cheney had been Chief Executive, and following the invasion there was focus on reactivating the old Kirkuk–Haifa oil pipeline, first built by British Petroleum in 1935, in the hope that it would provide the US and Israel with cheap Iraqi oil, and cut Israel's energy bill by 25 per cent.

Reopening this oil pipeline was delayed by the instability of Iraq, and President Obama temporarily abandoned the plan, which has so far not been implemented. Nevertheless, the war seems to have been inspired by the temptation to acquire Iraqi oil.

David Rockefeller of the Syndicate got Khrushchev sacked over 'Rockefellers'' oil, and later asset-stripped the collapsed USSR and constructed oil and gas pipelines under the Caspian Sea
The Syndicate were very close to Russia. Karl Marx was related to the Rothschilds as a third cousin (via his grandmother, whose cousin married Nathan Mayer Rothschild) and is also reputed to have been employed by 'Rothschilds' in London.

We have seen that 'Rockefellers' supported Stalin, had a half-interest in Russian oil including Baku's oil (see p.6) and were behind Soviet Communism. David Rockefeller is reputed to have got Khrushchev sacked after Khrushchev blocked the export of 'Rockefellers'' half-interest in Russian oil from the USSR to China, where it was to be handled by 'Rockefellers'' new Hong-Kong branch of Chase Manhattan Bank, which he had personally opened six months previously.[6] Khrushchev phoned Rockefeller and pleaded with him to go to Moscow immediately.

There was a difficult meeting at which Rockefeller's daughter Neva took notes,[7] and in October 1964 Khrushchev was ousted by the Council of Elders (the Supreme Council of the Scottish Rite in Russia, which came to be known as the 'Supreme Soviet') to protect 'Rockefellers'' Chinese oil interests.

David Rockefeller seems to have been able to go to Moscow, demand the replacement of the Soviet leader for his own business reasons and secure it two months later.[8]

'Rockefellers' had links with Gorbachev. They had been deeply involved in piping Russian oil, and David Rockefeller was behind their asset-stripping of the collapsed USSR. In 1996 Boris Yeltsin's Prime Minister, Viktor Chernomyrdin, was in partnership with David Rockefeller and he sold the energy assets of the new Commonwealth of Independent States (CIS) to 'Rockefellers' for knock-down prices.[9] Gazprom, Russia's state-owned gas company, was sold in Moscow via banks that seem to have acted as fronts for 'Rockefellers' for $294 million, though valued at $3.4 billion; and United Energy Systems, the Soviet Union's power and utility generator, was sold to 'Rockefellers' for $467 million, though valued at $3 billion.[10]

By participating in the breaking-up of the USSR into independent republics 'Rockefellers' were able to pipe the oil and gas under the Caspian Sea to the west, south and east. Geologists have estimated there is $200 billion worth of oil under the Caspian Sea.

Gorbachev was linked with 'Rockefellers', and after he left office in December 1991 the Gorbachev Foundation was capitalised in the US with $3 million from the Carnegie Endowment for International Peace, the Ford Foundation, the Pew and Mellon Funds – and the Rockefeller Brothers Fund.[11] This suggests the 'Rockefellers' supported Gorbachev's *perestroika* (restructuring) and *glasnost* (openness), which may have been a 'Rockefellerite' policy to bring about new 'Rockefellerite' pipelines.

'Rockefellers'' and Russian oil pipelines from Baku
'Rockefellers', who owned a half-interest in Russian oil since 1925 (including Baku's oil), have long-planned alternative oil pipelines from Baku in Azerbaijan (further to part of their 1925 oil deal) to the vicinity of the Black Sea: Baku–Georgia–Supsa on the Black Sea, and Baku–Georgia–Ceyhan in Turkey.[12] Both pipelines are controlled by the British-led Azerbaijan International Oil Co. (AIOC), which is headed by the BP Group (created when British Petroleum merged with Amoco, formerly the 'Rockefellerite' Standard Oil of Indiana).

There are two Russian pipelines, additional alternatives: Baku–Chechnya–Novorossiysk on the Black Sea and Tengiz (Kazakhstan)–Novorossiysk. 'Rockefellers' funded Stalin's five-year-plans, as we have seen, and the links between 'Rockefellers' and Russia have always been strong.

'Rockefellers'' and three Russian pipelines from Baku,
two to the Black Sea

The Syndicate's 457 oil and gas pipelines
The Syndicate have progressed other pipelines. The world is now criss-crossed with pipelines. There are currently a staggering 121 oil pipelines and 336 gas pipelines on the world's continents. The vastness of the Syndicate's involvement in these 457 pipelines can be contrasted with the relatively tiny number of pipelines involved in the wars in Afghanistan and Iraq.

It can now be seen that to some extent the War on Terror was a cover for the Syndicate to loot the oil and gas reserves in former Soviet territories and pipe them to the west, south and east. Oil and gas pipelines have been good for humankind (although not for the earth's atmosphere), but for a self-interested group of people, a dynastic *élite*, to place their own interests above the interests of humankind is less good.

This covering of the world with 457 oil and gas pipelines was another levelling-down of the West (and levelling-up of some of the poorer countries in the East) as the pipelines crossed national borders and helped reshape the world into a supranational world government that supplies energy across borders to all nations.

Of these 457 oil and gas pipelines, the key pipelines are:[13]

- The US TAPI gas pipeline from Turkmenistan through Afghanistan to Pakistan and India, completion date late 2022;
- The IGI Poseidon gas pipeline from Greece to Italy, commissioned in 2007;
- The North-American Keystone oil pipeline from Alberta, Canada, to Illinois and Oklahoma, three phases in operation by 2015, the fourth failed to receive US government approval;
- The Russian gas pipeline from Mozdok in North Ossetia to

Azerbaijan, commissioned in 1983, attacked in 2010, scheduled to be operational in 2015;

- The Russian Altai gas pipeline from Russia to China, filled with gas in 2019, scheduled to be completed in 2022, subsequently rerouted farther east and renamed the Power of Siberia gas pipeline;
- The Russian South Stream gas pipeline from Russia to Austria and South East Europe, cancelled by the Russian government in 2014;
- The Russian Nord Stream 1 gas pipeline (major shareholder the 'Rockefellerite' State-backed energy giant Gazprom, see p.25) under the Baltic from Russia to Sassnitz, Germany, was completed in 2012; the Russian Nord Stream 2 (a subsidiary of Gazprom that controversially bypasses Ukraine and increases Russian influence on European gas) under the Baltic from Russia to Germany, was completed in 2021;
- The US Trans-Caspian natural gas pipeline from Turkmenistan to Azerbaijan, the Southern Gas Corridor began operating in 2020, beginning of the Trans-Caspian section imminent in 2021;
- The US White Stream gas pipeline from Georgia to Romania and West Europe, scheduled to be operational in 2016;
- The US Nabucco gas pipeline from Turkey to Austria and South-East Europe, scheduled to be completed in 2017 but Trans-Adriatic pipeline chosen to replace it;
- The SCO Growth Kazakhstan-China oil pipeline from Kazakhstan to China, completed, further portion scheduled to be completed in 2014;
- The ESPO oil pipeline from Russia to China and potentially Japan, scheduled to be completed 2014;
- The Iranian Pars gas pipeline from Iran to Turkey, scheduled to be completed in 2014;
- The Iran-Pakistan-India gas pipeline from Iran to India and Pakistan, scheduled to be completed in 2017;
- The Russian Trans-Ukrainian natural gas pipeline from Russia through Ukraine (Urengoy-Pomary-Uzhgorod in the Ukraine), also known as the Trans-Siberian pipeline, completed in 1982–1984 and several subsequent pipelines from Russia to Europe through Ukraine, some to the Black Sea; and
- The Mosul-Haifa oil pipeline from Kirkuk, Iraq to Haifa, Israel, begun in 1927, built by the British Iraq Petroleum Co. between 1932 and 1935, operational in 1935 and reactivated by the US Bechtel Co. after 2003.

The financial crisis, 2008–2009
The financial crisis burst into public attention with the collapse

and bankruptcy of Lehman Brothers on 15 September 2008. This triggered global panic. The underlying cause is nowadays attributed to deregulation in the financial industry, which permitted banks (including Lehman Brothers) to engage in hedge-fund trading with derivatives (financial contracts that derive their value from an underlying asset) and over-borrow – increase mortgages – to support their profitable selling of derivatives.

But behind this activity involving deregulation was a massive withdrawal of $550 billion from the American banking system between 9am and 11am on 11 September 2008, the seventh anniversary of 9/11, four days before the bankruptcy of Lehman Brothers. The US Treasury spent another $105 billion in propping up the currency, so the loss in two hours totalled $655 billion. The Treasury then stopped trading for the day; otherwise $5.5 trillion would have been lost by the end of the day, the US economy would have collapsed and the world economy would have followed the next day.[14]

The Treasury, Federal Reserve and President Bush agreed that the withdrawal should be kept secret. On 23 September 2008 Congress made available $700 billion to "buy toxic assets from many banks" – but in fact to replace the $655 billion. The haemorrhaging of $655 billion was a Syndicate withdrawal associated with 'Rothschilds', who then owned or controlled 187 central banks in the (then) 192 UN nations. When Bush attended Israel's 60th anniversary celebrations in May 2008 a group of rabbis connected with the Holy Temple and the Temple Mount movements based in Jerusalem (that seek to rebuild the Third Jewish Temple and the Temple Mount in Jerusalem) warned Bush in a scroll known as the Megillat Bush Scroll that there would be consequences if he did not change his two-state policy towards Israel. The sudden withdrawal of $550 billion and the precipitation of a world financial crisis seem to have been those "consequences".

As a result the governments of North America, Europe and Asia handed over trillions of dollars to Syndicate-controlled banks to tackle the credit crunch and so-called "toxic assets". As a further result, in spring 2009 the Bilderberg Group agreed to create a global 'Department of the Treasury', and the new President of the European Union, Herman Van Rompuy, distributed a paper to EU governments calling for a new region of "economic governance", which would put the EU in control of its member-states' economies.[15]

The Syndicate was clearly behind the financial crisis, which was about more than deregulation. It was about bankers' raking in trillions of dollars from governments and advancing towards a self-interested world government. This was another levelling-down of the West, this time financially, and resulted in a Great Recession.

Arab Spring, 2010–2012
The Arab Spring was a succession of unconnected populist uprisings or revolutions in the Arab world that began in North Africa and spread to the Middle East, toppling dictators and liberating countries. The uprisings expressed dissatisfaction with oppressive regimes and a low standard of living, and called for free elections and democracy. At the time they seemed spontaneous and to be spreading like a wildfire.

The uprisings began in Tunisia and spread to Libya, Egypt, Yemen, Syria and Bahrain. They also affected Algeria, Oman, Jordan and Morocco, and there were street demonstrations in Iraq, Iranian Khuzestan, Lebanon, Kuwait and Sudan. There were full revolutions in Tunisia, Libya and Egypt, as a result of which Zine El Abidine Ben Ali, Gaddafi and Mubarak fell. The only democracy to emerge from the Arab Spring slid back into autocracy in August 2021 when the Tunisian president refused to give up emergency powers and suspended parliament indefinitely.

In fact the Arab Spring implemented the thinking in the Project for the New American Century (PNAC), which promoted American global leadership and shaped the global security system in accordance with US interests. The thinking was based on a book published in 1997 by Zbigniew Brzezinski, *The Grand Chessboard: American Primacy and its Geostrategic Imperatives*. A section of the PNAC's 2000 position paper, *Rebuilding America's Defenses*, entitled 'Creating Tomorrow's Dominant Force', advocated a global *Pax Americana* unrestrained by international law and stated: "The process of transformation, even if it brings revolutionary change, is likely to be a long one, absent some catastrophic and catalyzing event – like a new Pearl Harbor." 9/11 was such an event, and so, in their own ways, were the uprisings of the Arab Spring.[16]

Brzezinski was a Syndicate man through and through. A 'Rockefeller' adviser and specialist in international affairs, he co-founded the Trilateral Commission, a Syndicate organisation, with David Rockefeller after writing about the need for a co-ordinated policy among developed nations in 1970. At the 1972 Bilderberg meeting he proposed the creation of a new body, the International Commission of Peace and Prosperity. This body became known as the 'Trilateral Commission' because it focused on North America, Western Europe and Japan.[17] Brzezinski served as a director on the Trilateral Commission from 1973 to 1976, and selected Jimmy Carter as a member. From 1976 he was Carter's National Security Advisor.

The Syndicate was thus heavily involved behind the scenes in promoting and spreading the Arab Spring.

To add a personal note to the Arab Spring, on 5 April 2011 I sent an email to the White House and posted to President Obama, whose picture was on the cover, a copy of my work *The Secret American Dream* with the list of bin Laden's 69 attempts to obtain nuclear weapons flagged, together with my works *The Libyan Revolution* and *The World Government*. On 2 May 2011, within a month, it was reported that bin Laden had been killed. On 23 March 2011 I learned from Eleanor Laing, Deputy Speaker in the House of Commons, that another copy of *The Libyan Revolution* had been passed to Liam Fox, UK Secretary of State for Defence until 14 October 2011, six days before the death of Gaddafi on 20 October, and was told that the book had influenced the NATO-led deposing of Gaddafi.

Civil wars in Syria, Libya, North Iraq and Afghanistan
The wave of revolution reached Syria, where President Assad, who had inherited the country from his father, stood firm and invited in the Russians, regarding the "liberating Arab-Spring" rebels as terrorists. He retained the coastal strip, having abandoned the interior to rebels, Islamic State and the Kurds.

Syria was part of the Project for the New American Century. Zbigniew Brzezinski argued in *The Grand Chessboard* that to maintain global supremacy the US needed to gain control of Central Asia and its vast petroleum reserves, and that a new Pearl Harbor would sway the US public into supporting the US's imperial effort to establish a global *Pax Americana*. The American plan was to democratise Afghanistan, Iraq, Lebanon, Syria, Iran, Russia and China. They had already democratised Russia following the fall of the Berlin Wall, but President Putin had reversed this gain. Democratising China had been postponed for a while.[18]

The popular uprisings were supposed to turn dictatorships into democracies, but this did not happen. There was a tendency for the uprisings to turn into long-drawn-out civil wars: Syria's civil war began in 2011 and Libya's second civil war began in 2014. Both were still continuing in 2021. The ISIS civil war in North Iraq lasted from 2014 to 2019, and ended with al-Baghdadi's death. But the civil war could restart if ISIS regrouped. The civil war in Afghanistan that began in 1978 lasted until 11 September 2021, when the Americans and the British (except for a small number of SAS special forces) withdrew after 20 years, leaving the Taliban victorious and taking over in Afghanistan.

At the same time all US combat troops were withdrawn from Iraq.

The truth is, the US – and its Syndicate help through PNAC, which ended in 2006 – did not achieve the results that were hoped for in 2001. The Americans lost in Vietnam, and have now lost in Afghanistan; and they look like losing in Iraq, Syria and Libya. All these civil wars were started by the Syndicate, either as a consequence of the US invasion of Afghanistan after 9/11 or as consequences of the Arab Spring, and, in Libya's case, of NATO action against Gaddafi. Their unsuccessful outcomes for the West indicate the fall of the levelled-down West from its post-war world dominance.

Again on a personal note, during events in Manila leading up to the 2016 awarding ceremony for the Gusi Peace Prize, I was asked by a Syrian diplomat, Issam Eldebs, to visit President Assad on a peace mission, and to write him a message in the front of a copy of *The World Government*, which I did. I was asked to write a peace plan, and in my hotel room I wrote out a 15-point peace plan,[19] and was told that I would fly into Beirut and would be taken into Syria in early 2017. The visit never happened as Assad suffered an unpublicised stroke, and for a while Syria was run by his brother.

Russia and Ukrainian Crimea
In 2014 Russia's Gazprom controlled a fifth of the world's gas reserves and supplied more than half Ukraine's gas and 30 per cent of Europe's gas annually. US gas companies Chevron and Exxon were accused of encroaching on Gazprom's regional monopoly. Ukraine is a crucial corridor for Russian gas to Europe (Germany) and Asia (Kazakhstan), and it holds 395 million barrels of oil reserves. Ukraine is important because it is a corridor for Russian oil and gas pipelines.

A conflict between Russia and the Ukraine began in February 2014, centring on the Ukrainian regions of Crimea and Donbas. The Russians removed the Ukrainian President Viktor Yanukovych on 22 February 2014, and Russian soldiers without insignias took control of the Crimea, which had always given Russia access to the Black Sea. After a Russian-organised referendum Crimea was annexed in March. In April pro-Russian separatists in Donbas declared two People's Republics. With the support of the Russian military Ukrainian forces were defeated in December. The ensuing war was still continuing in 2021.

In March 2014 the Republic of Crimea's Deputy Prime Minister Rustam Temirgaliev announced that Gazprom would take over the ownership of Ukraine's state-owned oil and gas company Naftogaz. On 1 April Russia's energy minister Alexander Novak said Gazprom would finance an undersea gas pipeline to Crimea. A trans-Black-Sea undersea pipeline from Anapa, near the Crimea, to Turkey, a joint venture including Gazprom, began in January 2020.

The Syndicate's pipelines were behind the Russian-Ukrainian war and the annexation of Crimea. The Syndicate was behind the invasion of Crimea as Sevastopol in the Crimea is central to the northern shore of the Black Sea and is very near Novorossiysk, the largest Russian port and the largest port in the Black Sea. The Crimea is a base that can protect the shipping and export of oil reaching Novorossiysk via the two Russian pipelines: the Russian Baku–Chechnya–Novorossiysk and the Russian Tengiz (Kazakhstan)–Novorossiysk pipelines. The Crimea also affords a Russian base from which to defend Russian pipelines that cross the Ukraine to Crimea and cross the Black Sea.

It has to be said that in 2021 the West is losing in this Syndicate-involved and commercially-driven occupation of Crimea.

Palestine's oil and gas, and Israel, 2000–2021
Israel's natural gas fields are offshore, and pipelines carry gas across Israel and into Jordan. Geologists and resource economists have confirmed that 'occupied Palestinian territory', Area C on the West Bank, lies above sizeable reservoirs of oil and natural gas.

The Syndicate's proposed oil and gas pipelines have hardened Israel's attitude towards the Palestinians. Israel does not want a two-state solution, and resisted it in 2008 by beginning the financial crisis, as we have seen (see p.28). Area C forms 61 per cent of the West Bank territory excluding East Jerusalem, and under the Oslo II Agreement in 1995 was to be "gradually transferred to Palestinian jurisdiction", but this did not happen. It is home to 385,900 Israeli settlers, and 300,000 Palestinians.

Resenting Israel's control over the West Bank and former Israeli Prime Minister Ariel Sharon's visit to the al-Aqsa mosque in Jerusalem, the Palestinians launched a second *intifada*, which lasted until 2005. The Israelis built a barrier wall round the West Bank. In 2013 the US tried to revive the peace process, but peace talks were disrupted when Fatah formed a unity government with Hamas (which had been designated a terrorist organisation by the US in 1997). There was a confrontation between the Israeli military and Hamas in 2014.

There were weekly demonstrations at the border between the Gaza Strip and Israel in 2018. President Trump tried to get an Israeli-Palestinian deal and relocated the US Embassy from Tel Aviv to Jerusalem, which was condemned throughout the Middle East. The "complete and united Jerusalem" is now the Israeli capital, whereas the Palestinians claim East Jerusalem is the capital of a future Palestinian state.

In 2020 Trump's "Peace-to-Prosperity" plan was rejected by Palestinians as it supported future annexing settlements on the West Bank by Israel and future Israeli access to the oil and gas resources under the West Bank. The UAE and Bahrain normalised relations with Israel, joining Egypt and Jordan. The Palestinian leader Mahmoud Abbas rejected the agreements ("accords"), as did Hamas. Amid fears that a third *intifada* could break out, in October 2020 an Israeli court ruled that Palestinian families living in East Jerusalem should be evicted by May 2021 and their land handed over to Jewish families. This led to clashes in Jerusalem's Old City, and Hamas launched dozens of rockets into Israel, which responded with air strikes. In May 2021 Israel and Hamas agreed to a cease-fire. In June Israeli politicians voted President Netanyahu out by 60 to 59 in favour of a diverse coalition, which is signalling that it will be strong: it has drawn up a £1-billion funding package to strike Iran's fortified underground nuclear sites, the nuclear centrifuges where Iran is attempting to build a nuclear weapon.

Both 'Rothschilds' and 'Rockefellers' are extremely influential in Israel, and the Syndicate's approach to the oil and gas resources under the West Bank in land promised to the Palestinians is behind the ongoing conflict between Israel and Palestine.

Myanmar and the Syndicate's Shwe pipeline
Myanmar (Burma) is exporting oil and gas to China when three-quarters of its population lack electricity. The oil and natural gas pipelines link the deep-water port of Kyaukphyu (Sittwe) in the Bay of Bengal and Kunming in China's Yunnan province. Talks began in 2004.

In 2008 the Shwe gas field was discovered in the Andaman Sea and developed by Daewoo, a South-Korean company that had gone bankrupt in 1999 with debts of US$50 billion. In 2004 it was linked with General Motors, and in 2008 operated alongside the French company Total and the 'Rockefellerite' Syndicate company Unocal.

Armed forces ruled the country from 1962 until 2011, and the contract for the Sino-Myanmar pipelines was signed under this military regime. The Myanmar section of the gas pipeline was completed in 2013, after the return of civilian rule. The oil pipeline was completed in 2014.

The Shwe (meaning 'Golden') pipeline will allow oil to be pumped from the Gulf States and Africa to China, and gas from Myanmar's Arakan state to Guangzhou in south-west China. The Arakan state is occupied by the Rohingya Muslims, and following tensions between the Muslim and Buddhist communities the Rohingya were persecuted by the military from October 2016 to January 2017, and again from August 2017 to the present. There was a military *coup* on 1 February 2021, and the elected leader Aung San Suu Kyi was detained.

The Syndicate were behind both the clearing from Arakan state of Rohingya Muslims (who could not be trusted to live alongside a pipeline) for the Shwe gas pipeline to China; and behind the military *coup*, which has pushed ahead with supplying China with oil and gas. The 'Rockefellerite' Unocal has been on hand to supply China with oil and gas.

Azerbaijan's oil and gas pipeline, Armenia and the Syndicate
In 1988 Armenians in Nagorno-Karabakh demanded that Karabakh should be transferred from Soviet Azerbaijan to Soviet Armenia. There was guerrilla warfare for three years, and after the collapse of the USSR in 1991 the first Nagorno-Karabakh war from 1992 to 1994, which ended in an Armenian victory. There was still conflict until war broke out again from September to November 2020, after Azerbaijan accused Armenia of trying to attack its gas and oil pipelines, especially the Baku–Tbilisi–Ceyhan oil pipeline from Azerbaijan to Turkey. The oil and gas pipelines are in the disputed region of Nagorno-Karabakh, which is inhabited mostly by ethnic Armenians. The brief war in 2020 resulted in a cease-fire agreement cementing an Azerbaijan victory.

The issue is the Baku–Tbilisi–Ceyhan oil pipeline, and the feared disruption to the pipeline by ethnic Armenians in Nagorno-Karabakh. The Syndicate want the flow of oil to continue uninterrupted, hence the long-drawn-out conflicts and wars since 1988. The ethnic Armenians are being treated aggressively like the Rohingya Muslims in Myanmar – it seems also at the instigation of the Syndicate.

Brexit and the Syndicate's European integration
In 2016 the UK succumbed to populist nationalism and withdrew from the European Union, a Syndicate project supported by 'Rothschilds' and 'Rockefellers' who were behind the 1954 Treaty of Rome and shared power in the Bilderberg Group. The UK went back to how things were before 1973, to the days when it still had an Empire – which was now no more. It was importing 5–6 per cent of its electricity via power links with France, Holland and Ireland, EU members, and around 40 per cent of its gas from Norwegian and 7 per cent from EU pipelines. It negotiated a thin trade deal with the EU and avoided reverting to World Trade Organization tariffs that would have added £500 million a year to its annual trade bill with the EU.

The aim of the European Union is the integration of its (now) 27 member states. European integration is the process of industrial, economic, political, legal, social and cultural integration of states wholly or partially in Europe or nearby. The European Union has complete economic integration of its member states through its single market and single currency which caused nationalists to be concerned about loss of sovereignty, and it still aimed for industrial, political, legal, social and cultural integration. The French refer to coming political integration as *"finalité politique"* ('political purpose'). One of the leading European integrationists is Emmanuel Macron, who in 2008 became an investment banker at the Syndicate bank Rothschild and Co. for four years before becoming a senior adviser to President Hollande.

The vision of a fully united Europe conflicts with national sovereignty and cultural identity, and the ultimate vision is of a

Vladivostok

Lisbon

The ultimate vision of a European Union stretching from Lisbon to Vladivostok, and including Russia – and the UK

"common space" between Lisbon and Vladivostok, an EU including Russia. This was proposed by Russian Prime Minister Vladimir Putin in a German newspaper in 2010 in a call for a "common economic space" and economic integration from Lisbon to Vladivostok,20 and he said it is quite possible that Russia will join the eurozone one day.[21]

The departure of the UK from the EU was a setback to this vision, and is regarded by integrationists as temporary. On the other hand, the UK have been persistently obstructive on further integration, and to the Syndicate it may have been a blessing that its taking a step back could allow the EU to proceed to political integration and become a full United States of Europe, like the United States of America, as a stepping-stone to a world government that will ideally be a world democracy. Further integration has been put on hold because of Covid, but, freed from UK obstruction, Scholz's German government pressed ahead with a plan to rewrite treaties to turn the bloc into a federal United States of Europe.

Trump's abnegation of world leadership, President Biden's commitment to the New World Order

President Bush Jr had pursued a policy of 'American exceptionalism', which placed the US above the rest of the world as a unique beacon of democracy, and from a position of American supremacy he tried to impose democracy by force in Afghanistan and Iraq, without success. President Obama pursued a path of benevolence, of "Life, Liberty and the pursuit of Happiness", to all humankind. He reached an agreement with Russia for a 30-per-cent reduction of deployed nuclear weapons by 2015 to 1,550 on each side. 'Rockefellers" adviser Kissinger supported him, saying his impact was "an important element in shaping a new world order", and surprisingly Obama was related to both Bush Jr (his tenth cousin) and Dick Cheney (his eleventh cousin).[22]

President Trump reverted to populist nationalism, 'America First', and pulled out of America's global role in an abnegation of America's world leadership. In 2017 he pledged to scrap the 12-country Trans-Pacific Partnership trade agreement, preventing it from coming into force, and reduced US engagement in the South China Sea – which was a gift to China. He demanded that all NATO members should pay more so America did not have to subsidise them. He pulled out of the Paris Agreement on climate change of 2015–2016, and of the World Health Organization (WHO). He withdrew from Afghanistan by 11 September 2021, so having opposed the Taliban for 20 years America was leaving the country to the Taliban and would also withdraw all US combat troops from Iraq. In December 2017 he moved Israel's capital from Tel Aviv to Jerusalem. In 2018 the Syndicate's Kissinger visited Trump at the White House and said (presumably thinking of what Trump had done for Israel in Jerusalem) it was a "moment when the opportunity to build a constructive, peaceful world order is very great". He announced that the American economy was going well, but in 2019 there was a deficit of $616.8 billion.

Trump met the North-Korean leader Kim Jong-un, who had tested a hydrogen bomb and ballistic missiles, in Singapore in June 2018 for a North Korea-US Summit. It pledged to end the Korean War of 1950–1953 by the end of 2018 and confirmed the goal of a nuclear-free Korean Peninsula through denuclearisation. Behind this accord was the reappearance of the idea of constructing a gas pipeline to bring Russian Gazprom gas through North Korea to South Korea, and the need to maintain the flow of oil from China through its Dandong-Sinuiju pipeline, which in 2020 delivered more than the limit of 4 million barrels specified in the United Nations Security Council's sanctions. Once again, the pipelines of the commercial *élites*, the Syndicate, have led to a warming of relations at the Summit meeting to advance their integrationist ambitions.

By and large Trump reduced American global leadership and further levelled down the West. His presidency could have meant the end of the West as 'the West' came into being following the American commitment to come to its allies' defence. The First World War was a European conflict until 1917, when America entered the war and the ideal of 'the West' (the European nation-states supported by America) was born. In April 1941 the concept of 'the West' was renewed when Churchill and Roosevelt met off Newfoundland and signed the Atlantic Charter. As Trump abnegated coming to Europe's aid, and endangered democracy by encouraging his supporters to invade the Capitol to keep him in power, the future of the West was at stake, and China was waiting to inherit the US's global role.

A populist nationalist like the UK's Johnson, Trump undermined the Syndicate's attempt to create a self-interested New World Order, and there was relief in the Syndicate when he lost the 2020 election. 'Rothschilds' funded the Democrats' election campaign, and this funding was instrumental in securing President Biden's victory. Trump claimed there was voter fraud, but FactCheck has found no evidence of election fraud: 'ballot-box stuffing', swing states stopping counting, postal ballots arriving after election day, dead people voting and so on. In fact, Trump showed no interest in containing coronavirus, and that may have swayed many votes.

Trump has claimed to be in the tradition of Nelson Rockefeller's "Rockefeller Republicans", and he was also regarded as being in the tradition of Barry Goldwater, who opposed the Rockefeller Republicans. Joe Biden has been committed to the New World Order for most of his political life, and is a 'Rockefellerite'. He paid tribute to Jay Rockefeller on 2 November 2013, and said he had been an inspiration to President Obama. Nelson Rockefeller was a Liberal Republican, and President Biden is in his tradition. He is against populist nationalism, and therefore on the side of the Syndicate. The Syndicate supported President Biden during the election campaign, and it has yet to come out whether individuals within the Syndicate were able to manipulate votes in President Biden's favour.

Key members of the Syndicate, 2000–2021
During the last 20 years, key members of the Syndicate in the 20th century have grown old, like Henry Kissinger, now 98, or have died, like David Rockefeller, who lived to be 101. The two families that had colossal wealth in the 1930s, 'Rothschilds' and 'Rockefellers', are still

immensely powerful but their wealth is presented as having shrunk to an unexceptional level.

Between 2003 and 2008 the British and French houses of the Rothschilds merged, and the Rothschild family business was unified under David René de Rothschild, the current French Chairman of N.M. Rothschild and Sons. He is credited in wealth lists as having £72 billion, and a net worth of £10 billion. Sir Jacob Rothschild, Lord Rothschild, has £65 billion (according to Investopedia) and $1 billion (according to Bloomberg). The combined net worth of the Rothschild family has been retracted from $500 trillion or $350 billion to $6.04 billion. The Rothschild family fortune of $6 billion in 1850 has been calculated, if it was invested at 4%–8% per annum, to a minimum of $1.9 trillion and a maximum of $491,409 trillion, and the family is behind 187 of the world's 'state-owned' central banks that lend to governments.

A new 'Rothschildian' generation can be found in Zac Goldsmith and his second wife Alice Miranda Rothschild. Zac Goldsmith is the son of billionaire Sir James Goldsmith – the Goldschmidt family is of German Jewish descent, originally from Frankfurt, like the Rothschilds – and Alice is granddaughter of Victor, Lord Rothschild and is an heiress to the Rothschild and Guinness families. They are linked to British Prime Minister Boris Johnson: Goldsmith is Johnson's Minister of State for Pacific and the Environment (covering China and COP26), and after losing his seat in the Commons in 2019 was given a peerage by Johnson so he could continue his ministerial career. Johnson spent a week at Goldsmith's £25,000-a-week Marbella estate in October 2021.

The head of the Rockefeller family now is David Rockefeller Jr. The Rockefeller family officially has $11 billion. The family's fortune of $6 billion in 1937 has been calculated, if invested, at about $200 billion now, and the Rockefeller Foundation is behind the implementing of sustainability set out in the 'Rockefellerite' *Global 2000 Report* and renewed in the 21st century (see p.71).

In comparison, the five richest American families are: the Walton family, whose net worth is $247 billion; the Koch family, whose net worth is $100 billion; the Gates family of Bill Gates (see p.41, the seventh cousin three times removed of Nelson Rockefeller, whose grandfather was the John D. Rockefeller who died in 1937 leaving $6 billion), whose net worth is $148.1 billion; and the Mars family, whose net worth is $94 billion. Jeff Bezos (allegedly the richest man in the world, having made his fortune from Amazon) has a net worth of $213 billion; and Elon Musk's net worth is $162 billion. Again, in comparison, the UK's Queen owns £72.5 billion (according to Forbes), and James Dyson £16 billion. The wealth of these Westerners varies from month to month and from year to year, and the above figures are a snapshot taken on one day, which will be out of date in a month's time.

The UN's Agenda 21 (1992)
The UN was 'Rockefellers'' initiative and the UN building was built on land acquired by 'Rockefellers' immediately after the Second World War. The UN has always had close ties to 'Rockefellers'. Agenda 21 was a UN action plan for sustainable development that came out of the Earth Summit (UN Conference on Environment and Development) in Rio de Janeiro, Brazil in 1992. Its aim was to achieve global sustainable development by 2000 (the '21' referred to the 21st century). In this respect it was an action plan to implement some of the goals of *The Global 2000 Report*, also a forward look to 2000 and beyond.

Agenda 21's sustainable development involved combating poverty, promoting health and consumption patterns in developing countries, and achieving a more sustainable population – which meant sustaining the world's population at 8 billion. It also dealt with protecting the earth's atmosphere, combating deforestation, controlling pollution, strengthening the roles of women, children and indigenous people, and implementing this agenda with technology and financial mechanisms. Agenda 21 was the UN reinforcing *The Global 2000 Report*.

Rockefeller Foundation and Lock Step (2010)
The Rockefeller Foundation followed up *The Global 2000 Report* (1980–1981, see pp.14–17), written by 'Rockefellers'' staff member Gerald O. Barney, with a report produced in conjunction with the Global Business Network: *Scenarios for the Future of Technology and International Development* (2010).[23] In an introductory letter the President of the Rockefeller Foundation wrote: "We believe that scenario planning has great potential for use in philanthropy to identify unique interventions, simulate and rehearse important decisions that could have profound implications, and highlight previously undiscovered areas of connection and intersection." The report stresses that "scenarios are not predictions. Rather they are thoughtful hypotheses that allow us to imagine, and then to rehearse, different strategies for how to be more protected for the future." There are four scenario narratives which cover until 2030: Lock Step; Clever Together; Hack Attack; and Smart Scramble.

The first scenario narrative, Lock Step, foresees "a world of tighter top-down government control and more authoritarian leadership, with limited innovation and growing citizen pushback". It foresees in 2012 an extremely virulent and deadly pandemic infecting 20 per cent of the global population and killing 8 million in seven months; having a deadly effect on economies, halting international mobility and goods, debilitating industries such as tourism and breaking supply chains; emptying shops and office buildings; with disproportionate numbers dying in Africa, South-East Asia and Central America.

The report foresees the virus spreading in the US, and China's quick enforcement of quarantine and sealing the borders. During the pandemic, "national leaders around the world flexed their authority and imposed airtight rules and restrictions, from the mandatory wearing of face masks to body-temperature checks at the entries to communal spaces like train stations and supermarkets".

The report foresees that after the pandemic there will be a more authoritarian and controlled world which will gain wide acceptance and approval. It foresees an acceptance of biometric IDs for all citizens. It foresees people growing weary of top-down control by 2025, and of letting leaders and authorities make choices for them.

Practical consequences of Lock Step are detailed: advanced MRI scanners at airports, smarter packaging of foods, health screening. Under Hack Attack we might see "new threats like weaponised biological pathogens", in other words: bio-weapons. Smart Scramble foresees an economically depressed world.

Face masks, temperature checks, empty offices – despite no mention of social distancing Lock Step looks like a very precise dress "rehearsal" (a word in Lock Step) for the lockdowns of Covid 2019–2021. The scenario does not overtly mention population reduction to stabilise the world population at 8 billion, but the implication is that the impact of the pandemic on Africa, South-East Asia and Central America will contribute to this stabilising, and so the thinking in Lock Step can be seen as an extension of *The Global 2000 Report*.

The UN's Agenda 2030 (2015)
The UN Resolution called the 2030 Agenda, widely known as Agenda 2030, focused on 17 Sustainable Development Goals (SDGs), "a blueprint to achieve a better and more sustainable future for all". These goals were set out by the UN General Assembly as the Post-2015 Development Agenda which was to replace the 8 Millennium Development Goals that ended in 2015. The 17 Sustainable Development Goals (SDGs) are:

1. No Poverty
2. Zero Hunger
3. Good Health and Well-Being
4. Quality Education

5.   Gender Equality
6.   Clean Water and Sanitation
7.   Affordable and Clean Energy
8.   Decent Work and Economic Growth
9.   Industry, Innovation, and Infrastructure
10. Reduced Inequalities
11. Sustainable Cities and Communities
12. Responsible Consumption and Production
13. Climate Action
14. Life Below Water
15. Life on Land
16. Peace, Justice and Strong Institutions
17. Partnerships

These goals are all very commendable, but missing is a sustainable world population of 8 billion, on which many of the goals depend. It is present by implication in, for example, Zero Hunger (as 1 in 9 of the world's population are undernourished) and Sustainable Cities and Communities (as 1 billion of the world's population are living in slums). Again, the closeness of 'Rockefellers'' thinking to the goals of the UN requires us to see Agenda 2030 as a further extension of the 'Rockefellerite' *Global 2000 Report*, which has been accepted by every US president since 1980.

Gates Foundation and Event 201 (2019)
We have already seen (see pp.16 and 38) that Bill Gates is the seventh cousin three times removed of Nelson Rockefeller, whose grandfather was the John D. Rockefeller who died in 1937 leaving $6 billion. The Bill and Melinda Gates Foundation was launched in 2000, and by 2020 had become the second-largest charitable foundation in the world, with assets of $49.8 billion. Its goals are to enhance healthcare and reduce extreme poverty throughout the world, and to expand educational opportunities (hence the Gates Cambridge Scholarships) and access to information technology in the US. Funding of research on vaccines for infectious diseases and funding of family planning feature in the Foundation's committed funding over the years. In 1999 the Foundation invested $750 million in the Global Alliance for Vaccines and Immunisation (GAVI) to provide a rotavirus vaccine, which has decreased the number of children who have died from the disease. The Foundation provided $4.1 billion for development in 2019, according to the OECD (Organisation for Economic Co-operation and Development).

In 2016 Bill Gates had a 65-page-long plan for the world for the next pandemic. It sets out that Gates would be working with the Coalition for Epidemic Preparedness Innovations (CEPI), which he founded in 2017 with Klaus Schwab of the World Economic Forum, who would announce the Great Reset in 2020 (see p.101). The business plan was called 'CEPI Preliminary Business Plan 2017–2021', and it states that the drug industry would incur no expenses during the coming pandemic, and discusses the development of RNA vaccines (which anticipate the mRNA vaccines used in 2020). The business plan states that Pfizer and Moderna were given billions of dollars from the US federal government through BARDA (Biomedical Advanced Research and Development Authority) and NIAID.

On 18 October 2019 the Johns Hopkins Center for Health Security in partnership with the World Economic Forum and the Bill and Melinda Gates Foundation (and the CIA), funded by Bill Gates, hosted Event 201, a global-pandemic exercise in preparing for a coming severe pandemic. There had been approximately 200 epidemic events each year that had disrupted health, economies and society, and a severe epidemic would be 'Event 201' and would require co-operation between industries, governments and international institutions. The scenario ends after 18 months with 65 million people dead. It was of course presented as a hypothetical approach to pandemics, but the timing of this event is remarkable. It looks like another dress rehearsal for coronavirus.

The Gates-funded Johns Hopkins Center for Health Security also had a SPARS pandemic exercise plan, a scenario narrative for 2025–2028 after the majority of the world has agreed to a coronavirus vaccine. This was completed in October 2017, and 'SPARS' is clearly extrapolated from SARS (Severe Acute Respiratory Syndrome), the first outbreak of coronavirus that was identified at the end of February 2003 in China. Again, this looks like a dress rehearsal for a virus that will arrive in 2025 after the world has agreed to a coronavirus vaccine.

An article by *Columbia Journalism Review*[24] revealed that the Gates Foundation has steered over $250 million to 19 major news outlets, including the BBC, NPR, NBC, Al-Jazeera and the *New York Times*, and 'fact-checkers', which have given no background information that might embarrass Gates during the pandemic and, in the case of 'fact-checkers', have branded critics of Gates as "conspiracy theorists" and silenced them.

The Gates Foundation, in conjunction with the Children's Investment Fund Foundation, pledged nearly £100 million to put into projects funded by the UK government before the controversial £4-billion cut to aid for one year, a cut that put at risk sexual reproduction health services – in other words, stabilising the world's population at 8 billion. As a world integrationist Gates seems to have sought to embarrass and shame Johnson into reversing the cut with this one-year aid donation.

Prescient World Bank and NIAID
To be 'prescient' is to have foreknowledge or foresight, the ability to see into the future. The prescient assumption made by the World Economic Forum and Gates (see p.42) in 2019 that world vaccination would have been largely completed by 2025, before a 'SPARS' epidemic, chimes with a prescient assumption in the World Bank's report on its 'Covid-19 Strategic Preparedness and Response Program' (SPRP), 2 April 2020.[25] (The World Bank is a UN organisation and works in over 100 countries.) On the Datasheet that follows the Contents there are boxes:

Expected project approval date	Expected project closing date	Expected program closing date
02-Apr-2020	31-Mar-2025	31-Mar-2025

The total project cost was given as $4 billion. The report begins: "On March 3, 2020, the Board of Executive Directors endorsed the World Bank Group (WBG) to take urgent action supporting client countries' response to the Covid-19 pandemic." The "expected project closing date" and "expected program closing date" are unexplained and are stated with remarkable certainty.

How did the prescient World Bank's Board of Executive Directors know in April 2020 that Covid would last five years – until 2025, when the 'SPARS' three-year pandemic is scheduled to begin as an imagined hypothesis?

An even odder instance of being prescient is that although China did not announce Covid until 31 December 2019, Moderna together with Dr Fauci's National Institute of Allergy and Infectious Diseases (NIAID) was reported as sending mRNA coronavirus vaccine candidates developed and jointly-owned by NIAID and Moderna to the University of North Carolina on 12 December 2019. The material transfer agreement was signed by Ralph Baric of the University of North Carolina, who was involved in the project.[26] Dr Fauci picked Moderna to be the front runner of an unproven, untested mRNA vaccine technology in the spring of 2020.

How did the prescient NIAID and Dr Fauci know that Moderna should develop and prepare a vaccine for Covid before the world had ever heard of it? FactCheck claims there was misreporting, the vaccine was for MERS-CoV, not SARS-CoV-2. (See p.89 for the full context for this.) Nevertheless, the evidence does not support this claim, which must be seen within Gates' funding of news outlets (see p.42), and the release of SARS-CoV-2 in Wuhan in late 2019 is what we must look at next.

At this point, members of the jury, regarding the Syndicate's having worked for a levelling of the West and East through pipelines and integrationist policy, I rest my case.

3

The Syndicate, China, Wuhan Institute of Virology and Evidence for the Origins of Covid-19

We have seen what the Syndicate and its commercial *élites* have been doing in all parts of the world in preparation for an authoritarian world government and the scenario narratives of Lock Step and Event 201 on preparing populations to live under more authoritarian governments. Now we can turn to what happened in Wuhan in 2019, what the Syndicate knew in advance, and how it came by this knowledge.

'Rothschilds', 'Rockefellers' and the rise of Communism and China[1]
We have seen (see p.24) that Karl Marx was a third cousin of the Rothschild family. Socialism was a response to the long working hours and squalid living conditions of workers during the British industrial revolution. 'Rothschilds' were at the origins of Communism, and it can be said that 'Rothschilds' created and funded Soviet Communism. The *New York Times* stated in 1937: "Rothschild and Marx were brothers in blood and in spirit."

'Rothschilds' wanted to create a central bank in the US, which was opposed by Lincoln and so they were heavily involved in the American Civil War. And they wanted to create a central bank in Russia, which was opposed by the Tsar and so they were heavily involved in the Russian Marxist Revolution. In the US Lincoln was assassinated in 1865, and 'Rothschilds' achieved their goal there by establishing the Federal Reserve Bank in a unified US in 1913. In Russia the Tsar was assassinated through the Bolshevik Revolution, which 'Rothschilds' funded, and 'Rothschilds' achieved their goal of owning the Russian central bank.

The Russian revolutionary Mikhail Bakunin recognised the link between socialism and a central bank in 1869:

This world is now, at least for the most part, at the disposal of Marx on the one hand, and of Rothschild on the other. This may seem strange. What can there be in common between socialism and a leading bank? The point is that authoritarian socialism, Marxist communism, demands a strong centralisation of the state. And where there is centralisation of the State, there must necessarily be a central bank, and where such a bank exists, speculating with the labour of the people will be found.[2]

'Rothschilds" presence in China goes back to the 1830s, when they set up a small gold-and-silver trading business. 'Rockefellers" presence in China goes back to 1863, when they were selling kerosene to China. In 1903 Yale Divinity School established schools and hospitals in China, and these were collectively known as 'Yale in China'. The 'Yale in China' schools were in fact an Anglo-American intelligence movement to destroy the republican movement of Sun Yat-sen, and Mao Zedong was one of 'Yale in China"s most important students. 'Yale in China' schools were funded through 'Rothschild' foundations, and later through the Rockefeller Foundation.

In 1913 the Rockefeller Foundation had founded the China Medical Board and invested in Chinese education and in 1935 it founded a rural reconstruction initiative (until 1947); and by 1937 it had spent over $37 million in China. In the first half of the 20th century the Rockefeller Foundation made philanthropic medical grants, and in the second half of the 20th century the NIH's (National Institutes of Health) extramural funding program took the place of the Rockefeller Foundation, which remained behind what the NIH was doing. Over 150 years 'Rockefellers' invested hundreds of millions of dollars in China. In 2011 'Rockefellers' set up a joint venture between a Chinese company and Steven C. Rockefeller III, a sixth-generation member of the Rockefeller family. The 'Rothschild' and 'Rockefeller' foundations were also funding Soviet Communism.

Mao Zedong had fought a civil war throughout the 1940s against Chiang Kai-shek's Kuomintang forces, and in 1948 the People's Bank of China was founded. In 1949 Mao assumed the leadership of China, and the Chinese Communist Party (CCP) led by Mao founded the People's Republic of China under the CCP. In 1953, 'Rothschilds" banks were the first foreign banks to establish relations with China after the Communist Revolution.

'Rothschilds' controlled Mao with funding, which was organised by Israel Epstein (1915–2005). Epstein was taken to China by his parents at the age of two. He began to work for China's revolution in 1933, and in 1947 he wrote *Unfinished Revolution*, which sided with Communist China. He served as editor-in-chief of the magazine *China Reconstructs* (founded in 1952, later renamed *China Today*), and became a Chinese citizen in 1957. He was also a chief propagandist and wrote Mao's *Little Red Book*, which was waved when the Cultural Revolution broke in August 1966.

On a personal note, I was in China in March 1966 and was the first non-Chinese to discover the Cultural Revolution (see p.xix). I discovered at Peking University that all students had been sent out into the countryside to learn from the peasants unless they were exonerated by having a health certificate. (See *My Double Life 1: This Dark Wood*, Appendix 4, 'The first evidence of China's Cultural Revolution', pp.505–516.)

During the Cultural Revolution Israel Epstein was arrested for plotting against Zhou Enlai [Chou En-lai] and imprisoned from 1968 to 1973.

Mao Zedong with Israel Epstein, who wrote Mao's *Little Red Book* (above and left), and (below) the complete picture showing CCP Chairman Mao Zedong with Israel Epstein (first left), Soviet agents Anna Louise Strong (third left), Frank Coe (second right), and Solomon Adler (first right). (Coe and Adler were also New Deal economists in the administration of President Franklin Roosevelt.)

In February 1972 President Nixon visited China, a visit arranged through secret meetings between Henry Kissinger and Mao Zedong in 1971. George H.W. Bush, later President Bush Sr, also visited China in 1972 as America's first diplomatic representative to China. Bush Sr was a member of Yale Skull and Bones (an undergraduate secret student society at Yale University also known as The Order) as were his father, brother, son (Bush Jr), uncle, nephew and several cousins.

The *Yale Daily* (issue 96) reported:

> Without Yale support Mao Tse-tung may have never risen from obscurity to command China. Jonathan Spence, Professor of Chinese History, was the first to discover Mao Tse-tung's connection with Yale. The Professor noted, "In 1919 Mao, aged 26, was in Changsha, having finished his middle school education. He visited Peking and while there received a serious introduction to Communist theory in Leeteuk Charles' Marxist study group."
>
> Mao, if he was to develop a reputation in socialist circles, had to find a form to propagate his views. At this crucial point the Student Union of Yale and China invited Mao to take over the editorship of their journal. Mao accepted the position and changed the format of the student magazine. It would now deal with social criticism and current problems and focus on 'Thought Reorientation'.

David Rockefeller visited China in August 1973 and met Mao's premier Zhou Enlai (Chou En-lai). In 1978 Deng Xiaoping declared China's 'Open Door' policy. In 1979 the Rockefeller Foundation visited China to rebuild China's medical infrastructure and life sciences, and link China to global scientific networks. Thanks to the continuing investment of 'Rothschilds' and 'Rockefellers' in the 1970s and 1980s China has emerged as an economic superpower by gradually reforming the market of its state-owned industrial sector.

In 1982 'Rothschilds' took control of the People's Bank of China and under their control it became China's official central bank. In 2021 it was reported that the People's Bank of China (under 'Rothschilds' control) had muscled in on London's stock market and then owned UK shares worth $17.1 billion (£12.4 billion), even though it was uncommon for central banks to own shares, and there were plans for a new stock exchange in Beijing.

The Gates Foundation (which has spent $53.8 billion on global health, poverty alleviation and other initiatives) set up its Beijing office in 2007 and has worked with the Chinese government on several domestic projects including poverty reduction. Bill Gates, who as we

David Rockefeller with China's Zhou Enlai (Chou En-lai), in 1973

have seen (pp.16, 38 and 41) is related to Rockefellers, has visited China more than a dozen times since the 1990s and is friendly with the top leaders. He was welcomed by the former Chinese President Jiang Zemin in March 1994 immediately before China officially gained access to the internet. China wanted to open up its economy and catch up with the West in technology and the trip helped Microsoft expand into the Chinese market more rapidly than it could otherwise have managed. Gates promised Jiang he would help China develop its software industry.

In 2006 Gates hosted Chinese President Hu Jintao for dinner at his home in the Washington state. In November 2018 the Gates Foundation made a grant of $499,944 to the Wuhan Institute of Virology for 14 months, the purpose being "to establish international research networks and data-sharing platforms as well as develop policy recommendations for improving the medical insurance scheme in China". In 2018 the Chinese Communist Party hailed Gates as "the Chinese people's old friend". In 2020 President Xi wrote to Gates to thank him for the support in fighting Covid. In 2021 it was announced that Bill and Melinda Gates were to divorce after 27 years of marriage.

The Gates Foundation has long supported family planning services and reproductive health in developing countries, in accordance with *The Kissinger Report* of 1974 and *The Global 2000 Report*. A large number of people believe that Gates is planning to inject the world's population with a fertility-blocking microchip to keep the world's population at a sustainable 8 billion, but there is no evidence of this. He has often publicly spoken of the benefits of slowing population growth through improved healthcare. He has also pledged billions to support vaccination programs, and the Gates Foundation has invested $1.75 billion in Covid vaccines.[3]

In 2012 Lord Jacob Rothschild's listed investment trust RIT Capital Partners bought a 37-per-cent stake in David Rockefeller's wealth advisory and asset management group Rockefeller Financial Services, and agreed to form a strategic partnership in which Lord Jacob Rothschild and David Rockefeller would be working together after five decades of a personal relationship. In 2011 RIT Partners had set up one of the first private equity funds in China to invest renminbi overseas and amass $750 million in the first year.

In 2021 Alexandre de Rothschild took over as Chairman of Rothschild Bank from his father David de Rothschild. In 2020 Alexandre de Rothschild had met the chairman of CEFC China Energy, and both sides agreed to strengthen co-operation in energy, financial services, aviation, infrastructure, construction, food and high-end property management. 'Rothschilds' have worked closely with China since the beginning of 2020, and a flow of Chinese books about 'Rothschilds' confirms China's fascination with the family.

After 2012 under President Xi China has turned expansionist and aggressive towards the West. China has seized islands in the South China Sea, has clamped down on Hong Kong in denial of agreements reached with the UK in 1997, persecuted the Uyghur Muslims in Xinjiang to make them conform, has a plan to invade Taiwan, and is building up to 145 nuclear missile silos in the desert outside Yumen, which can be seen in satellite images (see p.97).[4] And China's trade surplus for the first eleven months of 2020 was $468 billion as opposed to the US net trade deficit for 2020 of $678 billion.

China (through the 'Rothschilds'-controlled People's Bank of China) has been buying American debt. It has accumulated US Treasury securities, and by January 2021 owned $1.095 trillion of America's national debt of $28 trillion (about 4 per cent). Only Japan owns more ($1.28 trillion). If China called in the debt, US interest rates and prices could rise and US economic growth would be slowed.

The events in Wuhan must be seen within the context of decades of close contacts between 'Rothschilds', 'Rockefellers' and the leadership of China's Communist Party.

Outbreak of SARS-CoV-2 in Wuhan, animal-to-human transmission unproven

On 31 December 2019 China announced the advent of a new coronavirus, SARS-CoV-2, as we have seen (pp.43, 70 and 77). Officially it was an animal-to-human transmission, from bats or pangolins (ant-eaters), following research on a new coronavirus hunted down in caves in Yunnan, a thousand miles north of Wuhan.

Shi Zhengli, known as 'bat woman', had led virus-hunting expeditions into bat caves near Nanning, the capital of Guangxi, for sixteen years. She had worked on SARS-like coronavirus from bats, including horseshoe bats, in the laboratory in National Biosafety Level 4 (BSL-4) in the Wuhan Institute of Virology (WIV) since 2004.[5] The research bats were supposed to be destroyed after experiments, and there was talk that some may have been illegally taken out and sold to an animal 'wet market' selling wildlife for food, bats for bat soup. The 'wet market' is nine miles from the WIV.

Every virus has reached humans from animals: TB came from goats, measles from sheep and goats, smallpox from camels, leprosy from water-buffalo, whooping cough from pigs, typhoid fever from chickens, bubonic plague (or the Black Death) from rats, malaria from mosquitoes, flu from chickens, Spanish flu from birds, Russian flu from cows, the common cold from cattle and horses, 'mad cow disease' from cattle, Ebola from fruit-bats and monkeys, SARS from civets and bats, MERS from camels and bats, and (it was first presumed) SARS-CoV-2 (Covid-19) from bats and pangolins (ant-eaters).

However, in the case of SARS-CoV-2 there is no experimental data that proves transmissions from bats or pangolins to humans, or supports a 'spillover' of SARS-CoV-2 from any animal species; there are only strings of letters on a computer. Shi Zhengli and the WIV have had a long-standing collaboration with Peter Daszak, a British researcher based in New York, and the charity EcoHealth Alliance – Daszak is its $460,368-a-year president (besides being a member of the Center for Infection and Immunity at the Columbia University Mailman School of Public Health) – going back to 2004.

In 2012 six Mojiang miners working knee-deep in bat-droppings (*guano*) in a bat-infested Chinese copper mine fell ill with pneumonia-like symptoms, hacking coughs and high temperatures, and in the case of three of them a fatal infection that was suspected to have been caused by a novel coronavirus. Dr Jonathan Latham, Executive Director of the US Bioscience Resource Project, suggested in 2021 that Covid-19 may have evolved in the body of a Chinese miner infected in 2012, but there is no evidence for this speculation.[6] Shi Zhengli did research in the caves and thought that the three miners died of a fungal infection, but would have died of coronavirus in due course.[7] She discovered RaTG13 in Yunnan province, China, in 2013, a virus that is 96 per cent identical at whole-genome level to SARS-CoV-2. It has since been established that she has no physical proof for the existence of RaTG13, but only its sequence information, a string of letters on a computer screen. Animal-to-human transmission of SARS-CoV-2 therefore remains unproven.

Alleged leak of SARS-CoV-2 in Wuhan in 2019, unproven
Much has been written about an alleged leak of SARS-CoV-2 on the fourth floor of the National Biosafety Level 4 (BSL-4) laboratory in the Wuhan Institute of Virology (WIV). The WIV is part of the Chinese Academy of Science, which is in turn governed by the State Council of the People's Republic of China, which is under the ultimate control of the People's Liberation Army.

The first inkling of this was a report by NBC News that there was a "hazardous event" between 6 and 11 October in the Wuhan Institute of Virology. There was allegedly no traffic and all cellphone activity ceased at the high-security section of the lab from 7 to 24 October. Satellite images were alleged to show hospital car parks in six hospitals fuller than a year before. This report was debunked by *The Daily Beast* on 6 June 2021. Satellite images showed traffic was normal. Reports of roadblocks turned out to be roadworks.[8] Shi Zhengli also denied that there could have been a leak. If her RaTG13 virus only existed on screen, there was nothing to leak. However, she has denied many things and is alleged to have given ambiguous, defective or false information on a range of subjects to keep China's reputation in the clear.

Confusingly, there was also a US-funded program at the WIV to work on benign bat coronavirus for five years from 2014, to discover the aetiology of diseases. There had been research organised by the American NIH (National Institutes of Health) which involved gain-of-function work, combining viruses and adding functions to create a chimera.

Following concern by US scientists who formed a body called the Cambridge Working Group, President Obama imposed a moratorium[9] on gain-of-function research in the US in 2014. The White House statement dated 17 October 2014 stated: "During this pause, the US government will not fund any new projects involving these experiments." Dr Fauci, director of the American NIH (National Institutes of Health), who had funded more than 60 scientific projects at the Wuhan Institute of Virology over the previous decade, argued that "the benefits of such experiments and the resulting knowledge outweigh the risks".

Now that gain-of-function research on potential pandemic viruses such as avian flu, SARS and MERS, which might transmit diseases from animals to humans, had been temporarily banned, the NIH (which we have seen on p.46 was funded by 'Rockefellers') outsourced their program to the WIV in China, and continued the work there.

Because of decades of close contacts between Rothschilds, Rockefellers and the leadership of China's Communist Party and because the NIH took over from the Rockefeller Foundation in seeking the aetiology of global diseases, the NIH naturally saw China as a suitable place to continue gain-of-function research.

As regards the NIH's funding of the WIV, in 2014 the NIH made an original grant of $3.4 million (more exactly $3,378,896,[10] confirmed in an email to Reuters[11]) to an organisation "which aims to protect people from viruses that jump from species to species": EcoHealth Alliance (whose Director was Peter Daszak), which then hired the WIV with which they had collaborated since 2004 and paid it $598,500 over five years to work on protecting people from viruses that jump from animals to humans.

EcoHealth Alliance awarded the $3.4 million to three other institutions besides the Wuhan Institute of Virology: to The East China Normal University (Shanghai), The Institute of Pathogen Biology (Beijing) and Duke-NUS Medical School (Singapore). Between 2010 and 2019 the Wuhan Institute of Virology received $814,608 from EcoHealth Alliance. The NIH and US State Department approved the WIV to do the research.

The American NIH continued its program of ongoing gain-of-function research in China, beyond the reach of the Obama administration, under the leadership of Francis Collins, its Director. The NIAID were part of the NIH funding of the WIV. The NIH- and NIAID-funded gain-of-function research in China was carried out by two top Chinese researchers at the WIV, who, like all Chinese scientists, worked on behalf of the CCP (Chinese Communist Party). In 2015 a scientific paper[12] stated that gain-of-function researchers had the means to create a pandemic. Ostensibly the two Chinese researchers were making vaccines, but as coronavirus mutates no vaccine can suppress it for long as there are always new mutations and strains that can bypass existing vaccines. Whether they realised it or not, the NIH and NIAID (part of the NIH) were therefore actually funding biological weapons in conjunction with the Chinese.

It is clear that US and Chinese scientists worked together, and that the intermediary between the NIH and the WIV was EcoHealth Alliance under Peter Daszak, who was based in New York.

The US moratorium on gain-of-function research was lifted in 2017 under President Trump, who had taken over from Obama, with no explanation of the decision and no public debate. On 19 December 2017 the NIH announced it would resume funding gain-of-function research involving MERS, SARS, coronaviruses and influenza.[13] Dr Fauci did not tell his boss, Alex Azar, the US health secretary, who found out from the media. The NIH was now funding gain-of-function research in the US, *and* in China, where there were no oversight or safety checks to US standards.

In 2018 a US visit to the Wuhan Institute of Virology caused alarm. The visit has been reported by an Australian journalist with American nationality, Sharri Markson, who in May 2020, citing a 15-page document dossier from a Five Eyes intelligence source, claimed that the Wuhan Institute of Virology could be the source of Covid-19. In May 2021 she published excerpts from a 2015 book (discredited for promoting conspiracy theories) that showed Chinese military scientists discussed the weaponisation of SARS coronavirus five years before the Covid-19 pandemic began. It must not be forgotten that the Wuhan Institute of Virology's level-4 laboratory is under the direction of the Chinese Academy of Sciences, which is under the ultimate control of the People's Liberation Army.

Markson reports[14] that in March 2018 a US career diplomat, Rick Switzer, and the US Consul-General in Wuhan Jamie Fouss inspected the Wuhan Institute of Virology and sent a concerned cable from Beijing to the US State Department warning of poor safety practices. It warned that after the construction of the level-4 lab between 2004 and 2015 the WIV was completely China-run (ultimately by the People's Liberation Army) and without collaboration with the international community, and that China was doing its own version there of the Global Virome Project (GVP): "to identify within ten years virtually all the planet's viruses that have pandemic or epidemic potential and the ability to jump to humans".

The Wuhan Institute of Virology had hosted visits from the US NIH, National Science Foundation and experts from the Texas Medical Branch in Galveston within the previous year. As a 2006 paper set out, Shi Zhengli was trying to determine how coronaviruses gain the ability to jump from one species to another by "inserting different segments from the human SARS-CoV-2 spike protein into the spike protein of the bat virus" and experimenting to increase transmissibility and virulence and the ability to be airborne.

Leaked proposals by Daszak in 2018 show that scientists in Wuhan, a team including Shi Zhengli and researchers from the University of North Carolina and the US Geological Survey National Wildlife Health Center, were planning to release advanced gain-of-function airborne coronaviruses into the Chinese bat population to inoculate them against diseases that could jump to humans. The plan was to release skin-penetrating nanoparticles containing "novel chimeric spike proteins" of bat viruses into cave bats in Yunnan, and to create chimeric viruses genetically enhanced to infect humans more easily. They hoped to introduce "human specific cleavage sites" to bat coronaviruses that would make it easier for the virus to infect humans. This included mixing high-risk natural coronaviruses with more infectious but less dangerous varieties.

Daszak requested $14 million from the US Defense Advanced Research Projects Agency (DARPA). Leaks in October 2021 of the grant application to DARPA revealed that the scientists were planning to create an entirely new coronavirus that did not exist in nature by combining the genetic code of other viruses. DARPA turned the idea down but the research may have gone ahead anyway. When Covid was genetically sequenced scientists were puzzled by how the virus had evolved such human-specific adaptation at the cleavage site of the spike protein, which is why it had become so infectious.[15]

In 2019 the program was renewed for a further six years, with funding of a further $3.4 million from the American NIH and NIAID, which was under Dr Fauci and is a part of the NIH. In this program the experiments modified a benign bat coronavirus with gain-of-function add-ons to make benign bat coronaviruses more airborne by involving nanotechnology, attach themselves to the ACE2 receptors in lungs and enter human cells, and impair immune systems with an envelope protein from HIV (GP141).

The program was creating a pathogen, an organism that causes a disease and therefore a quasi-bio-weapon, to research into diseases. The wisdom of doing this can be questioned – the Obama administration clearly thought it unwise, hence its banning from 2014 – but out of the first program came Remdesivir, which was sponsored by NIAID, an antiviral drug used against Ebola and later promoted as a treatment for Covid-19.

The second joint US-Chinese research program, scheduled to last six years (until 2025, the date in the World Bank document and of Event 201's second virus), was terminated on 24 April 2020, when the NIH withdrew the grant from EcoHealth Alliance – and reinstated on 8 July 2020. In April 2020 the NIH withdrew the grant from EcoHealth Alliance and in July 2020 reinstated it with conditions Daszak found "absurd". It was to run until 8 June 2021. The NIH's letter to Daszak on 8 July 2020 offered to reinstate the grant if EcoHealth Alliance could allay its concerns as the WIV "has been conducting research at its facility in China that poses serious bio-safety concerns" and: "We have concerns that the WIV has not satisfied safety requirements under the award, and that EcoHealth Alliance has not satisfied its obligations to monitor the activities of its subrecipient."[16]

Dr Fauci of NIAID (National Institute of Allergy and Infectious Diseases), which worked under NIH on this gain-of-function research, now distanced the NIAID and NIH from the gain-of-function research, and from March 2020 Dr Fauci had Secret Service security, having received death threats. When questioned by members of the US Senate Health, Education, Labor, and Pensions Committee in May 2021, Fauci denied before Congress ever having funded gain-of-function research at the Wuhan Institute of Virology or elsewhere.

A research article written by WIV scientists, 'Discovery of a rich gene pool of bat SARS-related coronaviruses provides new insights into the origin of SARS coronavirus', acknowledges funding from the NIAID/NIH for research that meets the US Department of Health and Human Services' definition of gain-of-function research, and on 20 July 2021 Senator Rand Paul announced that he would ask the Department of Justice for a criminal referral of Dr Fauci for making false statements to Congress.

Freedom of Information Act litigation against the National Institutes of Health resulted in the release of more than 900 pages of documents detailing EcoHealth Alliance's subcontracting of gain-of-function research on bat coronaviruses to the WIV.[17] According to Richard Ebright, a biodefence expert at Rutgers University, "The documents make it clear that assertions by the NIH Director, Francis Collins, and the NIAID Director, Anthony Fauci, that the NIH did not support gain-of-function research or potential pandemic pathogen enhancement at the WIV are untruthful."

In an article on 31 August 2021 Paul Thacker,[18] writing about the UK's Channel 4 investigative documentary, 'Did Covid leak from a lab in China?' and its detailing of evidence that the pandemic may have started from a lab leak in Wuhan, questioned Fauci's denial before Congress, claiming that the UK documentary clarified that Fauci was involved in gain-of-function research conducted by the Wuhan Institute of Virology. In response to the denial of a lab leak, and seemingly in support of Dr Fauci, the WIV delivered the first SARS-CoV-2 genome sequence, which enabled the European Virus Archive to design the polymerase chain reaction (PCR) diagnostic test for Covid-19.

The situation is far from clear. There is doubt and confusion. Everyone has denied there had been an escape or leak during the US-Chinese gain-of-function research: the WIV, Shi Zhengli (who had worked on weaponising the SARS virus, the progenitor of Covid-19),

Peter Daszak (who in an email thanked Dr Fauci for playing down the lab leak, see p.62), the 'Rockefellerite' World Health Organization (WHO) and Western scientists.

The denials were greeted with some scepticism, and there was a view that they were all lying as part of a gigantic cover-up, like the lying that happened about the cause of the fall of the Twin Towers and WTC7 (which was not hit by a plane) after 9/11. Daszak denied that live bats were kept in the WIV, but a 2021 video released to Australian media showed live bats in a cage in BSL-4 at the WIV.

The denials were further doubted when it became clear that the WIV's viral databases had gone missing, taken offline, on 12 September 2019 (see pp.61, 99) before the virus started to spread. This was blamed on cyberattacks, but the databases were never restored. The WIV had collected 19,000 bat samples to study, with coronaviruses detected in 2,481 samples. Many were now unsure that RaTG13 was virtual and not actual. By early 2021 MI6, the CIA and the new Biden administration were all conducting their own investigations into the possibility of a lab leak.

The Wuhan Center for Disease Control (CDC) laboratories were moved in early December 2019 to within 500 metres of the wet market. They were also handling coronaviruses. In February 2021 Dr Embarek, the mission leader, led the World Health Organization's mission to investigate the origin of Covid-19 in Wuhan and found a lab leak "extremely unlikely". President Trump said in April 2021 that the WHO "should be ashamed of themselves [for not investigating China in February 2021]", when WHO staff spent just two hours in the Wuhan Institute of Virology's lab before ruling out a leak. China hit back by claiming that the virus was planted in Wuhan by US military officers in October 2019 (see p.69).

Dr Embarek said in June 2021 that he was worried that the Wuhan Center for Disease Control (CDC) lacked the same level of expertise as that shown at the Wuhan Institute of Virology, and that it was likely that a member of the CDC staff had contracted Covid-19. Embarek also said that patient zero could have been a researcher for a Wuhan laboratory "who was infected in the field by taking samples", and the idea that there was a bat infection in a Wuhan lab is still a speculative hypothesis.

What exactly had gone on at the WIV? In 2017 the Chinese Academy of Science, of which the WIV was part, admitted that ten years earlier no one in China had known how to do this biosecurity research. The French, who had helped build the lab, and presumably the US collaborators, taught the Chinese how, and after many clashes the Chinese threw the French out when the lab they had helped install was finished.[19]

Peter Daszak admitted he worked with Ralph Baric at the University of North Carolina to insert a virus into the backbone of another virus – gain-of-function work – and Ralph Baric was one of those who was named when Dr Fauci sent mRNA coronavirus vaccine candidates developed and jointly-owned by NIAID and Moderna to the University of North Carolina (see p.43). There was clearly a strong gain-of-function link between Dr Fauci, Peter Daszak and Ralph Baric, but at the University of North Carolina rather than the WIV.

At the time of writing, a leak of SARS-CoV-2 from the Wuhan lab remains unproven.

Bat-to-human transmission versus accidental lab leak, both inconclusive
As we review the evidence and evaluate and take stock of the data so far, even though both of them are at present unproven, it is not clear that we can eliminate either bat-to-human transmission or an accidental lab leak as the origin of Covid-19.

The Americans knew of the escape in November 2019, and alerted Israel that same month. Covid-19 seems to have reached the UK by early December 2019 as it arrived in Iceland in December via skiers from the Alps and travellers from the UK. It was probably active in the UK during the general election of 12 December 2019 – the date NIAID and Moderna sought to register its candidates for a vaccine (see p.43).

There is no evidence that Covid-19 began in a wet market; this is speculation. The outbreak in Wuhan was near the Institute of Virology, where the gain-of-function work was happening, certainly after 2019, under distant supervision from the US, including the University of North Carolina. A leak in the laboratory cannot therefore be ruled out. There were cover-ups both in the US and in China, the two parties to the joint gain-of-function research.

In the US, Dr Fauci and Peter Daszak initially said there was no evidence of a laboratory leak, but later, in an email dated 18 April 2020 in a cache of more-than-3,200 emails (see p.62), Daszak thanked him for saying that the scientific evidence supports a natural origin for Covid-19, not a lab release from the Wuhan Institute of Virology. In an interview with CNN Fauci said the email had been taken out of context by critics and he had "an open mind" about the origin of the virus.

In China, a whistle-blowing ophthalmologist, Dr Li Wenliang, was forced to sign a retraction of "untruthful statements" implicating the WIV, and Shi Zhengli herself backtracked from the idea of a leak in her laboratory.

Prof. Ian Lipkin, the US head of a unit at Columbia University's Mailman School of Public Health (which received grants worth $1.34 million from Daszak's EcoHealth Alliance between 2018 and 2020), told a documentary by the director Spike Lee that he learned of "the new outbreak" on 15 December 2019.[20] Lipkin worked in China for two decades and was tipped off by Lu Jiahai, a public health professor at a Guangzhou university, who said the epidemic could have been avoided if warning systems had functioned properly. Lipkin tracked the disease through friends at the Center for Disease Control and Prevention in Wuhan. He visited China in January and came out with Covid-19 soon after his return to the US. Lawrence Gostin, a US professor of global health law, learned from a friend in Wuhan in mid-December 2019 that there was "a novel coronavirus and it looks very serious".[21]

Nevertheless, the evidence for both bat-to-human transmission and an accidental lab leak is at present inconclusive, as the US-intelligence investigation into the origins of Covid-19 for President Biden has confirmed. We can park these hypotheses and consider whether there was a deliberate release of the virus.

Gain-of-function research in the US, and Wuhan
Shi Zhengli may have been doing more gain-of-function research on actual rather than virtual viruses than she admitted, but it seems that the really serious gain-of-function work was done in the US, at the University of North Carolina where Peter Daszak of EcoHealth Alliance and Ralph Baric inserted a virus into the backbone of another virus, making a chimera, and Dr Fauci had vaccine candidates in conjunction with Moderna on 12 December 2019 *before* the world had heard of Covid-19 (see p.43).

At the University of North Carolina (UNC) at Chapel Hill Ralph Baric is the William R. Kenan Jr Distinguished Professor in the Department of Epidemiology and Professor in the Department of Microbiology and Immunology at the UNC Gillings School of Global Public Health (see p.xxix). Most of the research in the Baric Lab uses coronaviruses to study the genetics of RNA virus transcription, replication, persistence, pathogenesis and cross-species transmission. Baric's emails to EcoHealth Alliance, Wuhan Institute of Virology, the US National Academy of Sciences and experts in biodefence and infectious diseases are in public records and focus on coronaviruses. They total 83,416 pages. Baric is a top expert in coronaviruses with hundreds of papers to his name.

In 2013 he approached Shi Zhengli, who had taken fistfuls of bat *guano* (droppings) in bat caves and detected a new virus, SHC014, one of the two closest relations of the original SARS virus. Baric had discovered a way of bringing a virtual virus to actual life from its genetic code, and he could mix and match parts of multiple viruses. He wanted to take the 'spike' gene from SHC014 and move it into a genetic copy of the SARS virus he had in his lab. The resulting chimera would demonstrate whether the spike of SHC014 would attach to human cells. This would help him develop universal drugs and vaccines against all viruses. Shi Zhengli sent him the genetic sequences for SHC014 and his team introduced the virus modified with that code into mice and into a Petri dish (a shallow covered dish used for the culture of bacteria) of human airway cells. The chimera exhibited "robust replication" in the human cells – evidence that Nature is full of coronaviruses ready to target people.

While Baric's study was in progress the NIH halted gain-of-function research and brought his work to a standstill. Baric felt his work was urgent, and the NIH allowed him to continue. In 2015 he wrote a paper, 'A SARS-like cluster of circulating bat coronaviruses shows potential for human emergence'. It was a *tour de force* but revived concerns. Baric wrote, "The potential to prepare for and mitigate future outbreaks must be weighed against the risk of creating more dangerous pathogens." The NIH agreed and, as we have seen, funded work similar to Baric's at the WIV, which soon used its own reverse-genetics technology to make numerous coronavirus chimeras in a laboratory that was not subject to the same standard of regulations as Baric's.

It is clear that there *was* bat-engineering going on with real viruses as opposed to virtual viruses that existed in strings of letters, by now, and this puts Shi Zhengli's claims that she was dealing with virtual viruses into question. Two Chinese defectors have said that China deliberately released the virus. Baric says in his emails that it is likely that SARS-CoV-2 originated in animals like all the other viruses (see p.51) – and he wrote in an email on 5 March 2020, "There is absolutely no evidence that this virus is bioengineered."

The genetic code of SARS-CoV-2 does not resemble that of any virus the WIV was known to be culturing in its lab, and for this reason Baric believes that a natural spillover from animal to human is the most likely cause of the origin of Covid-19. He signed a letter published in *Science* on 13 May 2021[22] calling for a thorough investigation into Shi Zhengli's lab, arguing there will be unknown viruses in *guano* (bat-droppings) or on oral swabs, and culturing a virus will result in novel strains dropping into culture cells, and some will grow. There could be recombinants (formings of new sequences).

Baric himself had used bioengineering on mice – and in 2013 he had sent a mouse with modified lungs to Shi Zhengli[23] – and in these emails he may have been covering up his own gain-of-function work. It is hard to work out what the participants genuinely believed and what is cover-up. Baric is a legend in his field, and it is not impossible that the virus had a natural origin in bats and was not the consequence of an escape in a lab.

On a personal note, I have been in properties that have been invaded by horseshoe bats – in one case I was asked to go next door where they were coming down a chimney and flying round and round an elderly woman's[24] sitting-room – and, sometimes with gloves, I have caught them gently and put them out into the wild. From their droppings the majority were identified as horseshoe bats, and some of them may have had a coronavirus, but I was never infected.

House of Representatives' further evidence that SARS-CoV-2 was developed by gain-of-function research in a laboratory
A report by the House of Representatives Foreign Affairs Committee published in September 2020 reached the conclusion that SARS-CoV-2 *did* originate in the Wuhan Institute of Virology and that it was genetically manipulated.[25] It dismissed the wet market as the source of the outbreak.

The Committee noted there had been several safety concerns in labs in the People's Republic of China since 2004. The Committee noted that the WIV's viral database was taken offline on 12 September 2019, and pointed to the likelihood that the release was before that date, hence the infections during the Military World Games in Wuhan in October 2019. The Committee stated, "It is completely plausible that one or more researcher(s) was accidentally infected and carried the virus out of the lab."

The Committee believed that it was a "viable hypothesis" that the virus was genetically modified. It noted the 16-year collaboration between Peter Daszak (whose name appears 125 times in the report) and Shi Zhengli since 2004, and that together they had "led dozens of expeditions to caves full of bats, to collect samples and analyse them". They had repeatedly engaged in gain-of-function research on coronaviruses designed to make them more infectious in humans.

The report states that in 2015 Shi gave Ralph Baric spike protein sequences and plasmids they identified from bat faeces in 2013, and that these were used by American researchers to create "a chimeric virus expressing the spike of bat coronavirus SHC014 in a mouse-adapted SARS-CoV-2 backbone. In other words, they removed the spike protein from SHC014 and inserted it into a SARS coronavirus that was genetically manipulated to better infect mice."

The Committee added: "Given the above, it is self-evident that Shi and her colleagues, with funding and support from Daszak, were actively genetically manipulating coronaviruses and testing them against human immune systems in 2018 and 2019, before the beginning of the pandemic."

In a separate presentation at the House of Representatives Select Committee on the Coronavirus, Representative Jim Jordan drew attention to Dr Fauci's changing narrative as a funder:

> He initially said the United States taxpayer money did not fund the Wuhan Institute of Virology. He later changed that, saying no, no we did fund it but it was through a sub-grant. He subsequently said no, no we funded it but we did not fund gain-of-function research. Then just last Sunday he said, well, we funded it, there was gain-of-function research, but it was a sound scientific decision. And then he said... it would have been negligent to not fund the lab in China.

In a section of the report by the House of Representatives Foreign Affairs Committee titled 'The Cover Up' the Committee set out evidence that Daszak pushed for a cover-up. When Fauci's emails were released under the Freedom of Information Act, an email from Daszak to Fauci dated 18 April 2020 came to light: "I just wanted to say a personal thankyou (sic) on behalf of our staff and collaborators, for publicly standing up and stating that the scientific evidence supports a natural origin for Covid-19 from a bat-to-human spillover, not a lab release from the Wuhan Institute of Virology." (See p.60.) And Jordan quoted testimony from Dr Jarrar, a former assistant secretary for health: "I believe it's just too much of a coincidence that the worldwide pandemic caused by a novel bat coronavirus that cannot be found in nature started just a few miles away from a secretive laboratory doing potentially dangerous research on bat coronaviruses."

Further justification for seeing a laboratory source for SARS-CoV-2 has come from two scientists called as witnesses to the House of Representatives Oversight and Reform Select Subcommittee on the Coronavirus Crisis hearing in Washington on 26 June 2021. They believed Covid-19 was leaked or released from a Wuhan laboratory as a result of gain-of-function research. One of the two, Richard A. Muller, Professor Emeritus of Physics at the University of California, Berkeley and a Nobel Prize winner, said, "We have a whistle-blower, the virus itself."

The virus carries genetic information about its origins. He gave five "compelling sets of scientific evidence" for a laboratory release, and Dr Steven Quay gave "six undisputed facts that support this hypothesis". Quay, a doctor and scientist with hundreds of articles and the inventor of seven medicines, believes that SARS-CoV-2 came from a laboratory in Wuhan after undergoing manipulation to encourage infectiousness in humans, as the virus "has the fingerprints of genetic manipulation".[26]

Quay's six undisputed facts are:

- Covid did not begin in Huanan Seafood Wet Market as none of the earliest Covid patients from the market were infected by the earliest version of the virus – the Covid patients who went to the market were already infected; and no environmental specimens taken from the market had the earliest version, but were brought in by people already infected. 457 animals from Huanan market tested negative for Covid, 616 animals from suppliers to the market tested negative, and 1,864 animals in Southern China of the type found in the market also tested negative for SARS-CoV-2.
- The virus has not been found in an animal host: 80,000 samples from 209 different species tested negative for SARS-CoV-2.
- No cases of Covid were detected in blood samples prior to 29 December – if Covid emerged from animal-to-human transmissions a small number of cases would be in circulation. 9,952 stored blood specimens in Wuhan hospitals from before 29 December 2019 tested negative for SARS-CoV-2.
- There is no evidence of multiple animal-to-human transmissions – in the SARS and MERS outbreaks 50 to 90 per cent of early cases were linked to animal-to-human infections, but the 249 early cases of SARS-CoV-2 were linked to human-to-human transmission.
- SARS-CoV-2 was the result of gain-of-function manipulation because it has a unique figure on its surface, called a furin cleavage site, and a unique code in the genes for that site called a CGG-CGG dimer. To gain entry to a human cell the virus must bind to an ACE2 or CD147 receptor on the cell, and its S2 spike protein subunit must be 'proteolytically cleaved' (cut), and without the cleavage the virus would attach itself to the receptor and get no further. The furin cleavage is why the virus is so transmissible and invades heart, brain and blood vessels. The furin cleavage is not found in natural coronaviruses and its existence proves SARS-CoV-2 was created in a laboratory. And the other group of coronaviruses to which SARS-CoV-2 belongs do not have a furin cleavage site or CGG-CGG codon (a 'codon' being a sequence of three nucleotides forming a unit of

genetic code in a DNA or RNA molecule). Since 1992, the WIV and other laboratories around the world have inserted furin cleavage sites into coronaviruses repeatedly during gain-of-function experiments to make viruses more infectious and understand diseases. Quay wrote: "Scientists from the Wuhan Institute of Virology provided the scientific community with a technical bulletin on how to make genetic inserts in coronaviruses and proposed using the very tool that would insert this CGG-CGG codon." Therefore anyone in the scientific and military community around the world (including the US) who had read this bulletin would know how to make the furin cleavage and turn the virus into a bio-weapon. Interestingly, on 3 February 2020, Dr Shi Zhengli published the pandemic's most influential paper in *Nature* tracing the disease back to bats, but did not mention SARS-CoV-2's furin cleavage site, which challenges the virus's natural origin.[27]

- The part of the SARS-CoV-2 virus that interacts with human cells was 99.5 per cent optimised for human transmission – the commonly used method being to humanise a mouse so it developed human-like pneumonia, a week later recover the virus and infect more mice, and so on until there is a virus that can kill all the mice. In 2013 Ralph Baric sent Shi Zhengli a humanised mouse (see pp.60–61) and the WIV acknowledged they had been working on humanised mice, the technique developed by Baric at the University of North Carolina at US taxpayers' expense. There are reports that parts of the WIV's gain-of-function research involved using humanised mice to determine which coronaviruses could infect humans, and to make viruses that could not infect humans able to infect humans. There are reports that the WIV carried out research on infecting humanised mice with novel bat SARS coronaviruses in 2019, and there was an earlier video of the WIV researchers working on live viruses without protective covering. In 2020 Dr Shi Zhengli at the WIV and Dr Ralph Baric, the number-one synthetic biologist in coronaviruses research at the University of North Carolina, published a paper about their work in 2019, saying that growing SARS-CoV-2 in transgenic (humanised) mice kills the mice and they get bone infections. Quay wonders if that experiment led to a spill through a laboratory leak.[28]

Muller agreed with Quay's evidence and added:

- The absence of pre-pandemic infections in more than 9,000 samples taken before the outbreak is highly suspect.
- In a letter in *The Lancet* on 7 March 2020, all but one of 27 scientists

close to the WIV and linked to its Chinese researchers,[29] including Peter Daszak who orchestrated the letter (and omitted Baric so he could distribute the letter in a way "that doesn't link back to our collaboration"), dismissed the possibility that coronavirus could have come from a lab in Wuhan and praised China for identifying the animal that hosted the virus, but this animal has not been found. (In September 2021 *The Lancet* published an "alternative view" from 16 scientists calling for an "objective, open and transparent debate" on whether the virus leaked from a Chinese laboratory.)

- The genetic footprint of SARS-CoV-2 is unique, as could be expected from gain-of-function research.
- The mutations in the SARS-CoV-2 spike protein are unique, and the spike mutation could only exist following a gene insertion in a laboratory.
- Natural viruses cannot be optimised to attack humans – this can only happen through gain-of-function work.

The above evidence confirms that SARS-CoV-2 had a gain-of-function origin in a laboratory.

At this point, members of the jury, regarding the evidence for the origin of Covid-19's being not an animal-to-human transmission but a laboratory creation that seems not to have been released accidentally, I rest my case.

4

A Syndicate Bio-weapon: The Pentagon, Patents, the Rise of China and Wuhan's Military World Games

If there is no evidence for an accidental release of SARS-CoV-2 as we have seen (p.59) then it could have been deliberately and intentionally released. On the face of it, no Chinese would have deliberately and intentionally infected China's own people in Wuhan, and the above evidence suggests that there may have been an American-Syndicate release of a gain-of-function manipulated SARS-CoV-2 in Wuhan.

The possibility that SARS-CoV-2 was developed by America, the Syndicate or China as a bio-weapon with a view to a deliberate and intentional release or a deliberate and intentional exploitation of an accidental release
We have seen (on pp.45–48) how deeply 'Rothschilds' and 'Rockefellers' were involved in China. Being integrationists they and the rest of the Syndicate were opposed to the populist nationalism of Trump in the US and of Johnson in the UK, and would have welcomed a pandemic that might infect Trump and Johnson and disrupt Johnson's general election on 12 December 2019 and Trump's general election in November 2020, and get the world used to authoritarian control and lockdowns in accordance with Lock Step and Event 201.

It can be assumed that the Syndicate was aware of the NIH-funded gain-of-function work at the University of North Carolina and had followed Dr Fauci, Daszak and Baric (without their being fully aware of this). It can be assumed that the Syndicate was aware of the joint gain-of-function research in Wuhan from 2019, and that its "military-industrial complex" – Eisenhower's cladding of the Syndicate, a description still used today, and its commercial *élites* and corporations using public projects (including vaccine candidates) for private, self-interested gain – had access to American and/or Chinese researchers in New York, North Carolina and Wuhan.

We have to consider all the possibilities and scenarios, including the possibility and scenario that the virus was released deliberately and intentionally, or that an accidental release was subsequently exploited deliberately and intentionally. Did either America, via the Syndicate, or China deliberately and intentionally arrange a leak to torpedo the other's global leadership and economic growth?

Or did the Syndicate quietly organise an escape to halt Brexit (in which case it failed, although Johnson caught Covid), to get replacing the European Union with an integrated United States of Europe on track (in which case it worked, as Germany under Scholz pressed ahead with a plan to rewrite treaties to turn the EU into a federal state), and to disrupt Trump's election campaign (in which case it worked) while covering its traces and blaming China as the outbreak happened on its patch? Did the Syndicate seek to level the West and the East into authoritarian lockdowns in preparation for a coming world government, and to lend from its trillions to 193 governments that desperately needed bailing out from trade deficits caused by lockdowns, furloughing, sealed borders, collapse of tourism and closed offices and shops – to create markets in which bankers could lend trillions at future rising interest rates?

'Rothschilds' and 'Rockefellers', and the Syndicate, had invested in artificial intelligence. They had spent $500 billion in creating a model automated city (Neom) in Saudi Arabia, and they had already got Estonian citizens carrying one digital card that fulfils the functions of a passport, ID and banking. They had invested too much to see it snatched away by populist nationalism, and the virus gave them the opportunity to raise unlimited funds for a world government, implement a new AI (artificial intelligence) program and bring in their New World Order for a self-interested world government that would promise worldwide control of all future viruses. We shall see that automated towns are part of the Syndicate's New World Order, 'the Great Reset' (see p.101).

If there was a deliberate and intentional release of the virus and a cover-up, who was responsible? The Americans (who stopped funding the WHO as its head was "pro-Chinese")? Or the Syndicate (which as a funder of NIAID was aware of the joint-research program and had a reason for sending Americans to Wuhan)? Or the Chinese (who are blaming the Americans)? If the Americans and the Syndicate's commercial military-industrial project were responsible for the deliberate and intentional escape as well as for the joint research, what were the Americans doing funding the creation of a pathogen, a quasi-bio-weapon, in China?

A Norwegian-British scientific report in *Quarterly Review of Biophysics Discovery*, written by two Norwegians, Andres Susrud and a vaccinologist Birger Sørensen, and a Scottish immunologist Angus Dalgleish, suggested that the virus is remarkably well adapted to co-exist with humans and is the likely result of a Wuhan laboratory experiment to produce chimeric (artificially-engineered man-made) viruses of high potency. Commenting on this view, the ex-Head of MI6,

Sir Richard Dearlove, suggested that scientists may have conducted gene-splicing experiments on bat coronaviruses when Covid-19 escaped through a lapse in biosecurity, and if this can be proved China may face the prospect of paying reparations for the deaths and economic catastrophe wreaked upon the rest of the world. He believed the pandemic was started by accident but points to the way people in China were arrested or silenced to shut down debate.[1]

In 2004 the Chinese let a lethal SARS virus escape a Beijing lab and infect nine people. This virus is a chimera – it contains genetic material of more than one virus – and this suggests it has been modified in a lab as a bio-weapon. It can attach itself to co-receptors on human epithelial cells, noses and lungs, and that suggests it was created in a lab.

Milton Leitenberg, an American academic specialising in arms control, weapons of mass destruction (WMDs) and biological weapons, said in the *Bulletin of the Atomic Scientists* that "the possibility of a laboratory escape of the pathogen was a plausible, if unproved theory". He said that in 2005 Wuhan Institute of Virology "initiated construction of novel chimeric coronaviruses" and used "gain-of-function experiments to make a virus capable of infecting a new kind of cell". He dwelt on the inadequate security in two Wuhan labs, especially at the Center for Disease Control and Prevention.[2]

The case for China's being the cause of SARS-CoV-2 is anticipated in the words of Dr Li-Meng Yan, a Chinese virologist who fled to Hong Kong and said: "It comes from the lab, the lab in Wuhan, and the lab is controlled by the China government. This virus is not from Nature." The WIV lab claimed to store 1,500 strains of coronavirus and, as we have just seen, is known to have engaged in the dangerous engineering of chimeric coronaviruses, as documented in a 2015 article in *Nature Medicine*.[3] The question has been asked whether the WIV was trying to create viruses designed to attack ethnic groups such as Uyghurs.

In January 2020 according to a posting on a heavily-censored website and according to the *South China Morning Post* (denied by Shi Zhengli), Beijing sent Major-General Chen Wei of the People's Liberation Army, China's top "bio-warfare expert", to head the P-4 lab at the National Biosafety Laboratory in Wuhan and lead efforts "to understand" the new virus. Speculation was rife that she was sent to clean up evidence of a leak or the existence of a weapons program.[4] Her appointment was a clear signal that the disease was not the result of a natural mutation, as the Chinese authorities were insisting. But in fairness, it could also have been to oversee a report on an outbreak from a non-Chinese source in Wuhan. (See pp.72–73.)

The case against China rests not only on how the coronavirus first infected humans, but on what President Xi Jinping did once the pathogen crippled China. Despite the evidence from Prof. Lipkin that he was told about the outbreak of Covid-19 on 15 December 2019 (see p.59), on 31 December 2019 China reported a cluster of cases of pneumonia in Wuhan. Taiwan alerted the WHO that there was a virus with human-to-human transmission at the end of December, but was ignored. The WHO was not told by China for 16 days after Taiwan revealed the outbreak. On 1 January 2020 Xi's government claimed that the outbreak was non-transmissible and was being contained.

On 12 January China publicly shared the genetic sequence of Covid-19. Xi concealed the true nature of the outbreak until Wuhan was placed under quarantine on 22 January as it might affect China's image. His cover-up for 13 days and delay in sharing his knowledge that the virus could be transmitted from human to human allowed 5 million Chinese to travel out of the city, and some to travel abroad and infect other countries – allowed the virus to spread. In taking these steps Xi knew, or should have known, that his actions would spread the disease beyond his borders, presumably to cover up its origin in China.

Xi's actions in not telling the world until 22 January 2020 made the infections and deaths outside China deliberate, effectively a 'biological weapon'. And there have been consequences. In April 2020 India filed a case against China at the UN Human Rights Council, accusing China of "surreptitiously developing a biological weapon capable of mass destruction". The think-tank Henry Jackson Society issued a report showing that China owes the UK £351 billion in coronavirus-related damages. A feeling was growing that China was to blame for the outbreak of Covid-19 because of an insecure laboratory.

The EU now share this view. On 21 October 2020 the European Commission replied to a written question that the EU has funded the Wuhan Institute of Virology, and that in 2015 the EU paid 73,375 euros and in 2019 87,436 euros to promote research. The EU paid 88,433 euros 75 cents for a virus epidemic monitoring project launched on 1 January 2020. On 3 November 2020 the European Commission replied to a written question that the European Virus Archive project was set up in 2008 to make a collection of viruses available to universities, public health institutions and industry, and has grown from a consortium of nine European laboratories to having partners in Africa, Russia, Turkey, Germany, Italy and China, including the Wuhan Institute of Virology which received 130,576.80 euros between 2015 and 2019, with nearly 90,000 euros earmarked for the period until 2023.[5] On 23 June 2021 the European Commission replied to a written question that the

EU has transferred funds to the WIV, which "was the probable source of the Covid-19 outbreak". The virus is most likely to have escaped as a result of 'gain-of-function' research.[6] This supported Trump's claim that the WIV was the source of the outbreak.

These reactions by scientists and expert observers focus on the possibility that the virus is a bio-weapon, a chimera, but stop short of saying there was a deliberate and intentional release.

Possible motives for American-Syndicate gain-of-function research
It is now time to widen our perspective. From the above evidence a deliberate and intentional release of the virus in Wuhan cannot be ruled out, but it has since been found that China's vaccine is not as effective as the American Pfizer, and if China had begun the outbreak deliberately and intentionally it might be expected that they would have accurate knowledge on what its gain-of-function manipulation did and that China would know better than America how to create an effective vaccine.

Americans had been working on SARS-CoV-2 before the Chinese in Wuhan and it seems possible that the Syndicate, through the Rockefeller-funded, Gates-funded NIH, were working on a gain-of-function chimera – or pathogen or bio-weapon – from 2005, in the aftermath of 9/11 and with fighting continuing in Afghanistan and Iraq; and that their work was being monitored and encouraged by PNAC.

Besides being a possible battlefield bio-weapon as (according to military researchers) the Spanish-flu virus of 1918–1920 that killed 500 million was intended to be, the coronavirus bio-weapon could be used to depopulate the world to achieve a sustainable world population of 8 billion. (In October 2021 the world population was 7.91 billion.) Event 201 forecast in 2019 that 65 million would die in a pandemic, approaching the 75 million thought to have been killed in World War Two.

US Presidents since 1980, and so throughout the 21st century, have implemented the 'Rockefellerite' *Global 2000 Report* (1980–1981), and Obama, and later Trump, would have paid attention to Rockefellers' scenario Lock Step (2010), as would the Rockefeller-funded NIH.[7] When the Obama administration put a moratorium on federally-funded gain-of-function experiments in America, the NIH moved the research to China, and paid Daszak of EcoHealth Alliance $3.4 million for it to continue with Chinese researchers, notably Shi Zhengli, from 2014 to 2019. The Obama moratorium was lifted in December 2017, a year after Trump's election victory, and NIH ramped up the gain-of-function program in conjunction with Dr Fauci's NIAID from 2019 to make coronavirus airborne, attach itself to lungs and impair immune systems.

The US and China were rival superpowers and there were indications of a new Cold War with competition in the South China Sea and conflict in Hong Kong. It is extremely unlikely for security reasons that the US military would have developed a bio-weapon in China in a joint-research program with the Chinese to use a bio-weapon against China. It is also extremely unlikely for security reasons that the Chinese military would have developed a bio-weapon in China in a joint-research program with the Americans, to use a bio-weapon against the US. Whereas the Syndicate's involvement in mounting the joint-research program feels right: 'Rothschilds' and 'Rockefellers' making use of the long medical-funding relationship with China, funding both the NIH and the Wuhan Institute of Virology, conducting a joint project outside the rivalry of the two superpowers bringing West and East together, a project involving commercial *élites*, companies and corporations in which the NIH was being funded by the commercial 'Rothschilds' and 'Rockefellers', the Syndicate using public funds and projects for self-interested ends.

The motive for the gain-of-function research in Wuhan was overtly philanthropic and medical: the NIH and the Wuhan Institute of Virology looking to discover the aetiology of diseases in a funded project. But it may also have been covertly military within the Syndicate's "military-industrial complex" in adapting a virus for possible future civilian rather than battlefield use, from which money could be made and a rival's economy could be set back, and which may also have covertly concerned depopulation, the stabilising of the world's population at 8 billion. As with *The Kissinger Report* and the work of the Rockefeller Foundation, there was an overtly laudable, philanthropic and medical aim, and a more hidden agenda to prepare for a world government and integrate the world through projects and pipelines. The US and China could work together to eliminate disease when directed by a philanthropic foundation, but could not work together to advance military power by developing a new bio-weapon. This consequence of the joint research had to remain hidden.

The US military's links to EcoHealth Alliance
It is now time to look at the US military links to EcoHealth Alliance following an investigation by an independent journalist, Sam Husseini.[8]

Peter Daszak wrote in the *New York Times* in 2020, "Pandemics are like terrorist attacks. We know roughly where they originate and what's responsible for them, but we don't know exactly where the next one will happen. They need to be handled the same way – by identifying all possible sources and dismantling those before the next pandemic strikes." In an online talk on 7 October 2020 organised by Columbia University's School of International and Public Affairs, Daszak appealed for more than $1 billion to support his Global Virome Project for virus-hunting and surveillance. He was then Chair of the EAT-Lancet Commission on the pandemic's origins, and on the World Health Organization's committee to investigate the pandemic's origins, and he has consistently dismissed the idea that Covid-19 has a lab origin, seeing Nature as a "terrorist" instead.

Trump's cutting of the NIH's $3.4-million grant when he heard that EcoHealth Alliance had funded bat coronavirus research at the Wuhan Institute of Virology was reversed by NIH in late August 2020, and increased to $7.5 million. But far more funding for EcoHealth Alliance has come from the Pentagon and State Department than the NIH. EcoHealth Alliance states in the EHA Grant Management Manual's 'Privacy Policy, EcoHealth Alliance Policy Regarding Conflict of Interest in Research' that it is the "recipient of various grant awards from federal agencies including the National Institute (sic) of Health, the National Science Foundation, US Fish and Wildlife Service, and the US Agency for International Development and the Department of Defense".

In fact, its two largest funders have been the Pentagon, which funded EcoHealth Alliance from 2013 to 2020 for just under $39 million, of which $34.6 million was from the Defense Threat Reduction Agency (DTRA), a branch of the Department of Defense which states it is tasked to "counter and deter weapons of mass destruction and improvised threat networks". The other major funder has been USAID, the US Agency for International Development (USAID, State Department), $64.7 million. Together these two military organisations contributed $103 million, and the total US government funding of EcoHealth Alliance up to 2020 was $123 million.

A policy adviser to EcoHealth Alliance has been David Franz, former commander of Fort Detrick, the US Government's main bio-warfare and biodefence facility, who inspected Iraq for alleged bio-weapons in 2003. Daszak has Syndicate connections: he is involved with Jeffrey Sachs (former director of the Earth Institute at Columbia University and an adviser to the UN), who appears in talks and seminars alongside George Soros; and he works with the World Economic Forum (see p.101).[9]

Daszak may have used military-terrorist analogies for the pandemic and may have worked closely with the military, but his official focus was to cure diseases in conjunction with the NIH. The fact that the Pentagon and State Department knew in detail of his work from 2013 suggests that the US military Establishment was aware of where gain-of-function research had led and, no doubt without Daszak's being fully aware of it, used the basis of the work at the University of North Carolina and Wuhan Institute of Virology to create a bio-weapon (wmd), knowledge of which may have been passed on to, or illicitly obtained by, a faction within the Syndicate, who may then have released the biological weapon in Wuhan (see p.86). The Chinese military Establishment was also aware of the gain-of-function research as there is evidence that the People's Liberation Army's Major-General Chen Wei took over the lab at the WIV in January 2020 (see p.69), and Daszak would clearly have been aware of this at the time, and that both America and China were aware of the military use as a bio-weapon of the pathogen that was being created in the laboratory at Wuhan Institute of Virology.

So it is plausible that American-Syndicate funding was overtly to do with the aetiology of diseases, but, given the Syndicate's record, was also covertly to do with cutting China down to size, disrupting China's economic growth and preventing China from becoming the number-one superpower.

The possibility of an American-Syndicate development of a pathogen bio-weapon while framing China

It makes sense to stick with the hypothesis of an American-Syndicate development of a bio-weapon – although the medics in the American and Chinese laboratories saw it as the noble development of a panacea for many diseases.

In an interview with *Speaking Naturally* Ronnie Cummins, Director of the US Organic Consumers Association, said: "Biofascism is what we are staring in the face now. And if we're not careful... we're going to be living in a global state that more closely resembles Communist China than it does a participatory democracy." He was speaking of "the military-industrial complex" (Eisenhower's words for the Syndicate) that "is not just a threat of a nuclear war.... They're designing things that will make SARS-CoV-2 look less threatening.... Scientists, as we speak, are manipulating the SARS-CoV-2 virus to where it will be able to survive the basic immune response of humans.... It makes it very difficult to talk about that.... The globalists now see that they can consolidate power and control from what looks like an accidental release..., do this with other varieties [i.e. variants]."[10] In other words, another deadly pathogen can be released and bypass existing vaccines, the scenario of Event 201 which envisages a new virus from 2025 to 2028.

The World Health Organization (WHO), tasked with identifying the origin of SARS-CoV-2 in February 2021, announced that the Biosafety level-4 laboratories in Wuhan, China, had nothing to do with the outbreak of Covid-19. It has since come out that China influenced the WHO by getting the long-term friend of China, Ethiopian former health and foreign minister Tedros Adhanom Ghebreyesus, elected as Director-General of the WHO in 2017 and getting him to appoint the Zimbabwean dictator Robert Mugabe, China's ally, to be a goodwill ambassador for the WHO.[11] Since then the Wuhan Institute of Virology deleted from its website all mentions of its collaboration with the American NIAID (National Institute of Allergy and Infectious Diseases), which is part of the NIH (National Institutes of Health), and other US research partners.

The WIV also deleted descriptions of its gain-of-function research on the SARS virus. At the same time it has been reported that staff members of the Wuhan Institute of Virology have all tested negative, suggesting no accidental release occurred in the laboratory. Also, Chinese like Shi Zhengli are saying that SARS-CoV-2 has never been found in the world and RaTG13 does not exist as a real virus, only as a sequence in a computer. It is a virtual virus which cannot leak from a laboratory, and there is no evidence to suggest it did.

It is Americans who have been saying the Chinese have been using gain-of-function research. What if the Chinese are right, and America has been framing China? It may be that a cover-up by the Rockefellerite WHO and the WIV is being perpetuated and China's gain-of-function research has been made to look worse than it is as part of the framing of China. It may be that the WIV's computers were hacked by the Syndicate to suggest WIV deletions and carry forward the framing of China. The US under President Biden is now investigating pre-deletion information from the WIV held by NIH, NIAID, the US Agency for International Development, the Defense Department, the Department of Homeland Security, EcoHealth Alliance and the National Science Foundation. The US investigation of the WIV may turn the spotlight away from America and the Syndicate and towards China.

But with the prospect that, regardless of whether the escape of Covid was accidental or deliberate and intentional, the Syndicate (the "military-industrial complex") are reported as working on another deadly pathogen that can depopulate and continue levelling the West and the East into an authoritarian, perhaps totalitarian world government that will bring commercial benefits to the dynastic *élites* from 2025, it is essential to take a close look at the superpower rivalry between the US and China during the last decade, to see if the pattern of historical events between 2009 and 2021 can absolve China from responsibility for the release.

US-Chinese relations since 2009
China sees an America full of political and economic weaknesses, an America losing ground in technology, infrastructure and education, torn by racial and income inequality and unable to co-ordinate government policies to accomplish national goals; an America in decline – as Trump saw ("Make America great again"), and President Biden ("Build back better"). Both the Trump and Biden administrations have followed a 'pivot-to-East-Asia' strategy – an integrated diplomatic, military and economic strategy from India to North-East Asia, and a determination that the US should have a leadership role in Asia for the rest of the 21st century. China sees this strategy as an American attempt to contain China and undermine Chinese growth and enforce the US's role as global hegemon, a position threatened by the continued rise of China.

This US global role in East Asia continues the US military Air-Sea Battle (ASB), which was adopted as US military policy in 2010 (first outlined in a classified memo in 2009). It is a doctrine to penetrate and defeat an Anti-Access/Area Denial (A2/AD) defence system like that mounted by China.

Since 2010 America has been preparing for war with China. In a paper in 2013, 'Who Authorized Preparations for War with China?'[12] Professor Amitai Etzioni asks why the US government began preparing for war with China when Obama, a Nobel Peace Prize winner, was President. This decision was made without any debate in the media or by elected officials.

In 2012, Etzioni adds, soon after assuming power President Xi Jinping abandoned his predecessor's commitment to the "peaceful rise" of China, took direct command of the Central Military Commission, and commanded the military to focus on "real combat" and "fighting and winning wars". The 2010 ASB and 2011 'Pivot to East Asia' resulted in a US attempt to surround China with military bases and troops, and in response in 2013 China began reclaiming islands in the South China Sea, which Xi saw as defensive actions to protect China from America's hostile military intent. Xi's idea was to surround the US military bases.

So, during a period of peaceful relations an aggressive military doctrine introduced in 2009–2010, and reciprocated in 2012, reshaped US-Chinese relations. In February 2011, Obama's Secretary of Defense Robert Gates said in a speech to West-Point cadets that a policy of boots on the ground in Asia was not the way forward, suggesting that China's growing military might excluded a conventional land war and opening the way for bio-weapons to disrupt China's economy and destabilise the Chinese Communist Party's political structure.

It seems that a decision was taken as far back as 2011 to counter America's decline by preparing for a US biological-warfare attack on China through the "military-industrial complex" of commercial *élites*[13] – the Syndicate – and that this was behind, or linked to, the origin of the American NIH's gain-of-function medical work which was subject to a moratorium in the US under Obama in 2014 – and led to the NIH (which was collaborating with the Gates Foundation) exporting its gain-of-function experiments to prevent diseases to Wuhan.

Given this 2009–2011 context of secret war with China, we may conclude that it is not beyond the bounds of possibility that the bio-warfare pathogen was created under US-Syndicate control. Hence Moderna's being ready with vaccine candidates on 12 December 2019, before China announced the existence of Covid on 31 December 2019. This would explain the initial insistence by all those involved – the NIH and NIAID, Dr Fauci, EcoHealth Alliance, Peter Daszak, the WIV, the WHO and other bodies – that there was no laboratory leak in Wuhan. What was at issue was not a series of medical tests to prevent diseases but a secret military bio-warfare program hidden behind prevention of diseases, whose existence had to be denied.

American-Syndicate bio-warfare attacks on China's Wuhan Military World Games and Iran's Tehran Parliament more likely than a Chinese bio-warfare attack on the Wuhan Military World Games
Ron Unz, an American publisher and editor of *The Unz Review*, argued, in an article on 31 May 2021 (which drew huge reaction from China) and then in 'The Covid BioWeapon: Made in the USA, Aimed at China', that for many decades America had done biological research and experiments on bat viruses and that these have been the central focus of America's huge bio-warfare program and US-funded laboratories. And that after decades of creating, modifying and stockpiling toxic agents and mass-produced bottle-ready biological weapons (whose funding in the 1950s was equivalent to the funding for American nuclear weapons), America – perhaps a rogue element associated with the Trump administration – was behind the outbreak of SARS-CoV-2 in China.

Unz points out that after China announced the outbreak of Covid-19 on 22 January 2020, by late February 2020 Iran had become the second epicentre of the global outbreak. America had assassinated Iran's top military commander on 2 January 2020, and a few weeks later a large number of Iran's ruling *élites* caught Covid – 10 per cent of the entire Iranian Parliament were infected, and a dozen of its officials and politicians died – and the Holy City of Qom was badly affected. Since then, as we saw on p.33, Israel's government has claimed there is no diplomatic solution to ending Iran's nuclear program and has set up a £1-billion funding package for strikes on Iran's nuclear sites. The overall situation suggests American bio-warfare attacks on China and Iran, Unz says.

The American bio-warfare attacks on China and Iran, if they happened, were probably a rogue operation orchestrated, Unz suggests, by the Deep State Neocons in the Trump administration, followers of Mike Pompeo or John Bolton, admirers of PNAC during 9/11, both of whom have contacts within the Syndicate. There is no evidence or suggestion that either of these two were personally implicated.

We have seen (on p.69) that the mainstream Syndicate of 'Rothschilds' and 'Rockefellers' was opposed to Trump and Johnson as they put nationalism above the authoritarian New World Order the Syndicate wanted to put in place. One release may have targeted all their opponents: China, Iran, Trump's 'America First', and Brexit.

Unz focuses on the staging in Wuhan of the Military World Games on 18 October 2019. The 284-strong contingent of American military servicemen visiting Wuhan would have provided perfect cover for America "to slip a couple of operatives into the group, and have them release the virus in the city". Unz asks, "What would Americans think if 300 Chinese military officers paid an extended visit to Chicago and immediately afterwards a mysterious, deadly viral epidemic suddenly broke out in that city?"

The outbreaks in China and Iran cannot be attributed to China. It is certainly odd to think that a Chinese working in a Wuhan laboratory would release in China a virus perfectly designed to damage the Chinese economy. Or to damage China's ally, Iran. Furthermore, no one in the Chinese government was aware of the outbreak until the end of December 2019.

But in November 2019 the US Defense Intelligence Agency (DIA) had distributed a secret report to Government officials warning that a "cataclysmic" disease outbreak was taking place in Wuhan. Israeli TV independently confirmed that the report existed and had been distributed to NATO allies and Israel. The DIA report was prepared in "the second week of November".[14]

On 23 June 2021 Representative Mike Gallagher, speaking in Congress, urged the Biden administration to investigate the Wuhan

Military World Games for over 9,000 athletes from 109 countries as a Covid-spreading event. A city of 15 million was in lockdown, "to make it easier for the Games' participants to get around". Many of the athletes said Wuhan looked "like a ghost town", and in early 2020 athletes from France, Germany, Italy and Luxembourg claimed they had contracted Covid-19 at the Games and had spread it to their loved ones. Athletes from Brazil and Sweden were also infected. Gallagher wanted to know if the group of 284 American athletes and staff[15] were tested for antibodies, and if the virus had spread at their bases when they returned to US soil.

The assumption behind the question was that the Chinese had allowed the Games to proceed when Covid was abroad in Wuhan – and perhaps that the military athletes of the West (of North America and Europe) had been targeted. However, Unz's suggestion that an American rogue bio-warfare attack happened at the Games is arguably a more credible alternative as China would not want to release a virus in Wuhan that would damage the Chinese economy. At the time of writing there has been silence about American athletes who had Covid, amid allegations that some had been told to say nothing, which suggests an American-rogue rather than a Chinese initiative. It is not known how many Chinese athletes fell ill. Wuhan could have been a "ghost town" after an attack on the metro, which could have infected many of the participants in the Games, who were out and about outside their athletic events.

Before we look at the Wuhan Military World Games in greater detail we need to set out more fully why an American-Syndicate release of SARS-CoV-2 in Wuhan is more likely than a Chinese release. We have seen (on p.76) that America and the Syndicate began to prepare for the contingency of a war with China in 2010, and that China got wind of the plan and countered with its own preparations for defence in 2012. Both sides knew that nuclear warfare was not an option as it would lead to immediate retaliation and destruction. Both sides would therefore have a motive to prepare for secret biological toxins, pathogen bio-weapons.

However, obvious questions suggest the likelihood of an American-Syndicate release in China. Would China share its military biological research, as distinct from its medical biological research, with Americans in Wuhan? This is unlikely; Chinese military research would be hidden from all Americans. Would the US share its military biological research, as distinct from its medical biological research, with the Chinese in Wuhan? Again, this is unlikely; America's actual military biological research would be hidden from all Chinese at Fort Detrick. But if Obama shut down America's military and medical biological research in 2014 and the only way it could be continued would be to hide America's military biological research behind and within a joint US-China medical project on diseases in Wuhan, would the US and the Syndicate take this route? If the military biological bio-warfare element was hidden from the Chinese while Americans and Chinese worked together to prevent diseases, perhaps. It is not impossible.

And this is where the Syndicate's commercial approach may have given the US military biological bio-warfare project some cover. It is possible that the US Pentagon and State Department did not just fund Daszak's EcoHealth Alliance. It is possible that the US outsourced its military biological bio-warfare development program via the NIH to Daszak/the Syndicate for three years, and hid it behind EcoHealth's work on the aetiology of diseases, until 2017. It is possible that as progress was being made, the US military were happy for the medical program to be renewed in 2019. The overt program was to advance US-Chinese understanding of the aetiology of diseases, and the covert, hidden program within it was gain-of-function manipulation of bat coronaviruses, not just to prevent diseases but to create a military biological bio-warfare weapon.

Further obvious questions reinforce the likelihood of an American-Syndicate release. Could Covid have been deliberately and intentionally leaked by an American or Americans, or their agent or agents, in the Wuhan Institute of Virology? Possibly, but this is unlikely as it would draw attention to the collaboration. Could Covid have been deliberately and intentionally leaked by a Chinese in the Wuhan Institute of Virology? Possibly, but this is unlikely as it would infect Chinese and be self-defeating for China. A Chinese might have leaked it in America, but not in Wuhan. Could Covid have been deliberately and intentionally leaked by an American or Americans in Wuhan City as distinct from the Wuhan Institute of Virology? Possibly. This is a more likely scenario than a leak in the Wuhan Institute of Virology.

In a sense, the question as to whether the initial leak or release was accidental or deliberate and intentional is not of crucial importance, for once the leak (or release) had taken place, the pathogen was out there and could be reinforced by deliberate and intentional releases and could be treated in the same way as if it had been deliberately released. The scenarios could be urgently activated: Lock Step (2010, the year in which the US began to prepare for a war with China) and Event 201 (2019, the year of the renewal of the gain-of-function program – and, indeed, the month of the outbreak of SARS-CoV-2 in

Wuhan). 'FactCheck', which had received large sums of money from the Gates Foundation, would deny that Event 201 was anything but an imaginary hypothesis whose similarity to actual events was completely coincidental. Such a reaction is predictable and is by the by.

Looking back on the evidence so far, we can see that no experimental data supports a 'spillover' of SARS-CoV-2 from any animal species including bats, even though Baric still considers this a possibility. Even though most other diseases originated in animals (see p.51), SARS-CoV-2 is a theoretical construction. In fact, an emerging disease is only recognised as such when it has reached an epidemic stage. Before that the virus *circulates* in the population and sporadic cases are not recognised as a novel disease but are confused with a known disease. Hence Baric's title of his 2015 paper, 'A SARS-like cluster of circulating bat coronaviruses shows potential for human emergence'. This is a latency or stuttering phase during which the disease is uncharacterised and the virus is undetected. A novel emerging disease cannot be identified until the epidemic threshold of the outbreak has been reached and the epidemic has started.

The argument that Covid-19 began from a circulation model rather than a spillover model has been made in a paper by Roger Frutos and others, 'Understanding the origin of COVID-19 requires to change the paradigm on zoonotic emergence from the spillover to the circulation model'.[16]

We now come to the event in Wuhan that fits this circulation model. It leaves out the Wuhan Institute of Virology and still assumes a deliberately and intentionally released military biological bio-weapon that was released by the American Syndicate in Wuhan at the Wuhan Military World Games.[17]

A possible bio-weapon attack at Wuhan's Military World Games, 18–27 October 2019

Following the 2010 ASB and the 2011 'Pivot to East Asia', the US has acted covertly, concealing its intentions from China, Congress and its electorate and working with the Syndicate, and has attempted to destabilise China. Something seems to have happened during the 7th Military World Games hosted by the People's Republic of China from 18 to 27 October 2019 in Wuhan, while Trump was still President.

The Games were titled 'Military Glory, World Peace' and 9,308 military delegates and athletes from 109 countries competed in 27 sports at 35 event venues. All the athletes took part in the opening and closing ceremonies at the Wuhan Sports Center (Zhuankou Stadium, with 54,000 seats), where the swimming and diving and women's volleyball were also held. Twenty-five countries sent more than 100 athletes. The Chinese government used 236,000 volunteers, 90 hotels and 2,000 drivers.

172 US athletes took part within a travelling group of 284 Americans who included administrators, doctors, coaches, trainers, equipment technicians and nutritionists. All the Americans stayed in the Wuhan Oriental Hotel 300 metres from Huanan Seafood Wholesale Market, where the pandemic is alleged to have begun, and eight miles from the Wuhan Institute of Virology.

Athletes travelled between the event venues on the Wuhan metro, which has 240 stations. Five of its nine lines are completely underground. Experiments in the New York City subway showed that an enclosed underground system is ideal for releasing a pathogen as it concentrates the agent and increases exposure time.

President Xi Jinping attended the opening ceremony of the Military World Games on 18 October 2019, the very same day as the opening of Event 201, sponsored by the Gates Foundation. The Wuhan metro would have been an ideal place for a biological attack aimed at initiating a Chinese pandemic that would destabilise Chinese society, undermine its political leaders and arrest China's growth. The pathogen could have been disguised as medical supplies, tinctures and ointments needed for the Games and could have been covertly shipped along with the equipment the athletes would need to use.[18]

Athletes and support staff fell ill in Wuhan during the Games. French, German and Italian athletes suffered Covid-like symptoms before Covid had been heard of (coughing and diarrhoea), as did 60 of Canada's 114 athletes and support staff. The French military airport to which the French athletes returned was the first site in France found to be infected by Covid.

An academic in charge of collecting data told a Chinese health journal that there were two cases of Covid on 14 and 21 November. Connor Reed, a 25-year-old Briton teaching in Wuhan, told the *Mail Online* that he fell ill on 25 November and his sickness was confirmed as Covid-19 two months later.

Documented cases of Covid in Wuhan in December 2019 suggest human-to-human transmission between mid-October to mid-November. What Lipkin was told (see p.58) could have been part of this same pattern.

We have seen (pp.58, 78) that the US secretly notified Israel of the outbreak of Covid in November 2019, and NATO including France and Canada received this same secret notification. The US military knew about the outbreak in November and appeared indifferent, and

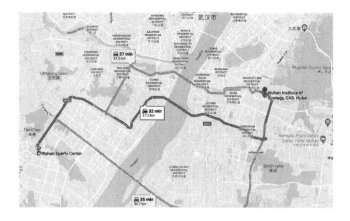

(Top) Map showing the distance (27.5 kms, 32 mins driving) between Wuhan Sports Center and the Wuhan Institute of Virology; (middle) map showing the distance (15.8 kms, 24 mins driving) between the athletes' village and the Wuhan Institute of Virology; and (bottom) map showing the distance (21.7 kms, 28 mins driving) between the Wuhan Sports Center and the athletes' village

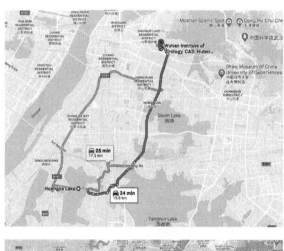

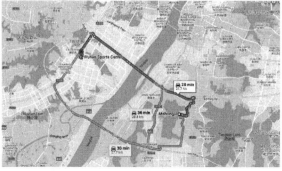

some infected US athletes were ordered to remain silent. Reports by US participants were removed from the internet in January 2020. In many ways the American cover-up mirrored the Chinese cover-up at the Wuhan Institute of Virology.

Understanding the outbreak of SARS-CoV-2 in Wuhan not as animal transmission or an accidental laboratory leak, but as a bio-weapon attempt to stop the rise of China

The Chinese New Year (Spring Festival) celebrations which began on 25 January 2020 have been seen as spreading the virus. An article in *The Lancet* says the first patient was infected on 1 December 2019, 56 days before the Chinese New Year.[19] A news article suggests the first Covid infection can be traced back to 17 November 2019.[20] These dates fit better with the Wuhan Military World Games than with the Chinese New Year (Spring Festival).

A 14-day incubation period from 27 October 2019, the last day of the Wuhan Military World Games, suggests that the first Chinese to have Covid would be identified on 10 November, which is confirmed by press reports. No athletes were in contact with pangolins or ate bat soup, no one went into the BSL-4 laboratories of the Wuhan Institute of Virology, so whether there was only a virtual virus on screen that could not escape was neither here nor there.

But a military biological bio-weapon released during the Wuhan Military World Games would account for all the subsequent evidence. A US-Syndicate attempt to disrupt China's growth and prevent the further rise of China and the fall of the West would seem to be the motive for the attack, if there was one. The discredited report that there was a "hazardous event" in the Wuhan Institute of Virology between 6 and 10 October and 14 and 19 October 2019, and the reports of roadblocks and full hospital car parks on satellite images, would be irrelevant if a bio-weapon was released before or during the Wuhan Military World Games, which began on 18 October. The possibility of animal-to-human transmission and of a lab leak at the Wuhan Institute of Virology would be set to one side if there was a deliberate and intentional release on the Wuhan metro.

At present there is no direct evidence, just Covid-like symptoms among many athletes and support staff – and a world pandemic.

Patents that prove SARS-CoV-2 was manufactured in the US from 2002, data that would have assisted an American-Syndicate bio-weapon

Hundreds of US patents show that SARS-CoV-2 is a man-made virus that has been tinkered with for decades. Much of the research was funded by the National Institute of Allergy and Infectious Diseases (NIAID) under the direction of Dr Anthony Fauci, and may have grown out of attempts to develop an HIV vaccine.[21]

The patents were found by Dr David Martin, whose company M·CAM International Innovation Risk Management is a business that has tracked patent applications and approvals since 1988. The company is used in underwriting for 168 countries, and has monitored biological and chemical weapons violations for the US Government following the anthrax scare in 2001. Martin says that more than 4,000 patents relate to the SARS coronavirus, and his company has reviewed the research involving manipulation of coronaviruses that gave rise to SARS.

Martin found a list of 120 patents relating to features associated with SARS-CoV-2, and these are referred to in two scientific papers.[22] Seventy-three of these patents describe the features that are said to be unique to SARS-CoV-2, and all were issued between 2008 and 2019. Numerous patents detail manipulation of the polybasic cleavage site, the spike protein and ACE2 binding, all three of which are unique features of SARS-CoV-2. When Baric published a paper in 2015 warning that SARS coronavirus was "poised for human emergence", the virus he was apparently referring to had been patented for commercial exploitation 73 times.

If the Syndicate's "military-industrial complex" had wanted to track the medical progress being made by the manipulations that created these three unique features of SARS-CoV-2 with a view to turning them into a military bio-weapon, then penetrating David Martin's research into the manipulation of coronavirus and the 73 patents associated with it would have immeasurably eased their task as they would have had an overview of ongoing American patented gain-of-function research. They knew of Martin's work on biological and chemical weapons violations for the US government, and without his being aware of it they could have remotely monitored his work on the manipulation of coronaviruses.

These patents go back to 1999 when coronavirus patients were in veterinary sciences (on diseases of farm and domestic animals), for example Ralph Baric's work on rabbit cardiomyopathy. The first coronavirus to use the S1 spike protein (for canine coronavirus) was patented by Pfizer in January 2000: American patent 6372224. It can be inspected on the United States Patent and Trademark Office's website.

In 1999 Dr Fauci of NIAID found the malleability of coronavirus to be a potential candidate for HIV vaccines, and he funded research at the University of North Carolina, Chapel Hill, where Baric has a laboratory, to create "an infectious replication-defective coronavirus" targeted for human lung epithelium (tissue), i.e. that attacks human lung cells. Patent 7279327 for this replication-defective coronavirus that attacks human cells was filed on 19 April 2002. It was issued on 9 October 2007, and it has three inventors listed: Kristopher M. Curtis, Boyd Yount and Ralph S. Baric.[23] It shows that the ACE receptor, the ACE2 binding domain and the S1 spike protein and other details of SARS-CoV-2 were engineered and could be synthetically modified by using gene-sequencing technologies. In other words, Martin says, "We [i.e. the US] made SARS" – or rather, Dr Fauci and the University of North Carolina did.

In the autumn of 2001, following 9/11 and the anthrax attacks, an "enormous number" of bacterial and viral pathogens were patented to the NIAID, the US Army Medical Research Institute of Infectious Diseases (USAMRIID) and their international collaborators. It is clear from this that a 2001 coronavirus was being seen not just as a vaccine vector for HIV, but as a candidate to be used as a biological weapon. Martin pointed this out before the outbreak of SARS in China in February 2003. Did Martin's pointing this out result in the Syndicate's remotely monitoring his company's research without his knowledge?

In April 2003, the US Centers for Disease Control and Prevention (CDC) tried to file US patent 7220852 for the entire gene sequence of the SARS coronavirus. This would have violated 35 US Code Section 101 (35 U.S.C. § 101),[24] which states that a naturally occurring substance cannot be patented. Two more patents associated with it, US patents 46592703P and 7776521, covered the gene sequence of SARS coronavirus and the means of detecting it by using RT PCR testing. Owning these three patents would give the owner complete control over the virus and its detection, all scientific and message control. The US Patent and Trademark Office rejected the first patent as it was 99.9 per cent identical to a coronavirus in the public domain.

In 2007 the CDC paid a fee to keep the patent private, and in 2007 the patent examiner's rejection was overruled and the CDC secured this patent. According to Martin, the gene sequence filed by CDC in 2003, 2005 and 2006 is 89 to 99 per cent identical to the gene sequence identified as SARS-CoV-2.

On 28 April 2003, three days after the CDC filed US patent 7220852, which was not passed until 2007, Sequoia Pharmaceuticals (founded in 2002, investors include the Wellcome Trust) filed US patent 7151163 on an antiviral agent to treat and control infectious coronavirus. So the treatment was patented in 2003 and the disease to be treated was patented in 2007.

On 5 June 2008 Ablynx (now part of Sanofi) filed a series of patents detailing the three features of SARS-CoV-2: the polybasic cleavage site, the spike protein and the ACE2 receptor binding domain. The first of these patents was issued on 24 November 2015. Between 2016 and 2019 a number of patents were issued to Ablynx and Sanofi covering the RNA strands and the sub-components of the gene strands.

Between 2008 and 2017 other patents were filed by: Crucell, Rubius Therapeutics, Children's Medical Center Corporation, Ludwig-Maximilians-Universität in München (Munich), Protein Sciences Corporation, Dana-Farber Cancer Institute, University of Iowa, University of Hong Kong and the Chinese National Human Genome Center in Shanghai.

A Rothschild's testing method for "Covid-19" first filed for patenting in 2015
There has been considerable interest in a vaccine manufacturer's testing method for Covid-19 patented in 2015. The patent numbered US20200279585A1 is headed on a Dutch website "System and Method for Testing Covid-19", and it is patented "with a Dutch Government organisation" in the US by Richard Rothschild with a "Prioriteitsdatum" (Dutch for 'priority date') of 2015-10-13: 13 October 2015. (See picture below.)[25] Was a testing method for Covid-19 really developed four years before the disease even existed?

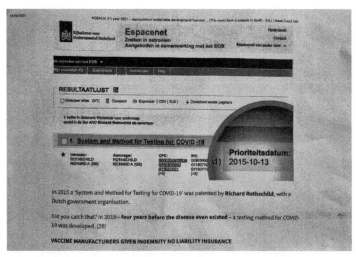

Patent filed by Richard Rothschild in 2015, mentioning Covid-19, issued in 2020

Reuters Fact Check[26] states that the patent for a system that analyses biometric data to determine whether the user is suffering from Covid-19 was not applied for until 17 May 2020. The "priority date" is the earliest filing date of a family of related patent applications or the earliest filing date of a particular feature of an intention. On 13 October 2015 Rothschild made a provisional application within this family of patents, predecessors to US20200279585A1. The CPC (Cooperative Patent Classification) is an extension of the IPC (International Patent Classification, established in the Strasbourg Agreement of 1971) and is jointly managed by the EPO (European Patent Office) and US Patent and Trademark Office, hence the mixture of Dutch and English on the application.

This patent application is nevertheless interesting as a system and method for testing coronavirus was being worked on at the earliest filing date of 13 October 2015, and it seems that if a Covid system is made in a laboratory and patented the patent can be undisclosed by law for 20 years, and no doctor can therefore be allowed to study the virus. It is interesting that the applicant named Rothschild has an early filing in 2015 for a patent finally applied for in 2020, which seems to reveal an intention to apply back in 2015, and it seems from the application that Covid-19 was made and patented in the USA.

Rothschild's testing method innovation was for acquiring and transmitting biometric data to determine, the 2020 abstract states,[27] if a user has "a viral infection, such as Covid-19". The method includes using a pulse oximeter to acquire pulse and oxygen saturation percentages – which I use and check every morning – and results are transmitted to a smartphone and uploaded to a cloud to determine whether a user is suffering from, or is likely to suffer from, "a viral infection, such as Covid-19". Medical staff can then be alerted if necessary.

There has also been interest in a patent for coronavirus owned by the Pirbright Institute of Woking, UK, which is funded by the Wellcome Trust and the Bill and Melinda Gates Foundation (patent 10.130.701 filed on 23 July 2015 and granted to Pirbright on 20 November 2018). The Pirbright Institute states[28] that it carries out research on infectious bronchitis virus (IBV), a coronavirus that infects poultry, and porcine delta coronavirus that infects pigs, and that it does not work with human coronaviruses. Reuters' and USA Today Fact Check[29] say this coronavirus is a weakened version of one kind of coronavirus that could serve for the development of a future animal vaccine, not Covid-19.

Clearly the 73 patents issued between 2008 and 2019 were registered for medical reasons, not for their military bio-warfare capabilities, but as we have seen, the three features of SARS-CoV-2 give it military bio-warfare capabilities as a side effect. And the issuance of these 73 patents means that they were publicly available for the Pentagon and State Department, and the "military-industrial complex" (the Syndicate), to study them from a military bio-warfare point of view.

A paper by Hong Zhou and twelve others,[30] 'A novel bat coronavirus reveals natural insertions at the S1/S2 cleavage site of the spike protein and a possible recombinant origin of HCoV-19' (2 March 2020), identifies the "novel" coronavirus that is SARS-CoV-2, but as we have just seen (on p.85), 73 patents issued between 2008 and 2019 describe these "unique" features. Patents have been filed for SARS-CoV-2's polybasic cleavage site, spike protein and ACE2 receptor binding domain.

There was therefore no 'outbreak' of SARS as it had been engineered in the US. And as we have just seen (on pp.81, 85), when Baric published a paper in 2015 warning that SARS coronavirus was "poised for human emergence", the virus had already been patented for commercial exploitation 73 times.

There are clearly medical and commercial aspects to the extensive patenting of coronavirus features in the US from 1999 to the present. From the outset Baric of the University of North Carolina and Dr Fauci of NIAID have been involved, looking for a vaccine for HIV, and patenting. The patenting involving Baric, NIAID and Moderna in November 2019 (see pp.39, 44, 58 and next paragraph), which FactCheck has dismissed as an earlier coronavirus, was clearly part of this process, and FactCheck's dismissal has to be read in the light of the above evidence that the three features of SARS-CoV-2 had been patented for nearly 20 years.

The commercial aspects of the profit motive of the patenting have been raised by Martin: "There wasn't a lab leak. This was an intentional bio-weaponisation of spike proteins to inject into people, to get them addicted to a pan-coronavirus vaccine." It is interesting that US patent 7279327, the patent issued on 19 April 2002 on the recombinant nature of the 'lung-targeting' coronavirus, was transferred from Baric's University of North Carolina, Chapel Hill, to the National Institutes of Health (NIH) in 2018. If the US Government has paid for research, it is entitled to benefit from it in accordance with the Bayh-Dole Act.

The NIH already had rights to the patent, but now took ownership of it and issued a Certificate of Correction to amend a typographical error in the grant reference. This was to make sure everything was correct to develop the Vaccine Research Institute's mandate, which was shared between the University of North Carolina, Chapel Hill, and Moderna in November 2019, when the University of North Carolina, Chapel Hill (Baric), NIAID and Moderna began sequencing a spike protein a month before the 'outbreak' of SARS-CoV-2. Again, FactCheck's intervention has to be read in the context of the previous 20 years.

It is also interesting that the slogan 'The New Normal' was first mentioned by Merck[31] at a conference titled 'SARS and Bioterrorism, Emerging Infectious Diseases, Antimicrobial Therapeutics, and Immune Modulated' on 6 January 2004. The slogan has since been adopted by the WHO, the Global Preparedness Monitoring Board (whose directors include Dr Fauci, Chris Elias – president of the Global Development Program at the Gates Foundation – and George Fu Gao, director of the Chinese CDC and a member of the Chinese Communist Party) and the pandemic virus industrial complex (the commercial Syndicate).

There is also a military aspect to this extensive patenting. Politicians and military seekers of new bio-weapons have had 20 years to follow coronavirus as a bio-weapon, and 73 US patents on the three features of SARS-CoV-2 were issued before 2019 when SARS-CoV-2 'first appeared'. Those focusing on finding cures for HIV and other diseases and patenting for profits might have been unaware they were under military surveillance by members of the commercial Syndicate – the commercial "military-industrial complex" – who were identifying SARS-CoV-2 as a potential military bio-weapon and obtaining samples for use in a coming biological war with China. They had ample time to absorb the military possibilities of SARS-CoV-2's three features and bring out Lock Step in 2010 as a coded dress rehearsal for a Syndicate bio-attack; and after more absorbing of SARS-CoV-2's three features to bring out Event 201 as a more advanced coded dress rehearsal for a Syndicate bio-attack. And then they could start a biological war with China by releasing SARS-CoV-2 in Wuhan, probably at the Wuhan Military World Games.

Even if new evidence subsequently comes to light that SARS-CoV-2 was released from the Wuhan Institute of Virology after all, despite the many denials, it is clear from its patent history – of 73 US patents – that it first appeared in America with the three main features of Covid-19 in 2002, and regardless of when it was released in China, began in the US.

How an American-Syndicate faction's release of SARS-CoV-2 to discredit and scapegoat China and stop its rise could have taken place on Trump's watch
To sum up, following the 2010 US decision to make contingency plans for a biological war on China and China's 2013 defensive expansion in the South China Sea, and Obama's 2014 moratorium on gain-of-function research, in 2014 the National Institutes of Health (NIH) – with US Pentagon and State-Department approval (see pp.74, 80) and US-Syndicate approval – funded gain-of-function research in the

Wuhan Institute of Virology, and Covid-19 was developed by 2019, after the moratorium was lifted in 2017.

On Trump's watch a faction within the US-Syndicate may have decided to disrupt China's growth and the rise of China, and may have released the virus, perhaps in the underground metro during the Wuhan Military World Games between 18 and 27 October 2019.

If so, this had long been planned, and Rockefellers' Lock Step and Gates' Event 201 alerted the public with coded scenarios as to how to react to a pandemic. Those who prepared Covid-19 also prepared a vaccine, which Moderna offered as a candidate vaccine on 12 December 2019.

Throughout all this, the Wuhan Institute of Virology may have been set up as a scapegoat so China could be blamed: the NIH/EcoHealth Alliance US-China joint project was encouraged so China could be blamed. Francis Collins of the NIH was awarded the Templeton Prize 2020 on Trump's watch for presiding over preventing diseases in Wuhan and unwittingly carrying forward the scapegoat agenda. And the blaming of China may have been accompanied by the idea there was a leak in the Wuhan Institute of Virology BSL-4 laboratory, which Chinese staff including Shi Zhengli deny.

President George W. Bush did not know about 9/11 while Vice-President Dick Cheney was shutting down the US air defence system; Bush was visiting a primary school when the Twin Towers were attacked. Similarly, President Trump – who was reckless in moving the capital of Israel to Jerusalem in defiance of Palestinian wishes, and in encouraging his supporters to invade and occupy the Capitol – may not have known about or sanctioned an attack during the Wuhan Military World Games, if it took place; and Event 201 was timed to begin as a bridge to controlling the public. Lockdowns were necessary as the US-Syndicate (and perhaps some Europeans) – the West – knew the virus may have been a bio-weapon, and all Westerners were asked to shield themselves by staying at home.

A cache of 32 emails between British and American health officials, including Sir Patrick Vallance (Chief Scientific Adviser to the UK Government), Sir Jeremy Farrar (Director of the Wellcome Trust) and Dr Fauci, about a secret teleconference held on 1 February 2020, at the beginning of the pandemic, has come to light under Freedom of Information laws – with all the content redacted (see below). The secrecy suggests there was something to hide. What did Western scientists have to hide in January–February 2020? Could it have been an American-Syndicate use of an engineered gain-of-function virus that began in an American lab?[32]

Redacted emails between Sir Jeremy Farrar and
British-American scientists dated 1 February 2020

The possibility of immediate retaliation and a self-inflicted wound that advanced the fall of the West

The idea behind the release of the bio-weapon, if it happened, was to avert the fall of the West. It did not work as China's prompt lockdown of Hubei province saw off the immediate threat, which rebounded and attacked the US and Europe, perhaps as a result of Chinese retaliation – China's making sure travellers took the virus to the West.

Trump, who may have been unaware of the release, if it happened, publicly scorned the virus, suggesting it could be treated with bleach. In public he played down the danger of coronavirus while privately saying it was very dangerous.

Neither the ending of the rise of China nor the fall of China happened. China became stronger: the Chinese trade surplus rose from $421.9 billion in 2019 to $460 billion after the first eleven months of 2020, and America's net trade deficit increased from $616.8 billion in

2019 to $678 billion in 2020.

On this view Covid was a self-inflicted wound on the West, and it advanced the decline of the West. The fall of the West was now a real possibility.

At this point, members of the jury, regarding a possible American-Syndicate deliberate release of a bio-weapon in Wuhan, I rest my case.

5

China's Preparations for War, the Syndicate's Great Reset and the Collapse of the West's Financial System

China prepares for war with the West
In a massive parade to mark the 100th anniversary of the founding of the ruling Chinese Communist Party on 1 July 2021 President Xi Jinping spoke in Beijing's Tiananmen Square to thousands of soldiers. He said China would not allow itself to be bullied, perhaps a veiled reference to the American-Syndicate bio-weapon, and that those who try to bully China would face "broken heads and bloodshed in front of the iron Great Wall of the 1.4 billion Chinese people".[1] He said China had restored order in Hong Kong following the anti-government protests in the city in 2019, and he reiterated Beijing's determination to bring self-governing Taiwan under the Communist Party's control so there is "a complete reunification" of China and Taiwan.

President Xi speaking on the 100th anniversary of the founding of the Chinese Communist Party on 1 July 2021

A Chinese magazine marked the ruling Communist Party's centenary by publishing a detailed outline of a three-stage surprise attack on Taiwan:[2] DF-16 short-range ballistic missiles would pulverise airports, early-warning radar, anti-air missile bases and command centres in Taiwan; YJ-91 and CJ-10 cruise missiles would be unleashed from land, warships and submarines and strike military bases, ammunition depots, communications infrastructure and key road junctions; and a warship bombardment would destroy remaining obstacles and pave

Three pictures of China's warlike parade in Beijing's Tiananmen Square on the 100th anniversary of the founding of the Chinese Communist Party, reminiscent of Nazi Germany in the 1930s

the way for an amphibious beach landing and then a land invasion involving military hovercraft. (See p.98.)

While President Xi Jinping was speaking, satellite images showed China was building 119 nuclear missile silos in the Chinese desert outside Yumen, in a nuclear expansion aimed at defending China against America. The total number of silos being built around China was 145.[4] It could not be said that these were defensive rather than offensive silos; the silos enabled nuclear missiles to be fired regardless of whether they were fired for defence or attack.

A satellite image showing one of the silo construction
sites hidden under a 230-foot dome cover

Thousands of troops and a threat that China will not be bullied – the feeling was of Hitler addressing thousands of troops in 1938.

After China flew a hypersonic nuclear-capable missile round the world, which can reach 3,850 miles per hour, five times the speed of sound, US politician Mike Gallagher warned that the US is on course to lose a new Cold War.

The Syndicate had been levelling the West down, and levelling up the East, to prepare for a world government, and now the rise of China looked unstoppable while the West was tottering.

House of Representatives' report blames China for Covid in a possible cover-up

On 2 August 2021 members of the Capitol's House of Representatives released details of an inquiry into the origins of coronavirus. The report claimed "a preponderance of the evidence proves that all roads lead to the Wuhan lab". Michael McCaul, the top Republican on the

STAGE ONE — KEY INSTALLATIONS ATTACKED

DF-16 short-range ballistic missile attacks will pulverise airports, early warning radar, anti-air missile bases, and command centres across the island.

Taiwan Strait

Tag Suao naval base

Taoyuan International Airport

Early warning radar

South China Sea

China's plan to invade Taiwan as announced on 1 July 2021: stage one, key installations attacked; stage 2, cruise missile strikes; and stage 3, warship bombardment. (Left and below) Stages one and two naming key targets, (bottom) all three stages with all the targets of stage one identified[3]

STAGE TWO — CRUISE MISSILE STRIKES

YJ-91 and CJ-10 cruise missiles would be unleashed from land, warships and submarines, striking military bases, ammunition depots, communications infrastructure and key road junctions.

Matsu

Ching Chuan Kang Air Base

CHINA

Taiwan Strait

TAIWAN

Kinmen

South China Sea

Penghu

STAGE THREE — WARSHIP BOMBARDMENT

Remaining obstacles destroyed to pave way for amphibious beach landing

STAGE ONE — KEY INSTALLATIONS ATTACKED

STAGE TWO — CRUISE MISSILE STRIKES

STAGE THREE — WARSHIP BOMBARDMENT

House foreign affairs committee, said: "It's our belief that the virus leaked sometime in late August or early September 2019." The report says: "Sometime before September 12, 2019."

Its reason for concluding this was a previously-unknown request by the Wuhan lab in July 2019 for a $1.5-million maintenance of its "environmental air disinfection system" and its "hazardous waste treatment system", even though they were less than two years old; and the Wuhan lab's scientists and officials taking their virus database offline in the middle of the night on 12 September 2019 and requesting more than $1 million for additional security. Republicans have long contended that China covered up a leak from the lab, and Trump referred to coronavirus as the "China virus".[5]

Relating our argument so far to this House foreign affairs committee report, there are two scenarios:

1. The NIH continued its gain-of-function research in Wuhan from 2014 to 2019 and again from 2019 to April 2020 and from July 2020 to June 2021, for which it paid Wuhan via Peter Daszak's EcoHealth Alliance, and before 12 September 2019 there was an accident or a deliberate leak from the Wuhan Institute of Virology for which the Wuhan Military World Games was an international vector.

2. One of the American contingent of 284 brought the virus to Wuhan in the pre-Games baggage for the athletes and released it in Wuhan apart from the Wuhan Institute of Virology so the Military World Games was an international vector, to discredit China's Belt-and-Road Initiative and limit the rise of China and its expanding trade. This scenario would explain why the staff of the Institute of Virology all tested negative.

The House report smacks of Republicans blaming China for the outbreak *before* the Military World Games and sees the Military World Games in Wuhan in October 2019 as being "an international vector spreading the virus to multiple continents around the world" as athletes returned home. The Report claims there was ample evidence that Wuhan Institute of Virology researchers were working to modify coronaviruses to infect humans. President Biden said three US intelligence analyses regarded the cause of the outbreak as being either an infected animal or "a laboratory accident", and the report would conclude it was a laboratory accident.

The report smacks of a cover-up as it ignores the indisputable fact that the three main features of SARS-CoV-2 were man-made in an American lab in 2002, and that between 2008 and 2019 there were

73 patents for these manipulations; and that no evidence for a leak has been found. If there was no leak, however much China wanted to replace the US as the world's number-one superpower, China had no motive in releasing a virus to scupper its own massive trade output, which gave it an annual balance-of-payments lead of $1 trillion over the US.

The report also ignores the outbreak of the virus in Iran in February 2020; and the possibility that the virus was released to target the Military World Games in Wuhan to limit the rise of China and its expanding trade through its Belt-and-Road Initiative in 140 countries, almost ringing the West. The report does not take into account President Xi's call before thousands of troops in Tiananmen Square to the US to stop bullying China or it will be faced by an iron wall of 1.4 billion people.

The Republicans ignored that coronavirus was modified in American labs between 2002 and 2019, and ignored the Syndicate's motives in levelling East and West to create a world government. They ignored that the Syndicate is seeking to discredit China by blaming it for an accidental outbreak – to cover up the American origins of the virus in the House report into the origins of coronavirus.

It is possible that this House report is part of the Syndicate's cover-up for its release of the virus in Wuhan – to make it look as if it could have been released during the American NIH-funded gain-of-function research at the Institute of Virology in Wuhan.

On the subject of cover-ups, the 9/11 Commission Report, the cover-up which whitewashed Syndicate involvement in 9/11, was controlled and shaped by Philip Zelikow, a Professor at the University of Virginia who was closely associated with Condoleezza Rice, George W. Bush, Dick Cheney, Paul Wolfowitz, Brent Scowcroft and others and has served in key intelligence positions in both George H.W. Bush and George W. Bush administrations. He was put on Obama's Intelligence Advisory Board in 2011.

Zelikow is now head of a Covid Commission Planning Group based at the University of Virginia, which is preparing for a National Covid Commission that will again cover up and whitewash Syndicate involvement in the origins of Covid. The group is funded by Schmidt Futures, the Skoll Foundation, the Rockefeller Foundation and Stand Together. Zelikow is a member of the Gates Foundation's Development Program Advisory Panel, and the Group will work with the Johns Hopkins Center for Health Security. Zelikow's involvement suggests a long War of Terror waged with military and medical weapons (instilling fear of terrorism and fear of viruses in the world's population) that will reflect the authoritarianism of the World Economic Forum's Great Reset. (See pp.42, 68 and below.) Zelikow seems to be a cover-up director appointed to clear a Covid cover-up group.[6]

On a personal note, on Sunday 2 June 2019 I belatedly celebrated my 80th birthday in the grounds of one of my schools, next to the cricket field where I batted during the 1958 season before crowds sitting four deep round the boundary. That day was close to the end of the old world in which masks and social distancing were unimaginable, a month before the new Biological Age began.

Schwab of the World Economic Forum, the Great Reset (a rebranding of the New World Order) and the Fourth Industrial Revolution

I have said (on p.97) that the Syndicate has been levelling the West down, and levelling up the East, to prepare for a world government, and that the rise of China looks unstoppable. We now need to get to grips with 'The Great Reset', which the US and the Syndicate hope will counter the rise of China and the decline of the West.

The World Economic Forum introduced the idea of a 'Great Reset' on capitalism in June 2020, and the IMF published its vision of a "Global Economic Reset", which promotes "an inclusive recovery" from Covid (healthcare that protects the most vulnerable, debt suspension for the poorest countries and tax reforms).

'The Great Reset' is in fact a rebranding of Nelson Rockefeller's New World Order (see p.10),[7] a new system of global centralised governance by unelected leaders drawn from the Syndicate. With it comes the "Fourth Industrial Revolution", which refers to the merging of digital, physical and biological systems, and to relying on technological surveillance to maintain public order – which means merging humans and machines. It advocates transhumanism, which uses technology to extend the length of human life and resist illness and disease in a mass transformation of the human condition.

Klaus Schwab is the founder (in 1971) and executive chairman of the World Economic Forum (WEF), and only he or an immediate family member can designate his successor (an echo of 'Rothschilds'' and 'Rockefellers'' approach). Schwab is the key figure in the Great Reset and the Fourth Industrial Revolution. His book titles speak for themselves: *The Fourth Industrial Revolution* (2016); *Shaping the Fourth Industrial Revolution* (2018); and *COVID-19: The Great Reset* (2020).

The Great Reset is about centralisation of control into fewer hands, globalisation and transformation of society through surveillance technologies. As Schwab says in *COVID-19: The Great Reset* (2020):

When confronted with it, some industry leaders and senior executives may be tempted to equate reset with restart, hoping to go back to the old normal and restore what worked in the past: traditions, tested procedures and familiar ways of doing things – in short, a return to business as usual. This won't happen because it can't happen. For the most part, "Business as usual" died from (or at the very least was infected by) COVID-19.[8]

The pandemic is instrumental in making the Great Reset happen, a reset to a new system of global centralised governance by unelected Syndicate leaders. It was noted in a World Economic Forum article of 21 July 2020 that the economic devastation caused by pandemic shutdowns "has the potential to hobble global prosperity for generations to come". Countries can move forward by developing their infrastructure, by "building back better" and by following Alexander King's Club of Rome and going over to green energy, part of which involves shifting to an all-digital, centrally-controlled currency system that can be used as a means of social control. The central bank digital currency (CBDC) will be controlled by the central banks (i.e. 'Rothschilds'), and smart contracts will allow banks to control all human lives.

One of the Great-Reset proposals is that by 2030 (a date that keeps cropping up) citizens will own nothing but will lease or rent, and society at large will own everything as in the first Communist state that 'Rothschilds' and 'Rockefellers' helped to create. In fact, the Syndicate will do the owning; the citizens will supply their services with no human rights or personal freedom. Some would say this is slave labour, enslavement.[9] It is certainly not the democratic World State I have envisaged.

(Supporters of Biden's administration and of Johnson's Brexit government will recognise their support in their speeches for developing infrastructure, "building back better" – Biden's campaigning slogan – and the Green Revolution, and it may be that their governments are being run on Great-Reset thinking, and will result in centralised ownership of everything. Biden and Johnson have become Orwell's Big Brother.)

Schwab was the son of a Nazi collaborator who used slave labour and aided Nazi efforts to obtain the first atomic bomb, and the Schwab family was involved in the European eugenics movement and in South-Africa's illegal nuclear program.[10] Detractors of population reduction have linked it to Nazi eugenics. Detractors of the Great Reset see Covid-19 gene modification injections as creating the first generation of transhumans, as genes can be updated by an injection of mRNA.

Members of the World Economic Forum include world government leaders, corporate leaders, non-governmental organisations (NGOs), journalists, activists, cultural leaders and artists, all of whom promote the WEF's technocratic and transhumanist mission.

The Syndicate's organisations have technocratic goals: the Club of Rome, which inspired the WEF, the Aspen Institute, the Trilateral Commission, the Atlantic Institute, the Brookings Institute and other think tanks. As we have seen (p.11), the Club of Rome, a scientific think tank that promotes global governance led by a technocratic *élite*, focused on reducing the global population before *The Kissinger Report*. It held that population reduction would receive more popular support if there was a common enemy: "pollution, the threat of global warming, water shortages, famine and the like". This climate-change threat, the brainchild of Alexander King, was originally designed to allow population reduction to happen without opposition becoming resistance.

It is possible that the Syndicate is using the Covid pandemic to make the world population have vaccines that contain atomic and molecular matter that can be controlled and manipulated by nanotechnology (controlling matter at the nanoscale, at dimensions between 1 and 100 nanometers for industrial purposes), which turn human beings into devices that can be programmed by 5G (fifth-generation technology networks). The President of Chile, Sebastian Pinera, has said: "5G will read your thoughts and also inject thoughts and feelings. 5G will become the nervous system of our society, determining what we think and feel. And we will make sure this reaches every house." Schwab has said: "You will own nothing, have no privacy,... and be happy!" The happiness may be a state of mind programmed by 5G, a form of brainwashing.

I am reminded of being taken to tea in March 1966 with Mr Liu, the son of the former match king of Shanghai who was under house arrest, having had his fortune of £140 million impounded by the Chinese Communist State and having been allowed to live off its interest. As I described in *My Double Life 1: This Dark Wood*, pp.194–195, he told me: "I have had to unlearn my capitalist ways, I have been remoulded. These Americans call it 'brainwashing', which is the process of seeing things in their right perspective. It takes a long time and patience."

He had studied at Cambridge and spoke like a Westerner, but in mid-sentence the reconditioned, remoulded mechanism took over and, like a gramophone record repeating, cut in: "Thanks to Chairman Mao I have my life, my interest and a chance to understand Communism. Thanks to Chairman Mao I can take part in the new China from this house." I was nauseated at the way Mr Liu had been treated as material, as a device, as a machine to be remoulded.

Technocratic control of the brain can have positive medical benefits: many medical conditions involving the brain, including strokes, blindness and deafness, can be cured by 5G in conjunction with nanotechnology. There are however negative possibilities, most notably the capability of brain control through 5G to end a person's life, and in ruthless hands this could be used to keep the world population below 8 billion. The President of Chile has said that the medical benefits outweigh the negative side. This may be a reckless judgment based on a misunderstanding of what the technocracy behind the Great Reset is seeking to achieve, and there will need to be international legislation under international treaty (see p.126) to protect the brains of all humankind from negative, abusive use of brain control by 5G.

It is now possible that, now we have been vaccinated against Covid, 5G can supply a form of programming – remoulding or brainwashing – that can control the entire world population, and that those of us who have already received two doses of vaccine and a booster may already have atomic and molecular matter within us that can be manipulated by nanotechnology that just needs the 5G of the Great Reset, which all countries (like Chile) are installing, to programme us technocratically into having our brains controlled. It is possible that our brains can then transhumanly overcome their deterioration or, in the case of some judged to be "useless eaters", be switched off (put to death) so that the world population can be reduced and kept below a target figure; and those of us allowed to live, the contributors to society, will all become servile devices or machines.

It seems from all this that the Syndicate used the Covid pandemic to roll out a technocratic and transhumanist agenda as a post-Covid "reset", which the WEF is driving forward. As the Syndicate's "reset" project for technocratic world governance gained impetus from Covid, it is even more likely that SARS-CoV-2, which enabled the "reset" to begin, was an artificially man-made chimera to make a planned "reset" possible, and that it has not come from bats but had an American-Syndicate release in Wuhan.

The Syndicate origin of the Great Reset and the planned collapse of the West's GDP and financial system
The Great Reset, which was given impetus by Covid, had a Syndicate origin. It grew out of the 1930s' Technocracy Movement at Columbia University, New York, where Zbigniew Brzezinski and David Rockefeller collaborated with technocrats and planned a new energy-based economy

(our Green Movement) rather than a price-based economy:[11] a planned collapse of the West's financial system.

In 1970 Brzezinski wrote *Between Two Ages: America's Role in the Technetronic Era* and revived the doctrine of technocracy with David Rockefeller and Klaus Schwab, whose mother was a Rothschild (Marianne Rothschild), by creating the World Economic Forum (WEF) to hold meetings with world leaders at Davos. Schwab has said[12] that the first meeting in Davos in 1971 was to present the Club of Rome's report *The Limits to Growth* (see p.11).

Brzezinski, Rockefeller and Schwab were all members of the Club of Rome, the Bilderberg Group and the Trilateral Commission, Syndicate organisations, out of which grew UN Agenda 2030 with its 17 Sustainable Goals (see pp.40–41), the Green New Deal and the Great Reset with its 'Fourth Industrial Revolution'. Schwab and Brzezinski nurtured trade relationships with Chinese leaders to normalise the US relationship with China in 1973, the year David Rockefeller visited China, from which 'Rockefellers' benefited as we have seen (pp.45–49). Schwab and Brzezinski normalised relations with China so technocrats could draw on cheap Chinese labour for the Fourth Industrial Revolution.

The Great Reset, which is effectively Schwab's 'Fourth Industrial Revolution', is characterised by a fusion of technologies, such as AI (artificial intelligence), gene editing and advanced robotics, that is blurring the dividing lines between the physical, digital and biological worlds. It is a Reset for a new Biological Age (see pp.143, 144, 147). The Great Reset will disrupt nearly every industry in the West as it will end the price-based economy of small businesses and free enterprise globally for a society that lives in technocratic urban environments, 'smart cities' like the one trialled in Saudi Arabia (see p.68).

The Great Reset includes stealthily moving from shareholder capitalism to "stakeholder capitalism" by 2030. Under stakeholder capitalism the power of corporations is increased and the Syndicate's corporations should not serve shareholders but be custodians of society for customers, suppliers, employees and communities – and have more power than democratic institutions, a move towards corporate authoritarianism, a form of Fascism. The Syndicate's corporations will be more powerful in global decision-making than governments, and no one will own anything but pay for the right to use everything while they are alive.

Stakeholder capitalism has been advocated by David Rockefeller's associate Klaus Schwab for decades, and it spearheads the WEF's Great-Reset plan that was announced in June 2020. It is linked to the Great Reset's Global Redesign Initiative to redesign global governance.

Governments and non-governmental organisations such as the WEF would be equal stakeholders and will have a say in how nations are governed. Corporations (and the Syndicate) will become the main stakeholders; governments will take a back seat.[13]

The Great Reset is interwoven with the 17 Sustainable Goals of UN Agenda 2030 (2015). On 19 June 2019 the UN and World Economic Forum signed a deal to accelerate the 17 Sustainable Goals of Agenda 2030, 'The Strategic Partnership Framework'. The two who signed were António Guterres, the UN Secretary-General, and Klaus Schwab of WEF. The UN have tried to fulfil these 17 Goals by using the threat of Climate Change to shut down the price-based economy of boilers and non-green heating and energy. Following the pandemic's lockdowns people are being urged to give up their freedoms in order to save the world, and pandemic legislation fulfils the aims of Climate Change and the 17 Sustainable Goals.

A consequence of green heating would be a move away from oil and gas, and therefore from the Syndicate's 457 oil and natural-gas pipelines, which will have to be replaced by offshore energy (power from windfarms and waves). And a new generation of the Syndicate's families can be expected to harness and control this offshore energy.

However, as the Syndicate at present controls 457 pipelines, some of which took more than 20 years to negotiate and put in place, it will want to keep the income from these pipelines coming in. At COP26 oil and gas were not even on the table. It has embraced going green as there are trillions of dollars more to be made, and interest on loans from 'Rothschilds'' central banks to flood in, by lending to governments to assist with going green (replacing boilers and fuel-driven cars). The surprising rapprochement between China and the US at the very end of COP26 suggests that this was prearranged as part of a long-term Syndicate plan to bring East and West together.

The Syndicate's pipelines can be expected to be phased out slowly and replaced by income from going green so as not to reduce, but rather to increase, the Syndicate's capital, and the reluctance of the world's main polluter China (whose central bank is controlled by 'Rothschilds') to move forward its net-zero target of 2060 is a part of this pattern.

The WEF says the pandemic "has presented a great opportunity to bring about social change that will re-engineer the whole of society" (into a State that resembles Communist China), and Schwab has said, "You will own nothing, and you will be happy." The WEF website says that GDP is of the past and will be replaced by a new economy based on green taxes and data-driven surveillance using 'impact investing' and 'human capital bonds', akin to the Chinese credit system – a move towards uniting with China, slashing Western GDP (see pp.121–122, 141) and reflecting the idea in Event 201 of a pandemic requiring a global vaccine. Lockdown caused the biggest collapse of GDP in the UK for 300 years, and, as it has taken place within the Great Reset and given it impetus, the pandemic seems to be a planned crash of the global economy to bring about universal dependence on hand-outs from the State, which will control society and appear to undermine capitalism – and all this has been happening under Covid.

The Great Reset to a green utopia is being called a technocratic dystopia in which human beings and AI merge in 'The internet of bodies'. The Great Reset's slogan 'Build Back Better', often quoted by the Syndicate's follower the UK Prime Minister Johnson, assumes that the existing capitalist and financial system and its property-owning will be destroyed – as is happening to small- and medium-sized businesses which have been forced to close following lockdowns.

The Great Reset needs to exploit a catastrophic incident, the Covid pandemic, to advance its agenda and bring in what has been called a transhumanist world under transnational governance that prioritises technocracy over elections. The Great Reset is Brzezinski's and David Rockefeller's Syndicate legacy of a smashing of the old order to create a New World Order in a planned abrupt collapse of the West's financial system that will bring about the fall of the West.

The Great-Reset thinking that is advancing the fall of the West
In 2019 the US trade deficit was $616.8 billion, and the Chinese trade surplus was $421.9 billion. The US President Trump had been following the position and insisting that the UK end its relationship with Huawei.

The Syndicate could see how things were going from such commercial decisions and attitudes. There was a trade gulf between the two superpowers of more than $1 trillion per year, and this would widen exponentially unless something was done. How to stop China overtaking the US and becoming the number-one superpower?

The Syndicate wanted the West levelled down and the East levelled up to prepare for a centralised world government by unelected leaders, making good use of the 457 pipelines it had put in place, but did not want the East to rise too high; otherwise the imbalance would make a centralised world government unachievable. There was a debate as to how to stop the rise of China and its economic growth.

In 2013, seeing the growing gulf between the US and China and reacting to China's defensive island-snatching in the South China Sea,

President Obama imposed a moratorium on gain-of-function research and gave the National Institutes of Health an excuse to start a joint project with China. The NIH had the approval of the US's military Establishment, the Pentagon and the State Department, which funded EcoHealth Alliance (see pp.74, 90). Gates had an ongoing relationship with the NIH and was close to China and made visits to Chinese leaders that cemented this joint project. (He may have been unaware of any military effect of his visits.)

In 2019 President Trump was reckless as all saw from his recognising of Jerusalem as the capital of Israel in December 2019 (and his 2020 encouragement of the invasion of the Capitol). Gates had an ongoing relationship with both the NIH and Dr Fauci of the NIAID, who had advised all the Presidents since 1980 and was Trump's adviser. Working within the NIH, Fauci oversaw the gain-of-function medical experiments on coronavirus in Wuhan. Probably without his knowledge (or Daszak's or Baric's), the overt medical gain-of-function work in Wuhan, which the US military Establishment were funding (see p.74) and which Fauci would have reported on to Trump, opened the way for a hidden military gain-of-function creation of a pathogen, which could be used by a faction within the Syndicate as a bio-weapon.

This military work may have taken place within America and not Wuhan and may have involved scrutiny of the 73 patents for the three features of SARS-CoV-2 which had been researched by David Martin, again leaving the medics Fauci, Daszak and Baric unaware of this hidden dimension to the work at the WIV. With meetings taking place on how to arrest the rise of China and a nuclear stalemate disqualifying any use of nuclear weapons, it is possible that a faction within the Syndicate explored how to make use of the military biological bio-weapon that had come within their reach.

It is possible that by 2019 the WIV had been set up to be a scapegoat so it could be blamed for any release of a bio-weapon in China. It is possible that a faction within the US-Syndicate was ready to act as China's trade surplus was getting larger and larger, and the trade gap had reached $1 trillion per year. The commercial leaders of 'Rothschilds', 'Rockefellers' and the Gates Foundation would have mixed feelings on a US-Syndicate biological war with China as they were trading with China as bankers, investors and software sellers, but the 'Rockefellerite' Great Reset had been planned for decades and the 'Rockefellerite' scenario of Lock Step in 2010 had presented the Syndicate with a model for how to link it to a pandemic. Syndicate voices may have urged an update to Lock Step.

This update may have happened in Event 201, which took place on the opening day of the Military World Games in Wuhan, 18 October 2019. It is possible that a hidden faction within the Syndicate arranged for a military biological bio-weapon to be released at the Wuhan Military World Games.

It is possible that the pathogen was released in Wuhan's metro. It has been estimated that the number of Chinese infected in the course of the outbreak was ten times what the Chinese government announced. The effects of the bio-weapon may have been contained by China, which acted promptly, putting Wuhan and Hubei province into lockdown, implementing Draconian measures and following the 'Rockefellers'' Lock-Step approach. Lock Step may have been followed in the 2020 lockdowns.

(If the West's leaders have *not* been implementing the 'Rockefellerite' Lock Step in 2020, it was unfortunate that on 9 August 2021 a spokesman for 10 Downing Street should have excused Johnson's threat to remove his Chancellor Sunak by saying that they were both "in lockstep": "They have been in lockstep throughout this incredibly challenging period for the country."[14] If this does not mean 'They have been following the Lock-Step scenario' then the phraseology was extremely unfortunate as it suggested that the UK Government's approach to Covid-19 had been implementing the Lock-Step scenario.)

China's economic miracle continued. Foreign currency, mostly US dollars, had been flowing into China, and the Chinese government had kept sufficient dollar reserves to maintain an undervalued renminbi (literally 'people's currency' issued by the 'Rothschildite' People's Bank of China, its main unit being the yuan), which made exports cheaper and imports more expensive, reducing the demand for foreign goods.

In 2020 the US trade deficit was $678 billion and the Chinese trade surplus in the first eleven months of 2020 was $460 billion. The US's position had worsened; China's stature had grown even though there was international disquiet at the lack of information about the outbreak of Covid in Wuhan.

The Syndicate may now have wanted to cover up the 2019 release and go with the Great Reset, and the first thing was to get Trump out. In 2020 'Rothschilds', who had always had a strong relationship with China, funded President Biden's election campaign to put an emollient President Biden in charge of managing the aftermath of Covid-19, implementing the Great Reset and smoothing over an episode that, as many countries had borrowed money from them, would hugely benefit their central banks and which would soon further benefit them as the technocratic Fourth Industrial Revolution and the Great Reset progressed.

In 2019, analysts were trying to prevent the further fall of the West and the further rise of China. The Syndicate's centralised world government, the Great Reset (a rebranding of the New World Order) and the Fourth Industrial Revolution were all supposed to achieve that. In 2020 the West (America and Europe) were more badly affected by Covid than China, perhaps because China arranged for an immediate retaliatory release of SARS-CoV-2, perhaps among the American, Canadian and European athletes at the Wuhan Military World Games in Wuhan, and by 2021 the West had fallen further and China had risen higher.

In *Pro Sexto Roscio Amerino*, section 84, and *Pro Milone*, Cicero attributed to the Roman consul and censor Lucius Cassius Longinus Ravilla the question, '*Cui bono*?', 'To whose advantage was it?' To whose advantage was Covid?

If the release of Covid was deliberate and intentional due to the rivalry between two superpowers, either a faction in the US-Syndicate was trying to prevent the further rise of China, or the Chinese were trying to accelerate and precipitate the further fall of the West. We have seen that the evidence points to its being the first, not the second, as China would not have released SARS-CoV-2 in China since to do so would have infected its own people and damaged its own economy.

But China may have retaliated and spread SARS-CoV-2 in the US and Europe, perhaps via US and European athletes, and the Syndicate may have assisted this retaliation just as it assisted 9/11, as Covid-19 was used to create a pandemic that would level down both the East – sufficiently to arrest the rise of China – and the West – more drastically, to accelerate the fall of the West so it could be level with the East, and create a global centralised governance by the Syndicate.

The US may have been helped by 'in-betweeners', a hidden faction within the Syndicate, the commercial *élites* who had sold arms to both sides during the Cold War and now traded with both sides through philanthropic foundations and their supply of oil and natural gas through their 457 pipelines; and who wanted to prevent the further rise of China and accelerate the further fall of the West so their self-interested, centralised world government of unelected leaders could follow and there would be no pipeline borders anywhere.

Factions within the Syndicate had manipulated the invasions of Afghanistan and Iraq, were behind the Arab-Spring revolutions, the Russian-Ukrainian War and the seizure of the Crimea, the expulsion of the Rohingya Muslims and the military *coup* in Myanmar, to increase their wealth through pipelines (see pp.21–35). In their calculation, the release of SARS-CoV-2 would level down the world and require all governments to borrow hundreds of billions from the Syndicate's trillions – and pay the coming interest-rate rises caused by inevitable inflation, and perhaps stagflation, into the coffers of the Syndicate's banks.

The 'Rockefellers'' scenarios report in 2010 is about scenarios, hypothetical situations for which a philanthropic institution must be prepared. Nevertheless Lock Step is uncannily like 2020, a preparation for it, a rehearsal. If we did not know that 'Rockefellers' were behind *The Kissinger Report* and *The Global 2000 Report* on depopulation, we would not think of depopulation in relation to the 'Rockefellers'' scenarios or in relation to 'Rockefellers'' relative Gates' Event 201, as the word 'preparation' cannot be found in either. But once we know about 'Rockefellers'' involvement in *The Global 2000 Report*, which has been accepted by every President since 1980, then we cannot avoid seeing the scenarios in Lock Step and in 'Rockefellers'' relative Gates' Event 201 as an extension of *The Global 2000 Report*, and as a dress rehearsal in 2010 and 2019 for what would happen in 2020.

Similarly, if we did not know that 'Rockefellers' were behind the Great Reset and levelling the West's and the East's GDP, we would not think that Covid-19 was part of a plan to give impetus to the Great Reset. But once we know about 'Rockefellers'' involvement in the Great Reset and the slashing of GDP with green taxes, we cannot avoid seeing Covid as part of the Great-Reset plan that is inextricably linked to *The Kissinger Report* and *The Global 2000 Report*.

The 'Rockefellerites' have put forward scenarios, hypothetical situations. In the same spirit I offer my view of the Great-Reset thinking as a scenario, a hypothetical situation that draws on what the Syndicate has been doing in the 20th and 21st centuries and that fits the facts, in which the jigsaw pieces interlock without being forced in. Just as the 'Rockefellerites'' Lock Step and Event 201 scenarios and Great Reset present a hypothetical situation as a forecast, my scenario presents a hypothetical situation in retrospect that takes account of Cicero's '*Cui bono?*'

There is no hard evidence that Covid was deliberately released at the Wuhan Military World Games to arrest the rise of China. The outbreak of Covid-19 seemed like 9/11 all over again: an attack, leaders not telling the people the truth, the Syndicate again involved. In understanding how Covid-19 happened we have looked at every option, and without making any imputation against any living individual I present a scenario that shows that lockdowns in the West may have been self-inflicted as an act of Western-Syndicate aggression that karmically boomeranged back on the West as lockdowns in many Western countries; and that the fall of the West has been accelerated by the rivalry between the two major superpowers and by the Syndicate's levelling in preparation for a world government: by the hidden release of SARS-CoV-2 by a faction within the Syndicate.

It is possible to argue and justify the reverse scenario, that China deliberately and intentionally released SARS-CoV-2 in Wuhan at the Wuhan Military World Games so athletes could take it back to their bases and infect the military bastions of the West while making out that America, with help from the Syndicate, had released it, so that China could intensify its preparations for war and its coming invasion of Taiwan. But that does not explain the similar release in Tehran, China's ally, and asks us to believe that China would knowingly release within China a virus that would damage Chinese people and the Chinese economy.

So we are sticking with a possible American-Syndicate initial release ("made in America, aimed at China"), to discredit China's hold over 140 countries in its Belt-and-Road Initiative, its global trading project as we are about to see. We have seen what the Syndicate has been doing to integrate the world into a centralised world government, and we have a retrospective scenario of what the US-Syndicate might have done. We have seen that the alternatives can be ruled out, an initial Chinese bio-weapon attack on its own civilians in Wuhan, an accidental leak in a WIV lab and animal-to-human transmission in a 'wet market' – that although all other viruses were transmitted to humans from animals, SARS-CoV-2 is the exception, a bio-weapon created as a chimera that did not come from Nature, even though Baric insists (perhaps self-defensively) that it probably did. And we have seen that all these alternatives are side issues and irrelevant if (as China suspects) the US-Syndicate "bullied" it with a viral bio-weapon attack.

It is entirely possible that China realised what had happened at an early stage and in retaliation deliberately infected American and European athletes at the Wuhan Military World Games, and that there was thus a release of SARS-CoV-2 in Wuhan by both sides between 18 and 27 October 2019.

At this point, members of the jury, regarding the possible American-Syndicate deliberate use of Covid-19 to advance the Great Reset and bring about a planned collapse of the West's financial system, I rest my case.

6

The Tottering West: The End of American Supremacy, Deagel's Forecasts, China's Belt-and-Road Initiative and a New Biological Threat

Looking ahead from 2021, with SARS-CoV-2 still around and causing self-isolation, and with quarantining of travellers and a feeling that the West cannot get back to normal, I think of the depopulating plagues of the past, and whether the West faces a similar depopulation now from a new plague.

Plagues as causes of civilisations' decline
The powerful Athenian Empire (which, after the defeat of the Persian invasion, was prosperous under the Peace of the Delian League from 478BC) plunged into decline from 430BC when a plague (typhoid or viral haemorrhaging fever) killed up to 100,000 Athenians including Pericles (out of a population of 350,000, just over one in three Athenians). The pandemic devastated the Athenian army, which never recovered, and ended the Athenian supremacy in 404BC, when Athens was defeated by Sparta. Although there was a second Athenian League led by Athens from 377BC, Greece fell into a long decline until it was annexed by Rome during the battle of Corinth in 146BC.

The mighty Roman Empire (whose *Pax Romana* began in c.27BC) plunged into decline from 165AD when a plague (smallpox) killed 5 million Romans including Marcus Aurelius. The pandemic devastated the Roman army, which never recovered, and ended the *Pax Romana* in 180AD (with the death of Marcus Aurelius), after which there was a long decline until the fall of the Western Roman Empire in 476AD.

The East Roman Empire was hastened into decline from 541AD when the Plague of Justinian (caused by the bacterium *Yersinia pestis* from the Tian Shan mountain range on China's border, the bacterium responsible for the Black Death of 1347–1351) devastated Roman Egypt. The pandemic infected the Byzantine Empire (especially Constantinople, including Justinian I, who recovered in 542AD), spread round the Mediterranean until 544AD, persisted in Northern Europe and the Arabian Peninsula, wiped out half the population of the East Roman Empire, contributed to its shrinking borders and hastened its slow decline.

In the same way, following the *Pax Britannica* of 1815 to 1914 and the subsequent loss of the British – and European – Empires during the 20th century while the *Pax Americana* took the *Pax Britannica's* place, Covid-19 has plunged Western civilisation into a further decline and destroyed the old order of liberal globalism and replaced it with popular nationalism's and authoritarian orders and travel bans. By October 2021 Covid had caused 4.91 million worldwide deaths, 728,000 American, 139,000 British and 1.288 million European deaths, with the UK having the highest number of deaths in Europe and leading the world in new infections (with a new Delta strain, AY4.2, looming). Like a latter-day Thucydides or Galen, in this work I describe a plague that has shut down Western economies and societies and seems more cataclysmic than the plagues of the past.

There is a Western perspective and an Eastern perspective on what will happen. I must start with the Western perception of coming events.

Western perspective of the end of the Pax Americana
A *Pax Americana* was spoken of soon after the First World War. It really came into its own at the end of the Second World War, after the two atomic bombs America dropped to end the war with Japan. America was then supreme throughout the world as the only nuclear power, organised the $13-billion Marshall Plan for European recovery, put the UN in place through 'Rockefellers' (who owned its site and provided the building and many of its original staff), and established NATO. The *Pax Americana* held, its visible symbol being NATO, but the Cold War divided Europe at the Berlin Wall, and the USSR and Eastern Europe were beyond its reach. The spreading of Communism into China in 1949 meant there was a swathe of anti-Western territories from Moscow to Peking (Beijing).

In spite of the difficulties of the Cold War, including the Cuban Crisis in 1962 and the Vietnam War, which ended in a hurried US withdrawal from Vietnam in 1975, the *Pax Americana* continued to hold until 1992, after the end of the USSR and the pulling down of the Berlin Wall.

There were wars under both the *Pax Romana* and the *Pax Americana*, but both the Roman and Western civilisations were prosperous. The Peace (*Pax*) did not mean complete peace but prosperity in military, agricultural, trade and manufacturing enterprises. Zbigniew Brzezinski of the Syndicate wrote in *The Grand Chessboard: American Primacy and its Geostrategic Imperative* (1997): "American global supremacy is... buttressed by an elaborate system of alliances and coalitions that literally span the globe." He was thinking of the UN and WTO (World Trade Organization), the IMF and the World Bank.

The *Pax Americana* was still thriving after 9/11, during the wars in

Afghanistan and Iraq, and under President George W. Bush's War on Terror. Peter Bender in his 2003 article, 'America: The New Roman Empire?' wrote of how both Rome and America expanded to achieve security, how both rendered their enemies permanently harmless and became protective towards other states. Both stopped waging wars and liberated countries to create peace. It was felt (by Charles A. Kupchan) that the *Pax Americana* was over in 1998, and that the war in Iraq marked "the end of the American era", but in 2012 he saw America's military strength as being as central to global stability as in the past.

There is no doubt, however, that under President Obama America weakened, and that under President Trump America's global position weakened further as Trump withdrew America from the Paris Agreement on climate change and demanded that the NATO countries should pay more, and withdrew from the WHO (World Health Organization).

By the outbreak of SARS-CoV-2 in the US, the *Pax Americana* was being challenged. The American-Syndicate bio-warfare attacks on China and Iran (if they happened) backfired, and resulted (perhaps due to retaliation) in the virus infecting many more Americans and Europeans than Chinese. By October 2021 there were 45 million American cases of Covid against 92,462 Chinese cases in a world total of 241 million cases; and 728,000 American deaths against 4,636 Chinese deaths out of a world total of 4.91 million deaths. The Biden administration looked weak, and the American withdrawal from Afghanistan, and removal of combat troops from Iraq, by 11 September 2021, and its handing of Afghanistan to the Taliban after 20 years of fighting, looked like the end of the *Pax Americana*.

Facing a large alliance of 57 authoritarian countries, America stood for the world's democracies as it had done since 1945. There were 125 electoral democracies in 2017, according to a Freedom Ratings table.[1]

Albania	Benin	Chile
Andorra	Bhutan	Colombia
Antigua and Barbuda	Bolivia	Comoros
Argentina	Bosnia and	Costa Rica
Australia	Herzegovina	Croatia
Austria	Botswana	Cyprus
Bahamas	Brazil	Czech Republic
Bangladesh	Bulgaria	Denmark
Barbados	Burkina Faso	Dominica
Belgium	Canada	Dominican Republic
Belize	Cape Verde	Ecuador

El Salvador
Estonia
Fiji
Finland
France
Georgia
Germany
Ghana
Greece
Grenada
Guatemala
Guyana
Hungary
Iceland
India
Indonesia
Ireland
Israel
Italy
Ivory Coast (or
    Côte d'Ivoire)
Jamaica
Japan
Kenya
Kiribati
Kosovo
Latvia
Lesotho
Liberia
Liechtenstein
Lithuania
Luxembourg
Madagascar

Malawi
Malta
Marshall Islands
Mauritius
Mexico
Micronesia
Moldova
Monaco
Mongolia
Montenegro
Namibia
Nauru
Nepal
Netherlands
New Zealand
Nigeria
Northern Cyprus
Norway
Pakistan
Palau
Panama
Papua New
    Guinea
Paraguay
Peru
Philippines
Poland
Portugal
Puerto Rico
Romania
St Kitts and Nevis
St Lucia
St Vincent and

the Grenadines
Samoa
San Marino
São Tomé and
    Principe
Senegal
Serbia
Seychelles
Sierra Leone
Slovakia
Slovenia
Solomon Islands
South Africa
South Korea
Spain
Sri Lanka
Suriname
Sweden
Switzerland
Taiwan
Tanzania
Timor-Leste (or
    East Timor)
Tonga
Trinidad and
    Tobago
Tunisia
Tuvalu
Ukraine
United Kingdom
United States
Uruguay
Vanuatu

The Economist Intelligence Unit (EIU), linked to the weekly *The Economist*, has a Democracy Index of 110 democracies – 23 full democracies, 52 flawed democracies, and 35 hybrid regimes (nations with regular electoral frauds):

23 full democracies

Australia	Iceland	South Korea
Austria	Ireland	Spain
Canada	Japan	Sweden
Chile	Luxembourg	Switzerland
Costa Rica	Mauritius	Taiwan
Denmark	Netherlands	United Kingdom
Finland	New Zealand	Uruguay
Germany	Norway	

52 flawed democracies

Albania	Hungary	Philippines
Argentina	India	Poland
Belgium	Indonesia	Portugal
Botswana	Israel	Romania
Brazil	Italy	Serbia
Bulgaria	Jamaica	Singapore
Cape Verde	Latvia	Slovakia
Colombia	Lesotho	Slovenia
Croatia	Lithuania	South Africa
Cyprus	Malaysia	Sri Lanka
Czech Republic	Malta	Suriname
Dominican Republic	Mexico	Thailand
Ecuador	Mongolia	Timor-Leste
Estonia	Namibia	Trinidad and Tobago
France	Panama	Tunisia
Ghana	Papua New Guinea	United States
Greece	Paraguay	
Guyana	Peru	

35 hybrid regimes

Armenia	Honduras	Nepal
Bangladesh	Hong Kong	Nigeria
Benin	Ivory Coast	North Macedonia
Bhutan	Kenya	Pakistan
Bolivia	Kyrgyzstan	Senegal
Bosnia and Herzegovina	Lebanon	Sierra Leone
El Salvador	Liberia	Tanzania
Fiji	Madagascar	Turkey
Gambia	Malawi	Uganda
Georgia	Moldova	Ukraine
Guatemala	Montenegro	Zambia
Haiti	Morocco	

America is standing for the world's democracies against a large alliance of authoritarian countries including China and Russia, but in 2016 the USA was downgraded from a full to a flawed democracy. For the last five years it has not got into the EIU's table of full democracies and is still regarded as a flawed democracy. America's chances of returning to the status of a full democracy were not helped by the incident on 6 January 2021 when, as the US election results were due to be certified there, the Capitol was invaded and nearly sacked for the first time since 1814, when British soldiers sacked the building.

There are 57 authoritarian regimes listed by the EIU:

57 authoritarian regimes

Afghanistan	Comoros	Iraq
Algeria	Cuba	Jordan
Angola	Democratic Republic	Kazakhstan
Azerbaijan	of the Congo	Kuwait
Bahrain	Djibouti	Laos
Belarus	Egypt	Libya
Burkina Faso	Equatorial Guinea	Mali
Burundi	Eritrea	Mauritania
Cambodia	Eswatini	Mozambique
Cameroon	Ethiopia	Myanmar
Central African	Gabon	Nicaragua
Republic	Guinea	Niger
Chad	Guinea-Bissau	North Korea
China	Iran	Oman

Palestine	Sudan	Uzbekistan
Qatar	Syria	Venezuela
Republic of the Congo	Tajikistan	Vietnam
Russia	Togo	Yemen
Rwanda	Turkmenistan	Zimbabwe
Saudi Arabia	United Arab Emirates	

America, the leader of the world's democracies, has to stand up to Communist China and its allies: Russia, Iran and (since 2021) Syria. An anti-Western axis stretches from Moscow and Tehran to Beijing, and it is significant that the last two, Tehran and Beijing, seem to have suffered American-Syndicate bio-warfare attacks. The sheer might of the anti-Western coalition makes the British decision to base two Royal-Navy ships in the Far East as a bulwark against China seem the hollow posturing of Brexiteers' neo-imperial delusions that risks a serious collision with China. The same can be said of the British decision to send its £3-billion aircraft carrier HMS *Queen Elizabeth* (named after the Tudor Elizabeth I) to visit 40 countries when five out of six of Britain's destroyers and half its 18 warships were out of action for repairs for which there was no money, and China has 360 "battle-force" ships.

The hegemony of the West began c.1700 when English GDP per capita overtook that in China's Yangtze delta. The West's 320-year-old hegemony, taken from China, now looks over, and it looks as if China is taking it back.

There is a feeling that the *Pax Americana* has come to an end, that a new world is dawning and the US will no longer lead it from a position of supremacy. A shift of power between nations began at the end of the Cold War, and has been accelerating in the 21st century. America remains a powerful country, but America's global power has been eroding for some time, and the power of other countries has grown, giving them the ability to manage global affairs independently of the US's wishes. It feels that America is in decline.

This global trend indicates the end of 'American exceptionalism', that America is an exceptional nation, which Americans have always thought it was since the nation was founded. The American era of global domination that began about 1948 seems to be drawing to a close. The US continues to have the world's only global military capability, which can be deployed anywhere in the world – the US has troops in 140 countries and 800 military bases in 70 countries, and the Syndicate's 457 pipelines cover much of every continent – but its leadership was erratic and contradictory under President Trump and is co-operative but uncertain under President Biden.

The rules-based international order has weakened, and we have seen on p.95 that America and China are preparing for war against each other. No longer is America central to the international system, China has come up alongside it, and American diplomacy is no longer essential to multinational agreements on climate change, regional security and arms control.

At the time of writing there is a crisis in Western leadership. Biden has deteriorated rapidly and after reading out policy decisions answers no questions. No one else is capable of leading the West. Macron is busy trying to be re-elected, Merkel is retiring and Johnson is a gesturing, pretend leader who makes empty promises and goes missing at difficult times. The West is struggling, and Putin senses he can invade Ukraine and Xi senses he can invade Taiwan, and that the West can do nothing about either breach of the rules.

Countries from the East are acting independently of America. Japan has lifted moral restrictions on its defence spending and the deployment of its military in view of growing Chinese power. North Korea is pursuing nuclear power and behaves like a regional overlord. India is a growing economic and military power. Russia is behaving like a great power, being assertive and counterbalancing the power of the US. America lacks authority in handling such independent states. And America's own secret forecaster is forecasting a nightmare by 2025.

Deagel.com's forecast of the West's depopulation in 2025
America's most secret intelligence agency Deagel.com has made a series of predictions on the population numbers of each country in 2025 (the year the World Bank sees as ending Covid-19, and the year a new virus arrives in Event 201's scenario on 'SPARS').

Deagel has foreseen a massive drop in the West's population numbers in 2025, following Covid-19 and the Great Reset. From its disclaimer, as we shall see, Deagel foresees a nuclear war involving the US and its allies such as the UK and the main EU countries, and the China-Russia 'block' as a possible originator. Russia is trying to undermine the EU: throughout Europe, right-wing parties are funded by Russian loans and are calling for exiting the EU, and there is some evidence that Russia interfered in the 2016 British Brexit referendum and in the 2016 US presidential election won by Trump. But Deagel also foresees a collapse of the West as being a more likely scenario. Until April 2021 its predictions have been regularly updated. Since then Deagel has mysteriously removed the population figures from its website. I have retrieved some of them from a video based on 2017 figures.

Worldometer's projection of the world population in 2025 is 8,184,637,460 (the limit of 8 billion having been reached in 2023). In 2017 Deagel gave the world's population as 7.4 billion and forecast that in 2025 it would be 6.9 billion (0.5 billion down). The US would be down from 327 million to just under 100 million (227 million down, a 70 per cent decline in its population), Canada down from 36 million to 26 million (10 million down), the UK down from 66 million to 15 million (51 million down, a 77 per cent decline), Germany down from 81 million to 28 million (53 million down), and France down from 67 million to 39 million (28 million down).

Certain countries have cataclysmic population reductions, such as the US and UK (70 and 77 per cent), but many other populations remained roughly the same, such as those of China and Russia. The nature of the cataclysm affecting the West cannot simply be a climatic disaster but must be some form of warfare, and this may not be a nuclear war as Deagel suggest. It could be the new virus forecast in 2025 by Event 201.

Websites say that Deagel "predicts massive global depopulation of 50% to 80% by 2025".[2] However, 50 per cent to 80 per cent of 8.1 billion gives a world population of 1.7–4.09 billion, whereas the Deagel figure in 2017 for the 2025 world population is 6.9 billion. It looks as if Deagel is forecasting a massive drop in the population of the West.

As we shall see, Deagel forecast a cataclysmic event involving the collapse of the Western financial system and the wiping out of the standard of living of its people, putting an end to the stock market and pension funds and causing widespread migration from the US and Europe. Much of the American population will migrate to Latin America and Asia, and there will be a similar migration from the present European Union and the UK. There would be a stunning fall of the West, and ultimately of Western civilisation.

According to the video based on 2017 figures,[3] the contrast in the forecast populations of the US, leader of the West, and of China, Russia and India from the East in 2025 as opposed to 2017 can be taken in at a glance:

- The US population forecast for 2025 would be 99,153,100, not as in 2017 326,620,000 (and in 2020 331 million), a drop of more than 227 million. US GDP would be $2,445,124, not $19,360,000.
- China's population in 2025 would be 1,358,440,000, not 1,380,000,000 as in 2017, and its GDP would be $16,967,051, not $11,940,000.
- Russia's population would be 141,830,780, not 142,260,000 as in 2017. Russia's GDP would be $4,324,406, not $1,470,000.

- India's population would be 1,341,720,000, not 1,280,000,000 as in 2017. India's GDP would be $5,124,927, not $2,440,000.

Europe is affected by the depopulation blighting the US:

- The UK's population would be 14,617,860, not 65,650,000 as in 2017. The UK's GDP would be $197,472, not $2,560,000.
- Germany's population would be 40,771,740 (as opposed to 28 million in the previous prediction), not 80,590,000 as in 2017. Germany's GDP would be $1,049,572, not $3,360,000.
- France's population would be 45,876,080, not 66,550,000 as in 2017. France's GDP would be $1,289,233, not $2,420,000.
- Italy's population would be 47,214,320, not 61,850,000 as in 2017. Italy's GDP would be $1,505,180, not $1,820,000.

These population forecasts show a stark drop in the populations of the US and Europe – the West. There is clearly an event that is being forecast that will cause this. Deagel speak of a nuclear attack on the West, but as there would be immediate retaliation this is unlikely. Deagel's planning seems to be based on a worsening of the current pandemic and the effects of the Great Reset. It is clear that the Great Reset involves a shift of power from the West to the East, and affects the Western financial system, so it can be anticipated that if the Great Reset proceeds there will be a dramatic fall of the West.

As the Great Reset is gaining impetus from Covid (as we have seen on p.107), it is reasonable to assume that there has been a Syndicate plan for a Great Reset to run concurrently with Covid, which can be blamed on China following a deliberate release in Wuhan (most probably at the Wuhan Military World Games), and that Deagel, as America's most secret intelligence agency, is party to the plan and has reflected the plan in its population figures, masking it as a nuclear event. In short, the Deagel figures are not guesswork and do not assume a nuclear event, but take account of what is expected from the Syndicate plan.

How reliable is Deagel? Is Deagel indulging in dystopian fantasy, or does it know something we do not know?

Deagel is an intelligence organisation of the US government. It has been operating since 2003, the time of the Iraq War, and is secret – and said not to exist. It is routinely used by the CIA. It was used as reference material in a Stratfor report on the technological capabilities of the People's Republic of North Korea. Deagel's reports have been presented to the US President during presidential meetings and provide information that is then used by the intelligence communities and governments, including the National Security Agency, NATO, OECD, OSCE, the Russian Defense Procurement Agency, Stratfor, the World Bank and the UN.

Since 2015, one prediction of Deagel.com has not changed: China will be the largest economy on the planet in 2025. And this prediction may have been behind the possible bio-warfare attacks on China and Iran.

As regards its reliability, Deagel itself stated on its forecast page on 26 October 2014:

> Take into account that the forecast is nothing more than a model whether flawed or correct. It is not God's word or a magic device that allows to (*sic*) foresee the future.

But this may be a smokescreen to conceal the detailed planning that has gone into Deagel's forecasts, and in view of the above Deagel's forecasts have to be taken seriously and should not be dismissed as doomsters' dystopian whims.

Deagel has attributed the fall of the West's populations to an event that is compounded by the end of the West's financial system, partly caused by its printing of money, as an old system collapses. Covid-19 is a factor in the fall of the West and, looking at the sharp drop in forecast population figures for 2025, some have wondered: what if the vaccines are programmed to result in death a few years later, to deliver Deagel's figures? A nightmare thought, which I, for one, dismiss, trusting in the integrity of the vaccine researchers. However, a US war with China, which can now fire hypersonic missiles at 3,850 mph, does look increasingly possible, if not likely, and this may account for the falls in the populations of the US and Europe.

A senior commander in the US Space Force (General David Thompson) has admitted that America is lagging behind China's hypersonic weapons capability after China launched a hypersonic spacecraft carrying a nuclear warhead that successfully fired a missile into the South China Sea while travelling at five times the speed of sound. The Pentagon is uncertain how to launch a missile from a manoeuvrable spacecraft travelling at hypersonic speeds, and it is unclear whether the weapon is intended as an air-to-air missile or has been developed to destroy missile defence systems on the ground.

America's Dark Eagle weapon is also hypersonic and can travel at more than five times the speed of sound. To date there have been successful tests and one failed test in Alaska. Russia has its own hypersonic weapons and their long range has caused America to reactivate a nuclear artillery unit in Germany for the first time since the Cold War. America is up against both long-range Russian and Chinese hypersonic missiles. It is likely that Deagel were aware of a new impending hypersonic Cold War.

Deagel have stated: "In 2014 we published a disclaimer about the forecast. In six years the scenario has changed dramatically. This new disclaimer is meant to single out the situation from 2020 onwards." Deagel's 2020[4] disclaimer gives a number of clues to its thinking:

Talking about the United States and European Union as separated entities no longer makes sense. Both are the Western block, keep printing money and will share the same fate.

After Covid we can draw two major conclusions:

1. The Western world success model has been built over societies with no resilience that can barely withstand any hardship, even a low intensity one. It was assumed that we got the full confirmation beyond any doubt.

2. The Covid crisis will be used to extend the life of this dying economic system through the so-called Great Reset.

The Great Reset – like the climate change, extinction rebellion, planetary crisis, green revolution, shale oil... hoaxes promoted by the system – is another attempt to slow down dramatically the function of natural resources and therefore extend the lifetime of the current system.

It can be effective for a while but finally won't adjust the bottom-line problem and will only delay the inevitable.

The core ruling *élites* hope to stay in power which is in effect the only thing that really worries them.

The collapse of the Western financial system – and ultimately the Western civilisation – has been the major driver in the forecast along with a confluence of crisis with a devastating outcome.

As Covid has proven Western societies embracing multiculturalism and extreme liberalism are unable to deal with any real hardship.

It is quite likely that the economic crisis due to the lockdowns will cause more deaths than the virus worldwide.

The stark reality of diverse and multicultural Western societies is that a collapse will have a toll of 50 to 80 per cent depending on several factors but in general terms the most diverse, multicultural, indebted and wealthy (highest standard of living) will suffer the highest toll.

The only glue that keeps united such aberrant collage from falling apart is overconsumption with heavy doses of bottomless degeneracy disguised as virtue.

Nevertheless, the widespread censorship, hate laws and contradictory signals mean that even that glue is not working any more. Not everybody has to die. Migration can also play a positive role in this.

The formerly known as second and third world nations are an unknown at this point. Their fate will depend upon the decisions they take in the future.

Western powers are not going to take over them as they did in the past because these countries won't be able to control their own cities far less likely countries that are far away.

If they remain tied to the former World Order they will go down along Western powers.

There is a lot of bad blood in the Western societies and the protests, demonstrations, rioting and looting are only the first symptoms of what is coming. However a new trend is taking place overshadowing this one.

Six years ago [i.e. in 2014] the likelihood of a major war was tiny. Since then it has grown steadily and dramatically and today is by far the most likely major event in the 2020s.

Another particularity of the Western system is that its individuals have been brainwashed to the point that the majority accept their moral high ground and technological edge as a given.

This has given the rise of the supremacy of the emotional arguments over the rational ones which are ignored or deprecated. That mindset can play a key role in the upcoming catastrophic events.

Over the next decade it will become obvious that the West is falling behind the Russia-China block and the malaise might grow into desperation.

Going to war might seem a quick and easy solution to restore the lost hegemony to finally find them into a France 1940 moment.

If there is not a dramatic change of course the world is going to witness the first nuclear war. The Western block collapse may come before, during or after the war.

It does not matter. A nuclear war is a game with billions of casualties and the collapse plays in the hundreds of millions.

The last words suggest that Deagel's forecast of a population reduction of 0.5 billion to 6.9 billion in 2025 is based on the collapse of the West rather than a nuclear war, a fall of the West caused by Covid and the Great Reset as the Syndicate organise a drawing-together of West and East in an authoritarian world government.

The event connected with the end of the West's financial system and printing of money (see pp.122–123) may be connected with the Great Reset. It is possible that the population-reduction target can be met by nanotechnology, by 5G control of the brain. As we have seen (on p.104) the technocratic control of the brain has positive medical benefits in treating strokes, blindness, deafness and so on, but it also has negative possibilities: it can enable ruthless controllers to switch off (i.e. put to death) targeted brains to keep the world's population well below 8 billion. Deagel's unexplained predictions may be based on the Great Reset's policy of technocratic brain control.

Technocratic, as opposed to democratic, treatment of the brain requires international legislation under treaty (see p.104), like the US Biological Weapons Anti-Terrorism Act of 1989 (see pp.xvii, 145, 162) further to the international Biological Weapons Convention disarmament treaty of 1972, which is implemented by the United Nations Office for Disarmament Affairs (see p.161). Such a treaty will protect the brains of all humankind from State manipulation by 5G, with involvement from the UN (even though the current Secretary-General Guterres is in partnership with Schwab of the World Economic Forum, see p.106).

Deagel sees the West as tottering and the Great Reset as managing an inevitable fall that will bring West and East together in a technocratic authoritarian world government based on 5G and nanotechnology.

Deagel and The Kissinger Report
Looking back on *The Kissinger Report* (see pp.12–13) from Deagel. com's forecasts, we can see that the 200-page study by the US National Security Council under Henry Kissinger, *National Security Study Memorandum 200: Implications of Worldwide Population Growth for US Security and Overseas Interests,* falsely claimed that lesser developed countries (LDCs) such as India were a grave threat to US national security. *NSSM 200* was adopted as official policy in November 1975 by President Ford, and was a covert plan to reduce population growth in LCDs through birth control and also (implicitly) by war and famine, as we have seen. Brent Scowcroft, who replaced Kissinger as National Security Advisor, was put in charge of implementing the plan, and the CIA Director George H.W. Bush was ordered to assist Scowcroft, as were the Secretaries of State, Treasury, Defense, and Agriculture.

The Kissinger Report looked back to the UK's Royal Commission on Population, which King George VI created in 1944, "to consider what measures should be taken in the national interest to influence the future trend of population". The Commission found that Britain was gravely threatened by population growth in its colonies, the biggest being India, since "a populous country has decided advantages over a sparsely-populated one for industrial production". Increasing population and industrialisation in its colonies might have "effects on the prestige and influence of the West", especially on "military strength and security".

The Kissinger Report similarly concluded that the US was threatened by population growth in ex-colonies, the 13 key countries in which the US has a "special political and strategic interest" being: India, Bangladesh, Pakistan, Indonesia, Thailand, the Philippines, Turkey, Nigeria, Egypt, Ethiopia, Mexico, Brazil and Colombia. As these countries might quickly increase their relative political, economic and military strengths, what is known as "depopulation policy" came into being. The UN's Agenda 21 includes a British sterilisation policy and other policies implemented through the UN to keep nations under Anglo-American influence.

This approach is part of the West's financial system which is heading for a complete collapse, according to Deagel.com.

Deagel.com and UN Agendas 21 and 2030

The population forecasts in Deagel.com draw on Agenda 21 and Agenda 2030 (see pp.39, 40–41). They focus on world population within these two projects.

The UN's Agenda 21 (1992) focused on achieving global sustainable development in the 21st century, and this will come to an end in March 2025, the date the World Bank had as the end of Covid, when the developed world will be depopulated by 90 per cent.[5]

The UN Agenda 2030 (2015) focused on 17 Sustainable Development Goals (SDGs), and Deagel's more recent take is that five years after the depopulation of the developed world in 2025 Agenda 2030 will reduce the undeveloped world's population by at least 90 per cent.[6]

Summing up the Western perspective

Returning to the Western perspective of its immediate scenario, the West is dreaming that it will get through the pandemic and is looking to its companies and corporations to eke out its influence. It is preparing for the rebranding of Nelson Rockefeller's New World Order as 'the Great Reset', and is working towards centralised governance – a world government – by unelected leaders to bring authoritarian solutions to the problems of the West, notably the collapse of the financial system in a time of coming inflation. The West is lagging behind the East, the bio-warfare attack on

China (if it happened) did not work, and the gulf between West and East is startling, and, as in Deagel.com's forecasts, shocking.

The West will be relying on public surveillance, AI (artificial intelligence) and technological solutions to problems to bring digital, physical and biological systems together in a Fourth Industrial Revolution that will extend life and health and fight disease to create a transhuman life – and delay the fall of the West.

The Eastern perspective and China's Belt-and-Road Initiative (2013)
The Eastern perspective and scenario is centred around China's being the number-one world economy in 2025 as Deagel has forecast, having

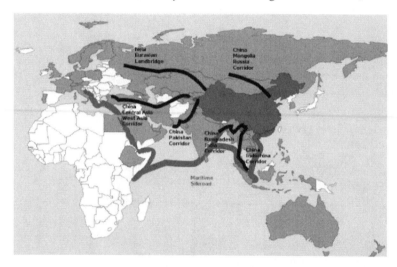

Two maps showing the land and sea routes of China's Belt-and-Road Initiative (2013), China's international-trade network extended its global lending program to Africa and Asia through its Belt-and-Road Initiative (or One Belt, One Road), a strategy adopted in 2013 as part of China's response to America's hostility after 2009–2010, to develop global infrastructure in 140 countries and 30 international organisations.

The Belt-and-Road Initiative (or the "Silk Road Economic Belt and the 21st-century Maritime Silk Road Development Strategy") was originally announced in 2013, the 'Belt' being short for "the Silk Road Economic Belt", referring to the land road and rail transport routes through Central Asia, and the 'Road' being short for the "21st-century Maritime Silk Road", referring to the sea routes through South-East Asia to South Asia, the Middle East and Africa.

The Belt-and-Road Initiative (BRI) was incorporated into China's Constitution in 2017. It is regarded by the US as a China-centred international-trade network, and Australia announced in April 2021 it would be pulling out. The Belt-and-Road Initiative is set to boost world GDP by $7.1 trillion by 2040, according to Global Consultants CEBR (Centre for Economics and Business Research), London.

The BRI project builds on China's traditional trade routes that connected China to the West, and include Marco Polo's route and the Silk-Road trade route in the north and Admiral Zheng He's maritime route in the south. China helps countries invest in infrastructure and construction materials, education, railways and highways, automobiles, real estate, power grid, and iron and steel. It is one of the largest-ever infrastructure-and-investment projects and in 2017 covered 68

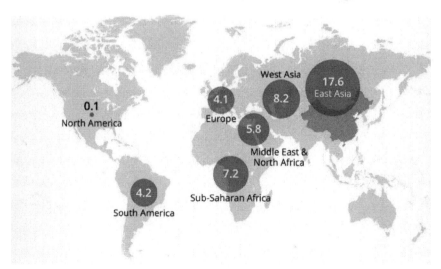

China's BRI investment by world region in 2020 (in billions of US dollars)

countries, 65 per cent of the world's population and 40 per cent of global GDP. In January 2021 it had expanded to cover 140[7] countries that have joined the BRI by signing a Memorandum of Understanding (MoU) with China.

The Chinese currency, the renminbi, is the currency of international transactions, and China's diplomatic relations with all the countries create new markets for Chinese products and allow China to export its surplus industrial capacity and to integrate countries rich in raw materials and commodities more closely into the Chinese economy. Whereas the West sees the project as extending and expanding Chinese influence, it in fact connects Asia, Europe and Africa and draws them together in a levelling-up the Syndicate want, and China is reducing the dependence of these countries on America.

The BRI project is the beginning of a Chinese global empire. In January 2019 there were 790 individual projects within BRI. Trade along the Silk Road could account for almost 40 per cent of world trade, and 63 per cent of the world's population is affected by BRI. The BRI project now dwarfs the post-war American Marshall Plan.

The Silk-Road Economic Belt is in fact three belts (see four maps on p.133): the North Belt runs through Central Asia and Russia to Europe; the Central Belt through Central Asia and West Asia to the Persian Gulf and Mediterranean; and the South Belt through South-East Asia, South Asia and Pakistan to the Indian Ocean. China will be integrated with Central Asia through an infrastructure program in Kazakhstan.

The Maritime Silk Road connects China (see maps on pp.128, 133) to Hanoi (Vietnam), Jakarta (Indonesia), Singapore, Kuala Lumpur (Malaysia), Colombo (Sri Lanka), Southern India, Malé (The Maldives), Mombasa (East Africa), Djibouti (Horn of Africa), the Red Sea, Haifa (Israel), Istanbul (Turkey), Athens (Greece), Trieste (Italy), Poland and the Baltic States (Central Europe) and Northern Europe and the North Sea.

There will also be an Ice Silk Road in which Russia and China (both close to 'Rothschilds' and 'Rockefellers') jointly build infrastructure along a north-sea route in the Arctic within Russia's territorial waters.

There is also to be a grid project (six electric grids) involving all Asia. A project involving Bangladesh, China, India and Myanmar has been dropped because of India's refusal to take part.

A consequence of all this is that China has invested billions of dollars in improving the infrastructure of South-Asian countries – Pakistan, Nepal, Sri Lanka, Bangladesh and Afghanistan – and a North–South road is being built in Armenia (where there have been pipeline problems involving the Syndicate, see p.34). China is one of the fastest-growing investors in India.

The financing of China's infrastructure comes from the Asian Infrastructure Investment Bank (AIIB), which had $160 billion of infrastructure projects in 2015, and the Silk Road Fund, a development fund of $40 billion which invests in businesses rather than projects. Sixty per cent of lending from Chinese banks is to developing countries. Covid has interfered with some of these projects, stopping work, and some projects have been scrapped, but China's prospects in the coming years are good.

China, which still has strong links with 'Rothschilds' and 'Rockefellers', sees its future as spreading further round the world through infrastructure projects and levelling up developing countries. A look at the map shows that just about all Asia, the Middle East, Africa, part of Europe, and Latin America can be in the BRI strategy in the coming years, and the only countries outside BRI are the West (the US and Canada, part of Europe and supporting countries with a Western way of life such as Israel, Australia and New Zealand).

The 140 countries[8] in the Belt-and-Road Initiative are spread across all continents:

- 40 countries in Sub-Saharan Africa;
- 34 BRI countries in Europe and Central Asia (including 18 countries of the European Union that are part of the BRI);
- 24 BRI countries in East Asia and Pacific;
- 17 BRI countries in Middle East and North Africa;
- 19 BRI countries in Latin America and Caribbean;
- 6 countries in South-East Asia.

The 140 BRI countries[9] that take part in China's Belt-and-Road Initiative in alphabetical order are (excluding China):

Afghanistan	Belarus	Cameroon
Albania	Benin	Chad
Algeria	Bolivia	Chile
Angola	Bosnia and	Comoros
Antigua and Barbuda	Herzegovina	Congo, Dem. Rep.
Armenia	Botswana	Congo, Rep.
Austria	Brunei Darussalam	Cook Islands
Azerbaijan	Bulgaria	Costa Rica
Bahrain	Burundi	Côte d'Ivoire
Bangladesh	Cabo Verde	Croatia
Barbados	Cambodia	Cuba

Cyprus	Liberia	Samoa
Czech Republic	Libya	Saudi Arabia
Djibouti	Lithuania	Senegal
Dominica	Luxembourg	Serbia
Dominican Republic	Madagascar	Seychelles
Ecuador	Malaysia	Sierra Leone
Egypt, Arab Rep.	Maldives	Singapore
El Salvador	Mali	Slovak Republic
Equatorial Guinea	Malta	Slovenia
Estonia	Mauritania	Solomon Islands
Ethiopia	Micronesia, Fed. States	Somalia
Fiji	Moldova	South Africa
Gabon	Mongolia	South Sudan
Gambia, The	Montenegro	Sri Lanka
Georgia	Morocco	Sudan
Ghana	Mozambique	Suriname
Greece	Myanmar	Tajikistan
Grenada	Namibia	Tanzania
Guinea	Nepal	Thailand
Guyana	New Zealand	Timor-Leste
Hungary	Niger	Togo
Indonesia	Nigeria	Tonga
Iran, Islamic Rep.	Niue	Trinidad and Tobago
Iraq	North Macedonia	Tunisia
Italy	Oman	Turkey
Jamaica	Pakistan	Uganda
Kazakhstan	Panama	Ukraine
Kenya	Papua New Guinea	United Arab Emirates
Kiribati	Peru	Uruguay
Korea, Rep.	Philippines	Uzbekistan
Kuwait	Poland	Vanuatu
Kyrgyz Republic	Portugal	Venezuela, RB
Lao PDR	Qatar	Vietnam
Latvia	Romania	Yemen, Rep.
Lebanon	Russian Federation	Zambia
Lesotho	Rwanda	Zimbabwe

China's challenge to the West

We are beginning to see why, from China's perspective, there can be a fall of the West before 2025. China and Russia contest America's global role, and a growing number of other countries are asserting a role in regional, economic and security fields that is independent of the West.

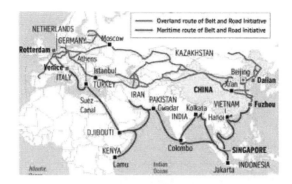

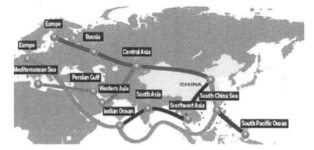

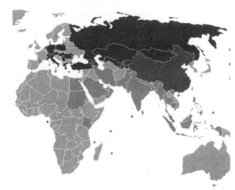

Four more maps showing China's Belt-and-Road Initiative and trade, and 140 countries in which China's influence is replacing the West's

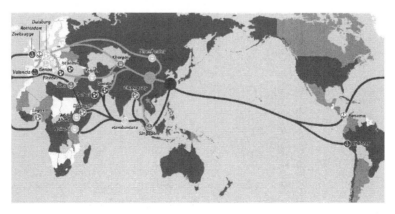

More and more countries are turning to China for financial support, and China had ploughed nearly £700 billion into members of the Commonwealth. China has persuaded Barbados to reject the Queen as its Head of State and to become a republic to rely on Chinese investment, with Jamaica set to follow. China's billions are buying up the Commonwealth: Commonwealth countries are now becoming in effect Chinese "client states".

In the Middle East, the US has sought to isolate Iran for decades, and John Bolton has continued this policy, but it is no longer working – hence the bio-warfare attack on Iran (if it happened). The Russians have a long-standing relationship with Assad, and are in Syria and the Middle East for good. Both the Russian and Turkish operations in Syria are independent of the US. The US failed to see that Saddam Hussein counterbalanced the power of Iran, as in the Iran-Iraq war, and in overthrowing Saddam in 2003 failed to create a stable Iraq that could influence events involving Iran and Syria.

American efforts to contain the rise of China have failed, and China

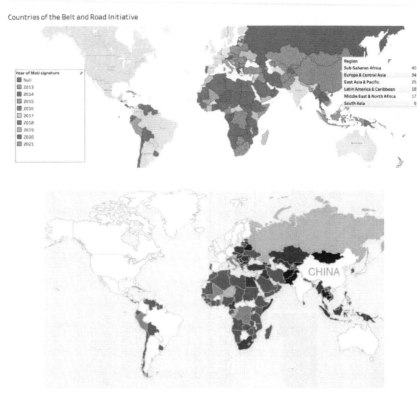

Countries of the Belt and Road Initiative

Two maps showing the West's southern and eastern borders
pressed by China's Belt-and-Road Initiative[12]

has armed artificial islands in the South China Sea and built a military base in Djibouti. China's global lending program, the Belt-and-Road Initiative, has strengthened its global role in climate change. China is spreading its political and economic influence into Africa and Latin America, and in 2021 Afghanistan, and the US has been unable to slow China's economic growth and contain its power. Hence the bio-warfare attack on China (if it happened). Hence there may have been, or may be, a semi-retaliatory biological, bio-warfare attack on the West – and that is what may have driven Deagel's forecasts for 2025.

We have seen (on pp.76–77) that America turned hostile towards China in 2009–2010, and that China took steps to manage this in 2012 and 2013, and the expansion of China's 2013 BRI into 140 countries is a stunning riposte to the US's hostility. It again looks as if the bio-warfare attack (if it happened) was about halting BRI by discrediting China in the eyes of the host countries.

The Syndicate's Council on Foreign Relations on the Belt-and-Road Initiative
How should America respond to the vastness of BRI? How can the West compete with this bloc of 140 countries?

The American Council on Foreign Relations (CFR), a Syndicate organisation (which David Rockefeller joined in 1941 and of which he was appointed a director in 1949),[10] has sponsored an Independent Task Force report on a 'US Response to China's Belt and Road Initiative'. And we can begin to realise just how Covid has affected BRI. The CFR report says:[11] "BRI have funded and built roads, power plants, ports, railways, fifth-generation (5G) networks, and fibre-optic cable around the world."

In practice BRI lends funds to unsustainable projects, adding to countries' debt burdens. The CFR report says: "It locks some countries into carbon-intensive futures by promoting coal-fired power plants, tilts the playing-field in major markets toward Chinese companies, promotes exclusive reliance on Chinese technology, and draws countries into tighter economic and political relationships with Beijing." The Covid-19 pandemic has "accelerated host countries' reckoning with the initiative, in many cases eviscerating their ability to pay for projects and forcing them to stall or cancel expensive projects. The pandemic has driven the Chinese government to pivot to a more slimmed-down, cost-effective and technology-focused BRI." This might be the reason for the American-Syndicate bio-warfare attack on China (if it happened), and the virus seems to have succeeded in slowing down the BRI project and the host countries' response.

The CFR report identifies China's willingness and ability to fill voids left by the US because of cutbacks in federal research, development funding and investments in advanced technologies. China has stepped in and moved ahead of the US in "the sale of 5G technology, the installation of high-speed rail, the production of solar and wind energy, the promulgation of electronic payment platforms, the development of ultra-high-voltage transmission systems, and more". The US's withdrawal from the Trans-Pacific Partnership and disinterest in multilateral trade agreements in Asia has allowed China to have a central position in regional trade.

The CFR is recommending that the US adopts a strategy that improves governance standards along the BRI and provides an effective alternative to BRI. It says the US should promote sustainable infrastructure, uphold high environmental and anti-corruption standards in foreign infrastructure projects, ensure that non-Chinese companies operate on a level playing-field in foreign markets, and assist countries to preserve their political independence. The CFR Task Force report offers a strategy to do this. It details steps to improve US competitiveness; specifies how the US can do more with allies, partners and multilateral organisations to better meet countries' infrastructure needs; and offers steps to detect US security interests in the 140 BRI countries. The US should not match China dollar for dollar or project for project, but should try to offer a compelling alternative to BRI that makes use of US strengths: cutting-edge technologies, world-class companies, pools of capital, tried international leadership, a role in setting international standards, and support for the rule of law and transparency in business.

The US response to BRI is to question the sustainability of many BRI projects and debt sustainability. Otherwise countries wrecked by the pandemic could be forced to choose between making debt payments and providing healthcare and social services to their citizens.

President Biden's squaring up to China
President Biden, who arrived after the biological attack (if it happened), is confronted by practical issues regarding China, the effects of Xi's aggressive, authoritarian one-party state: human rights abuses, cyberhacking, trade that conflicts with improving climate change, Taiwan, maritime disputes and the Indian border, all likely to cause military action in the near future. China is on a single-minded drive to replace America as the world's number-one great power and establish its authoritarian model of governance as the one that should be the norm for all nations.

President Biden has set limits on business and investment in China and retained trade sanctions. There are new penalties for China's treatment of Hong Kong and Xinjiang (the Uyghurs). President Biden has condemned Chinese cyberattacks, and 30 NATO members, the EU, Australia, New Zealand and Japan have endorsed his approach. He has worked for a united anti-Chinese policy at the G7 and NATO summits, and at Quad (US, Japan, Australia and India) and Five Eyes meetings and in conversations with other national leaders.

The reaction has been mixed. Germany and France are reluctant to start a new Cold War, and Hungary, Greece and Italy will have BRI projects which Berlin would not finance. And NATO, which is centred on the North Atlantic, is wondering if it should be active in Asia and the Pacific.

The US is competing with BRI and hopes to match Xi's global infrastructure plan in 140 countries and to match China's distribution of vaccines to Asia and Africa. On 2 August 2021 President Biden sent to Congress a request for a program of infrastructure projects (such as roads, bridges and airports) within America costing nearly $1 trillion.

It was announced at the end of September 2021 that in an attempt to counter Beijing's BRI with an alternative, Biden was planning to launch a $2.5-trillion infrastructure scheme known in the White House as 'Build Back Better for the World' (a slogan from the Great Reset), initially aimed at South America's Colombia, Ecuador and Panama. But no fewer than 19 governments across South America and the Caribbean had already signed up to the Belt-and-Road Initiative. Even more than before, the Great Reset included world infrastructure projects in both East and now West. However, it was uncertain that Biden would get his plan through Congress as his infrastructure plan for America, costing $1 trillion, did not get through – as radical Democrats wanted guarantees on the $2.5 trillion bill. By the end of October 2021 the $3.5 trillion spending spree had been cut to $2 trillion, with pressure to cut it again to $1.75 trillion (half of what Biden wanted to compete with China and fund the Great Reset).

It is now clear that the 2020 call by Klaus Schwab and the World Economic Forum for the Great Reset to include infrastructure projects envisaged at one and the same time China's Belt-and-Road Initiative infrastructure projects in 140 mainly non-Western countries costing $50.1 billion in 2020 (assisted by 'Rothschilds'' central banks) and now America's infrastructure projects costing nearly $1 trillion (and UK and European infrastructure projects such as the UK's High Speed 2 railway project).

It is clear that the Great Reset is already uniting the infrastructure projects of the West and the East and leading towards the Syndicate's world government. The World Economic Forum is in fact a Syndicate Forum.

On a personal note, on 7 October 2015 I chaired the Constitutional Convention of the World Philosophical Forum (WPF) that brought in the Universal State of the Earth (USE). I was told by Igor Kondrashin, the founder of the WPF, that he had founded it on the model of the World Economic Forum (WEF) which had met in Davos since 1971. I had personally advanced the drawing together of West and East in the USE, an interim undemocratic World State with roots in Plato's *Republic* – I brought in the USE in Athens not far from the ruins of Plato's Academy, where Aristotle was a pupil, one of the attractions to me of leading philosopher-kings into creating a World State – and so I too contributed to the Great Reset back in 2015, before the term was even known.

President Biden has ordered the Pentagon (which has funded EcoHealth Alliance since 2013, see p.74) to be ready for military conflict with China. His approach has alienated China and made it less willing to collaborate on climate change (preventing carbon emission), arms control and preventing future pandemics – controlling future viruses. President Biden said in his inaugural address: "Without unity there is no peace." The Syndicate is looking for unity between West and East. But the more America struggles to keep the West united, the more war between the West and China looks a possibility, or even likely.

The Syndicate's attempt to unite Western Pax Americana's *and Eastern BRI's infrastructure projects in a rebranded New World Order and authoritarian world government*
So the West is to work side-by-side with China in BRI countries offering alternative projects. This is a recommendation from the Council on Foreign Relations (see p.136), which, from 1927 on, was funded by the Rockefeller Foundation.[13] We must remember that China could not have developed its economic empire without finance from the Syndicate, particularly from 'Rothschilds' and 'Rockefellers'.

The Great Reset is a rebranding of the New World Order, and the Syndicate's view of the world is of the West and the East together, the 457 oil pipelines and the 790 infrastructure projects of the East coming together within a New World Order that is technocratic and digital – and under the influence of the Syndicate (including 'Rothschilds' and 'Rockefellers'). The Syndicate Council on Foreign Relations' recommendation is that the West and the East should work together in the 140 BRI countries.

The big question regarding the Syndicate's perspective is: can the levelling-up of the East through BRI and the levelling-down of the West end now, so East and West can come together? Or has there to be a further levelling-down of the West to give the reduced populations in Deagel.com's forecast? Are there plans for a nuclear or biological war to reduce the population of the West and complete the levelling-down and fall of the democratic West to prepare for an authoritarian world government of West and East? Is the laboratory-built SARS-CoV-2, an attempt by a faction in the Syndicate to arrest the rise of China through BRI and infrastructure projects, deliberately goading China into releasing a new virus, as forecast in the scenario of Event 201 when its new virus 'SPARS' appears between 2025 and 2028? Is the second biological virus ahead for the West in the Syndicate's plan, and will this reduce the West's population? Is Deagel.com party to the Syndicate's – 'Rothschilds" and 'Rockefellers" – plan?

If apparent conflicts are being reconciled by the Syndicate, it now looks as if, despite President Biden's opposition to Brexit because of its damage to the Irish peace process, the Syndicate wanted the UK to leave the EU so the UK could have 'a global role' in checking China's expansion, by having made arrangements with India and Australia that would limit China's power and by sending HMS *Queen Elizabeth* to the South China Sea to act as a check and balance there. It could be that Johnson was following Syndicate direction in sending HMS *Queen Elizabeth* to patrol the Far East, just as he was following the Syndicate World Economic Forum's Great Reset slogan, 'Build Back Better'. It could be that the Syndicate wanted Brexit so they could transfer Europe's financial capital from the City of London to Amsterdam, as has subsequently happened along with the West's implementing of the Great Reset.

The Syndicate's attempt to unify the West prior to uniting West and East may have been behind the UK's Brexit. The Syndicate had founded the EU in 1954 via the Bilderberg Group, and may have secretly encouraged Brexit to root out the UK's reluctance to integrate within an EU wanting a single foreign policy and army, and to root out the UK's dominance of the financial-services market from London. The financial-services market was left out of the Withdrawal Agreement, and by 2021 the EU had shifted the financial-services market to Amsterdam and had begun a fishing war with a view to banning EU trade with the UK (that amounted to 44 per cent of the UK's trade in 2016) and wait for empty supermarket shelves and massive shortages in the UK to lead to a UK clamour for trade with the EU to resume, a striking way of making it clear to the British people that leaving the EU has caused more damage than if they had remained in the EU. The Syndicate's plan may be to hope that Labour will overthrow Johnson and return to the EU in the future – without the City of London's dominance (which has already moved to the Continent), with a reformed UK attitude towards integration (which would be a condition of the UK's re-entry into the EU) and a UK readiness to replace sterling with the euro and accept a single EU foreign policy and army (which would be further conditions of re-entry). The EU may emerge as the long-term winner following Brexit, with the UK sharing a pan-European implementing of the Great Reset and the Syndicate's New World Order. The tweaking of the UK's long-term relationship with the EU may be part of the Great Reset, and by the end of the Reset the UK may be back in the EU, with the changes the EU always wanted to make having been made.

In the short term, the Great Reset tackles climate change, and the UK's Brexit means that it is not taking part in the EU's New Green Deal to improve long-distance cross-border train services in Europe in order to reduce air travel in view of the climate emergency. Only a few Eurostar trains from the UK go to five destinations in Europe while UK planes (with UK Government support) have increased their services to destinations all over Europe – and this when the UK is chairing the UN Climate Change Conference (COP26) to reduce carbon-dioxide emissions and pollution in Glasgow in November 2021.[14] Moreover, the emergency measures to manage post-Brexit lorry queues, which the UK adopted in October 2019 and extended in December 2020, are to be made indefinite to avoid ongoing disruption as the botched, over-hasty Brexit deal will leave long queues of lorries at Dover and other ports, empty shelves, frustrated businesses and Kent a permanent lorry park, for the foreseeable future, as long as the UK's Brexit lasts – with a huge increase in carbon-dioxide emissions and pollution.[15] The UK has cut greenhouse gas emissions by more than 40 per cent since 1990 by exporting British manufacturing to other countries, including China, and then importing the products manufactured in those countries, including China, the world's greatest polluter.

Is the Syndicate funding and encouraging China and the East, and at the same time funding and encouraging the West, to achieve a balance in the middle, where both sides can meet and agree a world government? Is this what the UK is supposed to be doing with its new independence? Containing China, despite BRI? Acting as a check on China's BRI and so achieving an East-West balance?

Between 2014 and 2018 China spent billions of dollars on infrastructure construction in Pakistan, Nigeria, Bangladesh, Indonesia, Malaysia, Egypt and the UAE, and investing in Singapore, Malaysia, the Russian Federation, Indonesia, South Korea, Israel and

Pakistan. As we have seen, China has engaged with 140 of the UN's 193 nation-states, and with 30 international organisations in BRI. Russia and China have 150 common projects, including natural-gas pipelines and the Polar Silk Road. This is all in opposition to the West.

There are criticisms of BRI's lack of environmental concerns, of building coal-fired power stations in Turkey, and adding to pollution. China is dependent on coal: its annual carbon-dioxide emissions (10.2 billion tonnes in 2019) are 28 times higher than the UK's when its population is only 21 times higher, and account for more than half the world's entire coal-power generation. And with the UN Intergovernmental Panel on Climate Change (IPCC) warning that the 1.5°C limit for a rise in global temperature above pre-industrial levels will be breached within two decades (causing even more flash-floods, wildfires, and drowned islands), the internal coal-fired power plants that power China's economy are under international scrutiny even though China has said publicly it will cease to base its BRI external infrastructure projects on coal-fired plants.[16] (In a last-minute amendment to the text of the COP26 agreement, India, with the support of China, watered down a commitment to "phase *out*" the use of coal to "phase *down*" the use of coal, allowing China, the world's worst polluter, to phase down/carry on polluting with coal-fired plants until 2070, with a climate catastrophe looming that will see the earth approach a rise in global temperature to 2.4°C above the pre-industrial level.) Chinese migrant workers sent abroad live in slave conditions without human rights.

There are concerns that China is engaging in neo-imperialism, and in debt-trap diplomacy – in trapping the countries benefiting from new infrastructure in debts to China, which, when they can't pay, China translates into support for her geostrategic interests. The EU signed an infrastructure agreement with Japan to contain Chinese BRI influence.

There is concern that the Great Reset of the West will create an authoritarian New World Order that is similar to the authoritarian centralised governance of China in a bringing-together of 'Rothschilds'' and 'Rockefellers'' investment in China and the East and 'Rothschilds'' and 'Rockefellers'' investment in the West into one global interlinked pre-world-government alliance. There is even greater concern that China is committed to its three-point-invasion of Taiwan and will be at war with the West, that the silos being created in China will be used by 2025 and that the US and Europe will be targeted while a new bio-warfare virus sweeps through the Western world, causes a dramatic reduction in the West's population and GDP, and brings about the fall of the West.

The most urgent immediate policy of the West's governments and intelligence services – in the US, the UK and the EU, especially Germany, France and Italy – is to make sure the West does not fall to a new virus before 2025.

The decline of the West and the Cultural Revolution
On a personal note, when I was a Professor in Japan from 1963 to 1967 I had a privileged position in the Japanese Government's hierarchy. I was a Professor at three universities in Tokyo; wrote speeches for the Governor of the Bank of Japan (including his speech at the opening of the Asian Development Bank); was tutor to Emperor Hirohito's second son Prince Hitachi, taught him world history and helped plan his State Visit to the UK in October 1965; and selected multilateral conference interpreters at the Ministry of International Trade and Industry. I was present with the Bank of Japan's Vice-Governor when Lord Cromer, Governor of the Bank of England, rang him and asked for a loan in 1965.

I could see at first hand from the centre of Japan's financial Establishment that the West was in decline. Coincidentally, as I said on p.xxi, in 1966 I was asked to deliver a series of lectures titled 'The Decline of the West' to the postgraduate students, and I based my lectures on Gibbon's *The Decline and Fall of the Roman Empire*, Spengler's *The Decline of the West* and Toynbee's *A Study of History*. Also in 1965–1966 I wrote poems on the decline of the West: 'The Silence'; 'Archangel'; and 'Old Man in a Circle'. These three poems were full of images of the UK's decline from the zenith of its imperial heyday in 1914.

Still on a personal note, in 1966, a key year for me, I visited China and discovered the Cultural Revolution in March 1966. (See pp.xix–xx, xxiv–xxv, 46–47, 172.) I have already described (on pp.xix–xx) how on 16 March I went to the University of Peking [Beijing] expecting to see 9,600 students, and found the campus virtually deserted, and was told by a professor that the students were "in the countryside": "It's socialist re-education." I visited a students' dormitory and a 5th-year student acted as spokesman for the dozen students there. Outside the dormitory I asked him why he was not in the countryside. He replied, "Because I have a medical certificate."

The students were being re-educated by the peasants to be anti-bourgeois. The re-education was compulsory, and this student was exonerated as he had a medical certificate. For two days I demanded to see the Vice-President of Peking University and on 19 March I was taken to see him. In an hour-long interview I managed to confirm that the students had been ordered to live alongside peasants by the Communist Party and that a purge of those who held bourgeois attitudes was ahead, which was why they had been sent to work alongside the peasants. See my work *My Double Life 1: This Dark Wood*, pp.505–516 for a full account of these meetings.

I took my discovery back to the West. No one believed there was a purge coming. Then the Cultural Revolution broke in August 1966, and squads of Red Guards waved Mao's *Little Red Book* and purged the bourgeoisie, and all I had said was now believed.

In 1966 I lived through a time of murk and evasion in China when the truth was not being told. The position is similar now, when there is murk and evasion regarding Wuhan and SARS-CoV-2, and whether a virus is about to be unleashed on the West. China has been evasive about Covid, but despite the gain-of-function experiments in the Wuhan laboratory I believe that if there was a deliberate release of SARS-CoV-2 and a bio-warfare attack, China was the victim, not the perpetrator.

Members of the jury, I now see signs of China reacting to a biological attack: the building of silos (see pp.50, 97), the plan to invade Taiwan (see pp.95, 96), and the suspiciously heavy spreading of the virus in the US and Europe, which may be a hidden retaliation.

The Nuclear Age has given way to a Biological Age
I saw clearly in 1966, and I now see that a new era has arrived, a new Age. The Nuclear Age has passed as until now no one can use nuclear weapons without immediate retaliation and extinction (mutually assured destruction). (It remains to be seen if a Chinese hypersonic nuclear missile will trigger an immediate nuclear retaliation.)

Now that SARS-CoV-2 seems to have been human-engineered and funded by the US Pentagon and State Department among others, the suspicion is abroad – among the 6.9 billion in the world who side with China against the 1 billion Westerners – that a bio-warfare attack may have happened. That widespread suspicion is believed by 90 per cent of all Chinese throughout China and many of its Belt-and-Road beneficiaries. *Because* seven-eighths of humankind hold this suspicion and it is so widespread – regardless of whether Covid was actually released by an animal or as the result of an accident in a lab – that belief alone is enough to bring in a new Biological Age, in which a substantial majority of humankind believes that SARS-CoV-2 is the product of covert bio-warfare without the corroboration of conclusive evidence.

And so, assuming Chinese hypersonic missiles will trigger automated AI retaliatory attacks, the Nuclear Age has now been replaced by a

Biological Age in which wars will be fought with viruses rather than nuclear weapons. And the Great Reset reflects this Biological Age with its focus on the digital and biological. Members of the jury, before reaching your overall verdict, please consider whether you are now in a new Biological Age, and the West faces a new biological threat from an expanding China.

And so should we now expect a new bio-warfare attack that will bring about the depopulation of Deagel's forecasts and the fall of the West by 2025? Or is there another way that can avert the fall of the West for a while, a law of history? Has history a lesson that Deagel has ignored?

At this point, members of the jury, regarding Deagel's forecasts and China's Belt-and-Road Initiative being part of the Syndicate's levelling-down and Great-Reset plan and the resulting advent of a new Biological Age, I rest my case.

7

America's Withdrawal from Afghanistan, and the Syndicate's Planned Decline and Reset World Government

Both sides – America and China – would prefer to maintain that the outbreak of SARS-CoV-2 was an accident, as seeing it as a deliberate act will have consequences and brings with it the danger of retaliation. But the truth is, we are in new territory. With the Covid pandemic, regardless of whether or not there was a deliberate release, we have moved out of the Nuclear Age into a new Biological Age in which superpowers have the option of competing through bio-warfare.

Now there is a possibility that a gain-of-function manipulated bio-weapon SARS-CoV-2 has happened there is no going back, and both sides must be on their guard against possible new outbreaks. The most important thing is to understand what has happened, and how it happened, without making things worse. Hence this book. The second most important thing is, if there *was* a deliberate release, to work out 'Who dunnit': China or America-the Syndicate? And then what the West should do about it.

A World State to control the Biological Age
There are still many who believe, or want to believe, that SARS-CoV-2 came from China. There are others who think it came from America-the Syndicate, as NIAID-sponsored gain-of-function research was taking place at the University of North Carolina and being patented in 2002. Whichever it was – and I have concluded that the evidence indicates it may have come from America-the Syndicate – there is now no going back. The biological genie cannot be put back in the bottle.

As Dr Francis Boyle (see pp.xvii), the international bio-weapons expert who drafted the Biological Weapons Anti-Terrorism Act of 1989, said on 15 April 2020, "I personally believe that until our political leaders come clean with the American people, both at the White House and in Congress and our state governments, and publicly admit that this is an extremely dangerous offensive biological warfare weapon that we are dealing with, I do not see that we will be able to confront it and to stop it, let alone defeat it."[1]

We are now in a time when biological war can break out at any time when a state wants to achieve the blocking of another state's economy.

Therefore, there needs to be a democratic World State with power to control and end this biological nightmare.

Law of history: the rise and fall of 25 civilisations in 61 stages
I have said (on p.142) that when I was a Professor in Japan I was asked to teach a course to university postgraduates, actually for a year, on 'The Decline of the West' and that I based my lectures on Gibbon, Spengler and Toynbee. While doing this I saw a fourth way of regarding civilisations, which I thought of as my law of history. In 1991 I brought out *The Fire and the Stones*, a study of the rise and fall of civilisations, part of which I updated in 2008 as *The Rise and Fall of Civilizations*.

I studied 25 civilisations, including the European and North-American civilisations which form Western civilisation and are known as the West, and found that they have all progressed along 61 similar stages. I put these on a seven-foot-long chart, which I later displayed during a TV interview.

Nicholas Hagger and his seven-foot-long chart showing
the rise and fall of 25 civilisations, his "law of history"

My view of history is that civilisations grow round a vision seen by a mystic (such as Jesus, "the Light of the World", and Muhammad, who had a vision of the Fire or Light), round which gathers a religion (Christianity, Islam). A new civilisation expands geographically as neighbouring societies embrace its metaphysical Fire or Light and new religion. A new civilisation rises round its metaphysical vision and religion (belief), and declines when it turns secular (and loses its belief). When it ends it passes into another civilisation, just as the early Mesopotamian and Egyptian civilisations passed into the Arab civilisation, and almost overnight their god changed to Allah.

The North-American civilisation, founded at Jamestown in 1607, is now in stage 15, expansion into empire, the same energetic stage that generated the Roman Empire in the Roman civilisation.

The other living civilisations are all in advanced stages; China and the European Union are both in stage 43 (as are the Tibetan and Oceanian civilisations): loss of national sovereignty to a secularising conglomerate. The Chinese regions are like the European nation-states, living (sometimes reluctantly) under a centralised unity.

Another living civilisation, the Byzantine-Russian civilisation, was in stage 43 from 1917 to 1991, and then passed into stage 46, a federation of member states formerly in the Union. In stage 46 civilisations make a further attempt at a counterthrust under a foreign federalist influence (in the case of the Russian Federation, the influence of Russia).

The UK, part of the European civilisation since the Romans, was in stage 43 until it left the EU, and it will have declined to stage 46 if the United Kingdom breaks up into four federal nation-states. (If it were to return to the EU it would still be in stage 43.)

Many of the living civilisations – the Andean and Meso-American, the Arab, African, Indian, South-East Asian and Central Asian civilisations – are in stage 46. In stage 44 they have undergone syncretism (seeing the unity of all religions and merging them) and Universalism (seeing the unity behind the universe and all separate civilisations), and in stage 45 they have undergone a rejection of the present, a yearning for a lost past of their civilisation (like the Brexiteers' yearning for a return to the time of the British Empire when Britain was sovereign and independent). In stage 46 civilisations make a further attempt at a counterthrust under a foreign federalist influence, as we have seen – and this could be the Syndicate's New World Order, and could be a democratic World State.

The UK's Prime Minister Boris Johnson, in Rome for the G20 at the end of October 2021, the day before COP26 on climate change, said on television (and was reported in newspapers[2] as saying): "Humanity, civilisation, society can go backwards... at extraordinary speed. We saw that with the decline and fall of the Roman Empire... and we could see our civilisation, our world, also go backwards." He also said: "We can be conniving in our own decline and fall." According to my study of the rise and fall of civilisations, his going backwards is in fact going forwards into decline, and by leading the UK out of the EU he himself precipitated a decline to stage 45 and a looming stage 46, and contributed to the coming fall of the West that so alarms him.

Most of the living civilisations are in stage 46, and are already part of a federation, and they are therefore ready (in the sense that their stage is already a federal one) to be taken over by a US-created democratic, partly-federal World State for a while. Civilisations in stage 46 have the prospect ahead of foreign occupation in stages 49, 58 and 60 (after which a dead civilisation passes into a successive civilisation in stage 61).

The West is in decline and the US has been weak in surrendering Afghanistan and Iraq, and may not now seem capable of creating a World State. If the West can survive its present doldrums, there may be an opportunity for the US to create a democratic World State in the coming decades.

North-American civilisation the best able to organise a World State as it is the youngest civilisation

It is a law of history that can be confirmed from my seven-foot-long chart that in the past 5,000 years younger civilisations always triumph over older civilisations. The North-American civilisation, being in stage 15, will triumph in a conflict with the Chinese civilisation, which is in stage 43, in accordance with this time-honoured principle.

From this we may conclude that the North-American civilisation, being the youngest, is best placed to organise a World State and conquer some of the older civilisations. This runs counter to the thinking of Deagel, America's secret intelligence forecaster, which sees the North-American civilisation as on the brink of a fall that will also mark the fall of the West.

We have seen (p.101) that the Syndicate's Great Reset, its New World Order, will aim at depriving people of ownership so everything is rented, a state of affairs that can be achieved by following the digital procedures of the Fourth Industrial Revolution. It could be that the Syndicate will bring the present financial system and old order to collapse, that going over to the New World Order will be a more drastic and revolutionary change than people realise and will trigger migrations and population reduction.

Clearly, if the West and the East are to be united in one system, which can house both authoritarian China (and its trading partners in 140 countries) and America (along with the full, flawed and hybrid democracies), then to achieve unification under a world government either China will have to become less authoritarian or the West will have to become more authoritarian, or a bit of both must happen so they can meet in the middle. But at present there is no sign that China, whose leader President Xi warned the West that any country that bullies China will come up against an iron wall of 1.4 billion Chinese, is going to be less authoritarian.

Both 'Rothschilds' and 'Rockefellers' were behind Communism and are used to totalitarianism. It seems they have now decided that their Syndicate unification of West and East into a world government should be totalitarian.

American withdrawal from Afghanistan and the Middle East to pivot to East Asia (China)

As I write, the situation in Afghanistan is dire and Kabul has fallen. The Taliban, who oppose Western human rights, have ambled into Kabul unopposed by Western principles and strength in a self-inflicted Western humiliation. After 20 years, in the War on Terror the terrorists won. The West, under the US, has withdrawn from Afghanistan and has left it to the Taliban (along with 75,000 vehicles, 600,000 guns and 208 planes and helicopters worth in total $85 billion).

Such a withdrawal is in line with "pivoting" the US focus from the Middle East to East Asia (see pp.76–77) to build a coalition to challenge, and confront, China, and eventually to unite East and West as the Syndicate want. But the West seems in retreat, the *Pax Americana* ended. The West's advanced technology has been defeated by a 20-year-long 'barbarian' tribal insurgency backed by China – in a geopolitically important country for Western defences against Chinese expansion and Islamic terrorism, situated between Iran, Russia and China.

The Chinese foreign minister Wang Yi openly met a delegation from the Taliban in July 2021. A press release stated that Beijing expected "to play an important role in the process of peaceful reconciliation and reconstruction in Afghanistan". In other words there would be more Chinese Belt-and-Road infrastructure projects in Afghanistan. Afghanistan has rare earth metals worth $1–3 trillion, and a stable Afghanistan will protect China's $60-billion projects in Pakistan. As America and the West move out, China moves in.

For 20 years the West has been fighting a war against international terrorists who are based in Afghanistan. It has not been fighting in an Afghan civil war. America's international image and credibility have collapsed, and its role as leader of the free world is in doubt.

The American era appears to be ending; the American Empire appears to have overreached itself and has turned decadent, temporarily (since the presidencies of Trump and Biden) losing its appetite and will to be involved in the rest of the world and to be the world's policeman. It has turned inward-looking and insular like Trump and Biden. But it can rebound from this defeat in Afghanistan and its hegemony can still be restored under a new generation of leaders, and, ironically, through the commercial activities of the Syndicate which are continuing. The Syndicate are still very internationally-minded.

Trans-Afghan gas pipeline in the hands of the Taliban
The American withdrawal from Afghanistan meant leaving the gas pipeline in the hands of the Taliban. To understand why America would be prepared to do this we need to look back to 1996, when the Taliban seized control of Kabul, set up the Islamic Emirate of Afghanistan and ruled three-quarters of the country.

There have long been rumours that the Taliban were created by the CIA and Pakistan's ISI (Inter-Services Intelligence Agency) to guard pipelines that would carry gas and oil from ex-Soviet republics across Afghanistan to Pakistan. It had long been proposed that a natural gas pipeline should run from Turkmenistan (Dauletabad fields) through Afghanistan to Pakistan (Multan) and then India (Turkmenistan–Afghanistan–Pakistan–India, TAPI pipeline, see pp.22–23).

An understanding between Afghanistan and Pakistan was reached in March 1995 involving an Argentine company. The US company Unocal, the spearhead of 'Rockefellers'' Standard-Oil interests, and the Saudi company Delta signed an agreement for a separate project with Turkmenistan's president in October 1995. In 1996 the US Unocal led the CentGas (Central Asia Gas Pipeline) consortium, and worked with the Taliban, who chose to work with Unocal rather than on the Argentine project. In August 1998 American embassies in Nairobi and Dar es Salaam were bombed, and the US accused bin Laden of being behind the attacks and halted the pipeline negotiations. The Taliban's leader Mullah Omar announced the Taliban's support for bin Laden. Unocal withdrew from the consortium in 1998 and, according to some, the US was now looking for a pretext to invade Afghanistan and restart work on the pipeline. 9/11 may have justified that invasion. In December 2002 a new deal on the project was signed by Turkmenistan, Afghanistan and Pakistan, and in 2005 the US supported a resumption of the project. However, the project was shelved due to the instability of Afghanistan.

Construction on the TAPI natural-gas pipeline started in Turkmenistan in December 2015, and work on the Pakistani section was planned to start in December 2018. There was fighting in Afghanistan where the TAPI pipeline passed through Herat and Kandahar. Completion was expected in late 2022, and in February 2021 the Taliban vowed to guarantee the safety of the TAPI pipeline.

It was proposed that an oil pipeline should run from Turkmenistan (Chardzhou oil refinery) through Afghanistan to Pakistan and then

India, and be built by General Electric and Bechtel (which was linked to US Vice-President Cheney). In May 1997 Unocal secured a $2.5-billion pipeline deal with the Taliban, Turkmenistan and Pakistan. Unocal's adviser during the negotiations was Hamid Karzai, who was later installed by Bush as the new ruler of Afghanistan. In February 2001 Bush began to negotiate with the Taliban to get the oil-pipeline project resumed.

As I said in *The Secret American Dream* (2011),[3] the 2001 invasion of Afghanistan was partly motivated by an attempt to implement the Trans-Afghan pipelines. According to many, the Western-led invasion (provoked by the Syndicate-assisted 9/11) was to implement the gas and oil pipelines to break the Russian and Iranian monopoly on energy supplies to the region. Some argue that it was not a cause of the invasion as most Western governments have since preferred to receive oil from the Caspian via Azerbaijan, then Georgia and the Black Sea – but in 2001 this preference had not been established.

After 9/11 bin Laden ordered al-Qaeda to attack US oil and gas pipelines if either he or Mullah Omar were captured or killed, and as a result all locations were removed from websites. Iran competed by planning the Iran–Pakistan–India gas pipeline, which would avoid Afghanistan.

America's withdrawal from Afghanistan leaves the oil pipeline as a proposal that was never implemented, and the natural-gas pipeline in the hands of the (CIA-ISI-founded) Taliban who, following their guarantee of the TAPI natural-gas pipeline's safety, stand to receive large payments to guard the TAPI pipeline that may have partly been the cause of 9/11 and the 2001 US invasion of Afghanistan. The American withdrawal of Afghanistan in 2021 was based on a deal that the Taliban would guard the Syndicate's TAPI pipeline.

Withdrawal from Afghanistan a temporary setback and decline for the West
In a speech on the final day of the withdrawal President Biden said the war in Afghanistan had ceased to be in the US's national interests, that its original goal was to bring Osama bin Laden to justice, that it cost $300 million a day for two decades, and that in future US interventions and global engagement should have clear, achievable goals and be in the fundamental national security interest of the US, with no more remaking of other countries. In short, the US is no longer able or willing to intervene and will no longer be the world's policeman, seemingly leaving the way open for China.

In the evening of the last day of the American withdrawal the Taliban held a fake funeral. Film showed crowds carrying three enormous coffins draped in the US, UK and French flags and a placard proclaiming 'Death to the West', and supporters firing automatic weapons into the air all night, claiming victory in the 20-year war with NATO powers. Taliban fighters wearing abandoned US military uniform gloated and revelled at the $85-billion high-tech equipment abandoned by the US (most, not all, smashed and disabled to be unusable, and filmed being transported in a convoy of trailers carrying broken US military vehicles heading for Tehran). Taliban fighters pledged to turn Bagram Airbase into a terrorist-training camp to defeat the West by jihad.

The hasty withdrawal looked like the retreat from Vietnam in 1974, a fiasco and disaster, and Biden, having stripped the illusions from US foreign policy, looked the embodiment of America's current weakness, having squandered two decades of American sacrifice in weeks and seemingly uninterested in the Syndicate's New World Order.

Biden's execution of his withdrawal from Afghanistan without consulting American allies had consequences. It showed American weakness and reluctance to interpose American protection. It left Taiwan fearful that China will invade, Central Europe fearful that Russia will invade, and the Middle East fearful that Iran will invade.

This setback may be temporary and under a new leader there can be an American resurgence as the North-American civilisation is the youngest living civilisation and in the same stage that the Roman Empire was in. In 9AD, when the Roman Empire and the *Pax Romana* were still expanding, Emperor Augustus's Roman general Publius Quinctilius Varus lost three Roman legions when ambushed by 'pacified' Germanic tribes led by Arminius at the Battle of Teutoburg Forest while trying to suppress a revolt near the Rhine. This Roman defeat by 'barbarians' did not bring about the fall of the Roman Empire, which continued to pacify barbarians on its edges. Just as Germanic tribesmen put on Roman armour and gloatingly held captured Roman weapons and Rome then went from strength to strength, so the Taliban tribesmen put on abandoned American military uniforms and gloatingly held American weapons or sat in abandoned and disabled American planes and similarly America can still go from strength to strength under a new leader.

Afghanistan has not resulted in the fall of the West, but the *Pax Americana* (the rules-based system of international order and of America's mission to spread Western democracy and human rights round the world and remake countries) has begun to fracture from China's competitive expansion. China can now come into Afghanistan with Belt-and-Road projects and rebuild the country in return for mining rare minerals, including lithium, from the Afghan mine for which it has held a contract for the last 20 years; and the West has retreated and been overrun by the advancing Chinese tide, the Taliban having had a meeting with the Chinese foreign minister before the American withdrawal (see p.149) and having no doubt secured Chinese promises of infrastructure-funding during the coming years.

Just after I wrote these words the Taliban spokesman Zabihullah Mujahid claimed that Beijing was "ready to invest in and reconstruct" Afghanistan, raising hopes that China would provide a gateway to global markets, and that China would revive Afghan copper mining and production under its Belt-and-Road scheme (under which China provides large loans to other countries to invest in their infrastructure). China did not evacuate any staff from its Kabul embassy and seemed set to run Afghanistan behind the scenes.

It may be that Biden's positioning of America as having withdrawn from its role as the world's policeman and his resetting of America's posture, setting aside the US's military dominance, was a necessary positioning and resetting in a global reset – the Great Reset – that will advance the Syndicate's efforts to bring East (China) and West

(America) together in a world government and New World Order. And without mentioning the Great Reset and coming New World Order, Biden has paved the way for the Syndicate to follow up his American reset with their drive for an authoritarian world government.

Only four days after the 20th anniversary of 9/11 the UK, Australia and the US (three of the Five Eyes, Canada and New Zealand not taking part) agreed a new trilateral landmark partnership, now known as AUKUS, to boost their defences and share nuclear submarine secrets, which would give Australia a multi-billion-dollar fleet of conventional nuclear-powered submarines – as a defence against China, the first stage of the US's pivoting towards East Asia which includes the US infrastructure scheme that is an alternative to China's BRI (see p.135). The idea was to protect Taiwan from a Chinese invasion at the start of what looks like a new Cold War.

The partnership would also focus on new technologies – cyber-defence, artificial intelligence and quantum computing – that will advance the Great Reset, the Syndicate's coming New World Order.

The fall of Afghanistan long planned to dismantle American superpowerdom and precipitate decline, for the Syndicate's totalitarian New World Order
As William Engdahl (who features in my *Selected Letters*) has pointed out,[4] America's 'collapse' in Afghanistan was part of a long-term strategy to end the global influence of the US, destroy its economy from within and end the nation-state in preparation for the global totalitarian

model of the Great Reset, which is based on the authoritarian approach of 6.9 billion world citizens.

This plan has revolved round the shadowy Afghan-born Zalmay Khalilzad, who has shaped US foreign policy since 1984 when (after working with Wolfowitz and teaching at Columbia University) he joined the US State Department and worked closely with the Syndicate's Brzezinski. He was already a CIA asset, having been 'selected' in the 1960s by Thomas E. Gouttiere, who headed the CIA-financed Center for Afghanistan Studies at the University of Nebraska at Omaha.

The Taliban came out of a CIA project initiated by Brzezinski in 1979 to attack the Soviet Red Army in Afghanistan. Osama bin Laden, a Saudi-CIA asset, was brought to Pakistan to work with Pakistani ISI intelligence to raise money from Arab states for the war in Afghanistan. The CIA were weaponising political Islam within the Cold-War context, and supported bin Laden. Al-Qaeda and the Taliban were now intimately linked.

On a personal note, I believe I met bin Laden and spoke with him at a crowded gathering I hosted in the Palace of Westminster's Jubilee Room for the publication of Paul Gorka's anti-Soviet *Budapest Betrayed* on 4 November 1986 (see *My Double Life 2: A Rainbow over the Hills*, pp.246–248). A bearded man dressed like, and looking like, bin Laden appeared uninvited, with a similarly dressed Arab, and told me he was in London to arrange a supply of weapons to Afghanistan and was staying at the Dorchester Hotel. I have since confirmed that bin Laden visited London with his half-brother Salem in mid-1986 to purchase anti-aircraft missiles, and stayed at the Dorchester Hotel.[5]

As host I sympathised with his anti-Soviet mission. This was before he began his 69 attempts to buy nuclear weapons to use against the West in 1992 and continued until 2005, a threat to the West that had to be stopped even if it was motivated by Syndicate levelling-down of the West (see pp.28–29).

Following Khalilzad's arming and backing of the Mujahedeen and bin Laden to weaponise political Islam, the Taliban backed by Pakistan's ISI took control of Kabul in 1996. Khalilzad worked with the PNAC (Project for a New American Century) and shaped the military agenda of George W. Bush's Presidency.

It is not known whether Khalilzad organised the attack on the Twin Towers and arranged for Cheney to leave the US air space unguarded that day. Evidence of the CIA's monitoring of the attacks from the top floor of the WTC7 (World Trade Center 7) was destroyed in the mysterious collapse of the building – the third building to collapse in New York on 9/11 – without being struck by any aircraft.

After the 9/11 attacks in 2001 Khalilzad orchestrated Bush's war against the Taliban in Afghanistan, fought because the Taliban under Mullah Omar would not surrender their al-Qaeda ally bin Laden. Khalilzad then became Bush's Envoy to Afghanistan.

In 2002 Khalilzad, now Special Presidential Envoy to Afghanistan, installed his former classmate CIA asset Hamid Karzai as President of Afghanistan. Karzai's younger brother, warlord of Afghanistan's largest opium province, Kandahar, was paid by the CIA from at least 2001, as Khalilzad knew.

In November 2003 Khalilzad became the US Ambassador to Afghanistan. Meanwhile he had been made Ambassador at Large for Free Iraqis in December 2002 to prepare for a post-Saddam Iraq, and later became US Ambassador to Iraq. Khalilzad was behind the CIA-funded rise of Islamic terror groups, including the Taliban and al-Qaeda, in Afghanistan and Iraq.

The most recent President of Afghanistan, ex-President Ashraf Ghani Ahmadzai, who fled Kabul shortly before its fall, was a classmate of Khalilzad in the American University of Beirut in the early 1970s.

In 2018 former CIA head Mike Pompeo recommended Khalilzad to be US Special Representative for Afghanistan Reconciliation for the Trump administration. Khalilzad took part in US-Taliban talks with their envoys in Doha, Qatar, a pro-Taliban Gulf state that also funds the Taliban. Khalilzad pressed Pakistan to release the co-founder of the Taliban, Mullah Abdul Ghani Baradar, to lead these talks without the Kabul regime's being present, with Trump's approval.

In February 2020 Baradar signed a deal negotiated by Khalilzad and the Taliban, the Doha Agreement, which promised that Afghanistan would never be "a platform for international terrorist groups or individuals". This was the deal agreed by Trump that Biden also agreed, only changing the date for a final US pull-out to 11 September 2021.

The fall of Afghanistan had long been planned and was not a miscalculation by Secretary of Defense Austin or the Pentagon. With the involvement of Khalilzad Austin approved the American abandonment of Bagram Airbase on 4 July 2021, signalling there would be no more US air cover.

So the CIA asset Khalilzad helped create the 1996 CIA-backed Taliban's take-over, the 2001 destruction of the CIA-backed Taliban and the 2021 restoration of the CIA-backed Taliban – all so that American superpowerdom could undergo a great fall and economic collapse, "the fall of the West", that would serve the Syndicate's Great-Reset plan in levelling down the West to enter a totalitarian world government with the East.

If the Syndicate can plan to lose Afghanistan to level down American superpowerdom and the West in order to create a totalitarian New World Order, could they not also – is it not plausible they might – release a virus to reinforce this levelling-down into a New World Order? Members of the jury, you are getting ready to judge.

The Syndicate's planned totalitarian world government moves forward
America seems to have rejected its imperial burden and its willingness to lead the world and fight "forever wars" to maintain its hegemonistic position, and although this might be a lull in its imperial stage (like a lull in the expansion of the Roman Empire) that can be revived by a new president intent on confronting China's expansion, it may also be a further cover-up of the Covid bio-warfare of 2019 and a further levelling-down of the West required by the Great Reset. America's retreat may be what the Syndicate now wanted, requested to Trump and have achieved.

I was not taken by surprise by the American withdrawal from Afghanistan. Nor should the CIA and MI6 have been taken by surprise, and therefore nor should the American and British leaders and politicians. Acting as a one-man intelligence agency, I reviewed all the available evidence for what has been going on, much of which has not been in the news and has been covert rather than overt, and saw that "pivoting to East Asia (China)" from the Middle East means withdrawing from the Middle East and Afghanistan, as Trump negotiated. I saw that as 'Rothschilds' supported Biden's election campaign and Biden's election slogan was the Great Reset's 'Build Back Better', Biden would implement the Syndicate's "pivoting to East Asia", which Trump began.

Biden has diverted his attention from the Middle East and Afghanistan to China, which is delighted at the dismantling of American influence in the world. I could see this as inevitable under the circumstances, and was not surprised when it happened. Could not the CIA and MI6 have seen the withdrawal as inevitable and not been surprised when it happened? Pivoting towards East Asia will seek to protect Taiwan from a Chinese invasion at the start of what looks like a new Cold War.

If there were no Syndicate and there was a US disengagement from running the world as from Afghanistan without pivoting to East Asia, then great powers (including China, Russia and Iran) could be expected to jostle for predominance. Both the US and the UK have appeared weak. The UK left the EU's liberal democracies at the very time when the US was becoming a less dependable partner, and, lacking the clout to act by itself as in Afghanistan, diminished its ability to persuade others to act with it and increased its geopolitical impotence. Only the Syndicate in the immediate future can bring East and West together in this jostling Biological Age.

Intelligence report to Biden diverts attention from American gain-of-function engineering and patents from 1999

In May 2021, Biden asked the intelligence community for a report on the origins of coronavirus within 90 days after 18 leading scientists sent a letter to the journal *Science* claiming that both the natural spillover and leak theories were equally plausible, and saying that the WHO had not given a balanced consideration to both scenarios.

There was still a body of opinion among the scientists that coronavirus is not just a human virus as it is found in bats and pangolins, and it transfers from humans to mink every easily and has infected deer in the US. This body of opinion still asserts that it is a generalist or promiscuous virus.

This body of opinion believes the natural-spillover argument does not suit some political groups as it focuses on the causes of spillover in biodiversity loss, deforestation (bulldozing rainforests and clearing wildernesses to provide land for farms and gain access to mines) and trade in wildlife. The destruction of vegetation and wildlife sets loose species of virus and bacteria they hosted, which then seek new hosts such as humans and livestock. The body of opinion which sees a lab leak as the origin of coronavirus may be seeking, in some cases, to deflect attention from deforestation, which it wants to continue.

The classified analysis of the US spy agencies on the origin of the virus is said to be inconclusive. It criticised Chinese authorities for failing to share information and kept open the possibility the coronavirus escaped from a laboratory in Wuhan rather than jumped from animals to humans.

China's Wang Wenbin, a foreign-ministry spokesman, claimed that the report was meant to deflect attention from US failings. Fu Cong, a Director-General in China's foreign ministry, said, "Scapegoating China cannot whitewash the US," and that China would "counter-attack".

On the same day that Biden's inconclusive report was due for publication Ambassador Chen Xu, China's permanent representative to the UN, sent a briefing to the World Health Organization – aimed at the 6.9 billion non-Westerners as opposed to the 1 billion in the West – entitled 'Doubtful Points about Fort Detrick', Fort Detrick being the lab in Maryland at the centre of the US biological weapons program where the USAMRIID (US Army Medical Research Institute of Infectious Diseases) is still based. In 2003, research published by Ralph Baric's team showed that work to manipulate coronaviruses was already ongoing. There was a leak of toxic waste from Fort Detrick in 2016 which resulted in millions receiving compensation, and the lab was closed down in 2019 for safety violations. A petition in 2020 to ask the US government to disclose whether the shutdown was linked to Covid was not answered.

Ambassador Chen Xu called for a transparent investigation into the high-security laboratories in Fort Detrick and Baric's University of North Carolina, and claimed that an American lab leak at Fort Detrick or at the University of North Carolina was a possibility that could not be ignored. This view has spread across China and is believed by 90 per cent of Chinese.[6]

It was clear from the declassified summary of the report that the US intelligence community failed to resolve the debate within the Biden administration as to whether the origin of coronavirus was a lab leak. The intelligence community remained divided on the origins of Covid – four intelligence agencies said with "low confidence" that the virus was initially transferred from an animal to a human, and a fifth intelligence agency believed "with moderate confidence" that the first infection was linked to a lab (either as a result of an accident or by design) – but said Chinese officials did not know about the virus before the initial outbreak, even though they obstructed the investigation from the start and withheld critical information on the origins of coronavirus, Biden maintained.

A subsequent declassified report (released at the end of October 2021) from the Office of the US Director of National Intelligence, which updated the review ordered by President Biden, further stated that coronavirus was not designed as a biological weapon but could have leaked from a Chinese lab.[7] The Chinese Embassy branded the report as "a farce".

One further allegation of a gain-of-function origin in a Chinese laboratory, which surfaced after these two intelligence reports, has been made by Li-Meng Yan, a doctor who escaped from China to the US in April 2020 to expose what she thought might be the origin of the Covid-19 pandemic, that SARS-CoV-2 was manufactured in a Chinese military lab. The Third Military Medical University in Chongqing, China and the Research Institute for Medicare in Nanjing discovered a bat coronavirus, ZC45, news of which was published in early 2018. Yan believes ZC45 was used as a template and/or backbone to create a man-made SARS-CoV-2.[8]

Yan says that the Chinese Communist Party (CCP) wants Covid jabs and vaccine passports created as a result of Covid-19 to make the world accept the CCP's authoritarian system based on social control, and she is urging Americans to realise the destructiveness of Communism. She says that China wants world domination by 2035 and has spent decades developing bio-weapons.

It has to be said that this speculative, unevidential and unproved hypothesis – suggestion – does not make clear how the virus allegedly moved from Chongqing or Nanjing to Wuhan, where the outbreak took place. It has to be said that Yan's allegation would be welcomed by those in the US intelligence community who seek to exonerate America and accuse China of a Covid cover-up.

All options, then, were still on the table, including a seafood market, a mine and a lab, and – although American analysts do not believe the virus was *"designed"* or *"developed"* (as distinct from being misappropriated and used) as a bio-weapon – for the sake of completeness a deliberate act of biological warfare that released Covid as a bio-weapon to arrest China's growth and dominance.

However, neither of the two reports (some might say, conveniently) confronts the evidence that gain-of-function research on viruses was happening in US laboratories from 1999, that it was patented and that some of it was funded by the Pentagon and State Department to create a bio-weapon for future military use – to disrupt a rival's economic growth, to stop China becoming the number-one superpower. Just as Biden denied mishandling the withdrawal from Afghanistan which ex-UK Prime Minister Tony Blair called "imbecilic", so the two reports may be diverting attention away from gain-of-function bio-weapon research by presenting a binary focus on spillover versus lab leak (with no human engineering and focus on bio-weapons even being considered).

The intelligence assessment needed to ask the following questions.[9] Did Baric hide the relationship between SARS-CoV-2 and his lab-created SCH014-MA15 in his 2015 paper, 'A SARS-like cluster of circulating bat coronaviruses shows potential for human emergence'? (Baric says it bears no resemblance to SARS-CoV-2.) Did the US government collude in hiding evidence that SARS-CoV-2 was genetically engineered? How did US funding contribute to the origin of SARS-CoV-2? What can US personnel who attended the Military World Games in Wuhan tell about the first cases in October 2019? And can the US rebut Chinese accusations that SARS-CoV-2 came from Fort Detrick?

In short, coming soon after the American "pivot-to-East-Asia" out of Afghanistan (see pp.76–77), the two reports look like a smokescreen for a coming confrontation with China to prevent it from becoming a number-one superpower, and cover-ups for a possible release at the time of the Wuhan Military World Games, where many athletes were infected with Covid-like symptoms. And having been written by the intelligence community (who were aware of the Pentagon's and State Department's funding of US gain-of-function research) rather than by scientists or medics who were focusing on preventing diseases, the two reports' omission of the funding and patenting of US gain-of-function research is glaring. It is as if the two reports were denying that we have moved into a new Biological Age.

Did a release of a gain-of-function virus in Wuhan break the UN's Biological Weapons Convention, and should gain-of-function research now be banned?
In fact, the appearance of coronavirus after gain-of-function research was funded by the Pentagon and State Department raises questions about the UN Biological Weapons Convention (BWC), or Biological and Toxin Weapons Convention (BTWC), a disarmament treaty signed on 10 April 1972 by 109 signatories, that came into effect on 26 March 1975 with 183 states or parties, and was ratified by 22 states including the three depositories: the US, the UK and the Soviet Union.

Biological warfare loomed long before the BWC treaty. It goes back to the siege of Caffa in the Crimea in 1346 when Italian troops released the plague, the Black Death, on 15,000 Mongols. International restrictions on biological warfare began with the 1925 Geneva Protocol, a "no-first-use" agreement. The Soviet Union began a bio-weapons program almost immediately. From 1943 to 1945 the US spent $400 million on biological weapons, and in 1965 the Johnston Atoll, which was under US dominion, was the location for large-scale bio-weapons development. According to the chief of product development at Fort Detrick, Maryland, one jet spraying a bio-weapon would cause more deaths than a ten-megaton hydrogen bomb.

America's bio-warfare system was terminated in 1969 by President Nixon, who issued his statement on Chemical and Biological Defense Policies and Programs at Fort Detrick. The US budget for *offensive* biological weapons programs was then $300 million a year. The BWC was negotiated in the UN's Conference of the Committee on Disarmament in Geneva from 1969 to 1972. Soviet scientists were reported to have conducted gain-of-function research from 1972 to 1992, until just after the Soviet Union collapsed. The Soviet Chimera Project combined DNA from encephalitis and smallpox, and Ebola virus and smallpox.

To be absolutely clear, while *offensive* bio-warfare research was ended in the US in 1969 as we have just seen and both the US and China signed up to a treaty banning the development of bio-weapons, *defensive* bio-weapons research was – and is – still allowed. The US and other countries are therefore permitted to manufacture and study toxins (such as SARS-CoV-2) that could be used against them by an enemy. The National Center for Medical Intelligence (NCMI) based at Fort Detrick to focus on outbreaks of global diseases is reported to have warned that Covid-19 would become a global pandemic at least a month before it was declared one.

The BWC treaty effectively bans biological and toxin weapons by prohibiting their development, production, acquisition, transfer, stockpiling and use. The BWC treaty does not itself ban the use of biological and toxin weapons but reaffirms the 1925 Geneva Protocol, which prohibits their use. The BWC treaty does not ban the possession or development of chemical or biological weapons, or biodefence programs. The treaty mandates that states or parties should consult with one another and co-operate to solve concerns. Its 15 articles include undertakings "never under any circumstances to develop, produce, stockpile, acquire or retain biological weapons", to "destroy" them "or direct them to peaceful purposes", and "not to transfer, or in any way assist, encourage or induce anyone to manufacture or otherwise acquire biological weapons".

The United Nations Office for Disarmament Affairs (UNODA), whose Geneva branch implements the Biological Weapons Convention, states: "Biological weapons disseminate disease-causing organisms or toxins to harm or kill humans, animals or plants. Diseases caused by such weapons would not confine themselves to national borders, and could spread rapidly round the world. The consequences of the deliberate release of biological agents or toxins by state or non-state actors would be dramatic. In addition to the tragic loss of lives, such events could cause food shortages, environmental catastrophes, devastating economic loss, and widespread illness, fear and mistrust among the public."

UNODA could not be clearer in seeking to prevent a new Biological Age that has been looming since the First World War and certainly 1925. But was what happened in Wuhan – a release of a gain-of-function virus – a violation of the 1925 Geneva Protocol and therefore, as it follows that Protocol, of the Biological Weapons Convention? This has been raised by Francis Boyle (see pp.xvii, 145), who drafted the US domestic implementing, legislation for the international Biological Weapons Convention known as the Biological Weapons Anti-Terrorism Act of

1989 that was signed into law by President George H.W. Bush. Should there not now be a worldwide ban on conducting and funding gain-of-function research until international and legally-binding standards are set under a treaty equivalent to nuclear-test treaties, as has been called for by scientists such as Simon Wain-Hobson, Professor of the Pasteur Institute, Paris? Gain-of-function work may now need to be declared illegal in an extension of the UN's BWC treaty at Geneva to control events in the new Biological Age.

The way forward in the new Biological Age
Because of the Nuclear and Biological Age we now live in, the fall of the West is a real possibility unless diplomacy can bring about a unification of West and East, of the US and China, of the 110 democracies and 140 BRI countries, so all the infrastructure projects go in one orderly direction and are not duplicated by West-East competition.

At the end of this reflection I come back to what I learned from Junzaburo Nishiwaki, Japan's distinguished poet, in 1965, when in a Tokyo *saké* bar, I asked him to sum up the wisdom of the East. Thinking of the *Tao* he wrote down on a business reply card among my papers on the table: "+A + −A = 0." I now see this wisdom including: "The West + the East = peaceful unity and prosperity in (eventually) a democratic World State, the Promised Land." But if we are not careful it could be: "The West + the East = annihilation, and the fall of the West."

At this point, members of the jury, regarding America's withdrawal from Afghanistan as a planned follow-on from Covid to bring in the Syndicate's reset totalitarian world government and bring about the fall of the West and its financial system, I rest my case.

8

The Fall of the West: The Syndicate's Totalitarian New World Order and a Future Democratic World State

End of Syndicate trilogy

I have now completed my trilogy on the Syndicate.

In *The Syndicate* (2004) I identified who was in the "military-industrial complex", and what they have been doing to the world since the beginning of the 20th century, how they meet and their plan for a world government. I came to the conclusion that a democratic world government would be better than the Syndicate's authoritarian centralised world government. As the Syndicate were behind both Soviet and Chinese Communism, their world government would be mixed with Communist authoritarianism.

In *The Secret History of the West* (2005) I examined the roots of the Syndicate in Freemasonry and the long undermining of the West through Freemasonic revolutions.

And now in *The Fall of the West* (2022) I have shown that the features of SARS-CoV-2 have been known and patented since 1999, and that the Syndicate had the time to turn it into a bio-weapon and bring out dress rehearsals for a pandemic – Lock Step in 2010 and Event 201 in 2019 – and that the pandemic has been a Syndicate event to advance their world government.

In this work, the third in my trilogy, I have spread out all the evidence regarding the Syndicate, Wuhan and coronavirus on my desk like pieces of a tipped-out jigsaw puzzle, and I have done all the connecting-up so all the pieces of evidence fit together. I am now looking at the picture, and I regret to report that it shows an American lab rather than a Chinese lab responsible for the first gain-of-function research that resulted in SARS-CoV-2.

The Syndicate's New World Order and Great Reset

We have looked at the evidence in a balanced way, including the evidence of the patents, and, members of the jury, I think you will now agree that we have lived through 20 years of American gain-of-function experiments that may have resulted in coronavirus's being turned into a bio-weapon and possibly an American-Syndicate bio-attack on China that backfired, perhaps having provoked immediate retaliation. The totalitarian Chinese may be echoing Hitler's totalitarian thought (in the tradition of Alaric the Visigoth and Genseric the Vandal who sacked Rome in 410 and 455AD): "The present world is near its end. Our only task is to sack it."[1] The Syndicate turned against Trump, and this withdrawal of support may have been part of their cover-up after the bio-attack (if it happened), which has resulted in the death of 728,000 Americans to date against 4,636 Chinese (which many believe is an understatement).

The Syndicate wanted emollient President Biden in place of divisive, abrasive Trump in resetting the world in the new Biological Age. It may be that the Syndicate, working behind the scenes, 'stole' the 2020 election. 'Rothschilds' certainly funded Biden's campaign and he is, by his emollient actions in withdrawing from Afghanistan and withdrawing combat troops from Iraq, denationalising the world and preparing for a coming world government, 'the Great Reset'.

In *The Syndicate*[2] I described what the Syndicate's New World Order would be like: "It would be a socialist state in which there would be a redistribution of wealth and a reduced standard of living for all Westerners.... There would be regimentation and restriction on movement, with no freedom of worship, no freedom to buy or own private property, no free speech, and no freedom to publish." We have been approaching such conditions during the pandemic of 2020–2021. And in Appendix 4 at the end of *The Syndicate*, 'The Syndicate's New World Order as a global phase in the evolution of the North-American civilisation',[3] I wrote of the world appearing unipolar (the US) and becoming multipolar with Russia, China, India and Europe all powers,[4] and since then it has become more bipolar, with America (only just) and China a tier above the rest.

The Syndicate's New World Order has been outlined in a letter (which David Lorimer sent me) allegedly by the Head of the Rothschild family, Jacob, Lord Rothschild (born 1936), son of Victor, Lord Rothschild who ran British Prime Minister Heath's think-tank, to a blogger concerned at the coming New World Order's authoritarian nature, within a religious context (Christians and Jews). I have doubts about the authenticity of this letter as it is extremely unlikely that the Head of the Rothschild family, long known for its silence on controversial matters, would write at length to a blogger. I am evidential and require evidence of the letter's genuineness, and until then I must make it clear that I regard the letter (https://prepareforchange.net/2021/12/19/the-alleged-jacob-rothschild-letter-and-a-third-option) as a very intelligent spoof written by a blogger pretending to be Lord Rothschild to parody the Syndicate's narrative and make key points with chilling effect. But it sums up the Syndicate's New World Order in a number of telling sentences, and I quote these for the succinctness of their ideas and the light they throw on the Syndicate's coming New World Order, and not as ideas expressed by the Head of the Rothschild family:

> None of the people heading up institutions directly or indirectly under the control of my family, including the British Crown, the Vatican, the Masons, and the major oligarchs and corporations of the world care what you think or say.
>
> We control the major finances of the world but also your governments, the major media networks, most jobs on the planet, and even the money in your bank accounts. These are the facts which you cannot change....
>
> *World management requires a material leveling and depopulation*
>
> In maintaining your control there is a tremendous burden of responsibility placed upon you where you have to make decisions to resolve a never ending array of very difficult problems, such as mentioned above – pollution, competition, exploitation, overpopulation, etc. Jacques Attali is a faithful disciple of our New World Order projects which come down to a global control over many things, with a world government, the means of which unfortunately require those very things your sentiments abhor which is a material levelling (*sic*) for equality and a radical reduction of the population of the world....
>
> *The burdens of total power*
>
> We have worked exceedingly hard with all heads of state, including the British Crown and the Vatican, as well as the leading families of the world, in carrying out the plans for a new order of world governance to replace borders and national restrictions...
>
> We see a future world without enough to go around, and therefore we must learn first to control it and then to share what is there as we deem most advantageous to those whom we choose. That is what power is for.
>
> What you are concerned about are the methods we are using to solve these problems, which you say are "totalitarian", and "communist". To us those are only abstract words like the words 'truth', 'freedom', and 'justice'....
>
> *Naivety*
>
> The vaccines you mention, you cannot even determine why are they are being forced on the public. Why you wonder, if they are so clearly unnecessary and useless in relation to the virus, which in any case was never a grave threat, or even very much anything more than an overture or an exercise to our culling potentials, would they do this?...
>
> Everyone must do the same. In all communist nations we have fostered, it is customary that for "equality" for the desired and planned

"leveling" in this new order, in order for people to have the same in their needs and wants, everyone has to be psychologically trained to obey the same commands.

In our prodigy nation of modern China, the people had to be cleansed of many of their differences and even such a small thing as everyone having to wear the same uniforms was crucial to instill cultural and material equality, or "sameness".

Of course the masks are totally useless for the virus unless you have a flu or cold and you sneezed or coughed without a handkerchief. However, it is the obedience and conformity to our top-down commands which is crucial, that "everyone" wear one subject to government mandate or command. It is like a uniform to make everyone "uniform". It is about instilling a sense of unity, conformity, obedience, and most of all "equality"....

Regardless of whether or not the vaccines are unnecessary and useless regarding the virus, or even harmful for many, they are the most uniform and concerted psychological weapon ever devised to control human behavior....

For the New World Order we needed a much deeper and lasting compliance....

In your efforts to protect your old and failing civilization we are dismantling, we find these means necessary. If people will allow such vaccines to invade their own bodies and their children's in order to comply and to be the same or "equal" to "everyone" else they most certainly will not object to or oppose their wealth, use of resources and life styles being equalized as well.

The Syndicate's unification of West and East to prevent war
I have said (on pp.148–149) that if the Syndicate is to achieve unification under a world government, then either the East and China, which is looked up to by 6.9 billion, will have to become less authoritarian or the West, which has just 1 billion of the world's population, will have to become more authoritarian. And if that happened, that would be the fall of the West as we know it, together with its freedom of speech, human rights and democratic values.

We have three possible scenarios:

1. America, being the youngest living civilisation by far, will organise a World State or New World Order, a global conglomerate, and rule it with Syndicate support so it is sufficiently authoritarian to make a home for China and its trade partners, and this conglomerate over a period of time may become more democratic as citizens living under

an authoritarian government want their voices to be heard rather than ignored.

2. China, which will have the most powerful economy in the world through BRI in 2025, will organise a World State or New World Order, perhaps also with Syndicate ('Rothschilds" and 'Rockefellers") support and will use biological war through a new virus to end the West's financial system and therefore end Western supremacy, and will include the post-collapse Western states in this global conglomerate.

3. Before this there can be a war between the West and China with bio-weapons.

There are two unknown factors to consider:

1. Has America the military strength, after losing in Vietnam and Afghanistan, to compel authoritarian China to follow the rules of living within a World State?

2. Has China the strength to continue its authoritarian rule without encountering an uprising from its own people demanding more freedom and free use of the internet? Soviet Communism lasted 74 years in power (from 1917 to 1991), and Chinese Communism has so far lasted 72 years in power (from 1949 to date, 2021). Could President Xi find that the 1.4 billion in China demand free elections, an Opposition and freedom of speech?

How can the West stand firm against the 140 countries whose infrastructure is being improved by the Belt-and-Road Initiative? Put bluntly, its democracies are completely outnumbered, and more and more are becoming flawed democracies (like the United States) rather than full democracies. Ideological compromises are already being made; authoritarian Big-State approaches are creeping into democracies. Despite America's arsenal of nuclear weapons, which are in practice unusable, China's authoritarian approach to its economy and to world supremacy is more successful than America's democratic and more chaotic approach at present.

However, despite the collapse of Afghanistan, America has troops in 140 countries, 800 military bases in 70 countries and no military presence in only 62 countries,[5] and the Syndicate has a total of 457 oil and natural-gas pipelines in every continent of the world;[6] and the US still has more of a global network of troops and pipelines than any other country, and given sound leadership could still safeguard the West. And crucially, the Syndicate controls the central banks of both the West (the US Federal Reserve Bank) and the East (the People's Bank of China). Both West and East listen to 'Rothschilds' and 'Rockefellers' as they are dependent on them for their governments' spending.

"Politics is the art of the possible, the attainable – the art of the next best," Otto von Bismarck famously said. This especially applies to international politics, and the Syndicate is bringing together the West's democratic 1 billion and the East's authoritarian 6.9 billion. An immediate unification of West and East is only possible by following the authoritarian approach of the 6.9 billion (a huge majority of the world's population).

Initially the West has no choice but to go along with the Syndicate's Great Reset, and go for a New World Order which has authoritarian elements. Chinese Communism has copied in many Western trading features. The democratic US can then try to democratise a rebranded New World Order with China in it, as people in China demand their liberty in future years and the Chinese monolith collapses into a federation, as did the USSR.

Therefore the democratic West has to follow the Syndicate into the Great Reset and New World Order, Bismarck's "next best", until a new bout of freedom from authoritarianism can loosen it into a democratic World State. The democratic principles of a partly-federal presidential World State are embodied in groups such as the Indian-based World Intellectual Forum (WIF, of which I am a founding member), which has formed the Global Network for Peace and Disarmament (GNET-PEDAD), and such groups may be able to help with the loosening. The WIF has also set up the International Commission of Inquiry into the Aetiology of Covid-19 (ICIAOC) to conduct a rigorous investigation into the origin of SARS-CoV-2.

It must also be remembered that the Syndicate ('Rothschilds' and 'Rockefellers') has funded both West and East throughout the 20th century, and that the Syndicate is able to influence and persuade both sides to adopt a central course: a centralised authoritarian world government that is less free than the present West.

What the funders and financiers of the Syndicate, the central bankers who have lent trillions to the 193 UN-recognised nation-states to survive Covid, say and do is a factor in the above scenario of a unified West-East world government.

We are in new territory. For 5,000 years recorded history has obeyed laws that have seen civilisations rise and fall according to their metaphysical belief at their outset, and the degree of their secularisation (lack of belief) and its consequences during their decline.

But the new Biological Age may sweep these rules aside. An older civilisation like China that is funded by the central bankers that funded the Soviet Union and the United States may be able to lead an attack that can sack a civilisation. The barbarian Goths and Visigoths were not even a civilisation, yet they were able to sack Rome in 410AD and 455AD before the West Roman civilisation finally fell in 476AD. The Yellow Peril of Genghis Khan and the Mongol invasions of Europe from 1236 to 1291 were an older Central-Asian civilisation pillaging a younger European civilisation. They did not overthrow the European civilisation, but like the Goths and Visigoths they were able to sack it.

Perhaps China could move in and sack the West through bio-warfare (and perhaps hypersonic missiles) and bring about its fall into a Chinese-run New World Order or World State, before facing uprisings throughout China and the splitting of China into federal regions?

It does not seem that President Biden is strong enough to arrest the Chinese advances through infrastructure projects. And it may be that the law of history broke down with the release of SARS-CoV-2, and it is now quite possible that China can destroy – with help from the Syndicate – key aspects of the Western financial system without affecting the Eastern banks.

The West's 9/11 was a Syndicate-assisted invasion of America's air space and public buildings.[7] And now a seemingly-Syndicate-assisted SARS-CoV-2 has invaded America's air and killed at the time of writing 728,000 Americans, more than the number of Americans killed in the Second World War (407,316).

Terrorists might try to create a new pandemic by developing a bio-weapon and releasing a deadly pathogen to destabilise the West in an act of bioterror, as Tony Blair has warned. As I write, authorities in India are racing to contain an outbreak since February 2021 of the Nipah virus after it killed a boy of 12 with a brain-swelling condition that has no cure, and has a mortality rate of 40 to 70 per cent, far higher than the 1 per-cent rate for coronavirus; and fear that it may become the next, more deadly pandemic.

An open and rational thinker would have to agree that it is quite possible for the fall of the West to take place through a further viral contagion, a biological attack, or a biological or nuclear war, and for the United States to become more like Communist China than democratic America.

However, as the Syndicate is involved with both sides, a centralised, authoritarian world government that can include China is a strong possibility. The leadership would be on a collective, rotational, representative basis rather than involve the democratic election of a

President, as befits an authoritarian and centralised world government following the Chinese core leadership model. (On a personal note, I know this is what the Chinese are seeking as a Chinese lawyer attempted to hijack my work *World Constitution*, alter my text to replace a democratically-elected President with a Chinese-style collective, rotational leadership without my knowledge, and publish it from Chinese funds.)

I must emphasise, my law of civilisations is clear: the younger civilisation always prevails over the older. The US, founded at Jamestown in 1607 and in stage 15, is much younger than the Chinese civilisation which goes back four millennia. But throughout recorded history there were no nuclear or biological weapons. Do these make a difference to my law? Can the Western civilisation abruptly fall in 2025, or to a second virus by 2030? I repeat, we are in new territory where the old laws of history may break down and collapse along with the old order.

The Syndicate's unification of West and East is better than the collapse of the West's financial system and the fall of the West
Again I must emphasise, the great hope under the circumstances is that both West and East will fall into a democratic World State – a democratic, presidential, part-federal world government that can replace the UN – before a nuclear or biological disaster happens.

I have already set out the details of what this World State will look like in *World State*: a UF (United Federation of the World), its seven federal goals, its structure and the benefits it would bring, detailing the constituencies for a World Parliamentary Assembly and a World Senate. I have supplied the data behind my calculations in full appendices. I have also written a world constitution in *World Constitution*: 145 Articles that detail the UF's structure and institutions at inter-national and supranational levels, and the rights and freedoms world citizens would be guaranteed. In these two books I have set out clearly how the whole world can be governed, with all countries initially continuing internally as they are, like American states, but linked democratically within a supranational federal system.

This may happen one day, but what about the next few years? Persevering with the present world structure in the new Biological Age is precarious. Some sort of international accord that will preserve world peace would be better.

The Syndicate has been levelling down in the West and levelling up in the East for its New World Order, for more than a hundred years. The Syndicate's New World Order, the Great Reset, will be more authoritarian, more like Communist China than what we know in the West, and pipelines and infrastructure projects will continue across the globe under their plan. They have 'Rothschilds' and 'Rockefellers' behind them, who were behind Communism from 1917 and who control China's central bank (pp.45–49) and funding. Can the Syndicate create an authoritarian World State – an authoritarian centralised world government – which is not as good as a democratic one but better than a nuclear or biological attack that will bring devastation and desolation and mass migration to a new environment?

Under the circumstances, as we look at BRI and China's authoritarian hold over 140 countries on the one hand and the 23 full democracies led by a flawed democracy, the US, on the other hand, the hope of any rational person must be that the Syndicate can create the world government for which it has striven for more than a hundred years, from the time when the British Empire was at its height, and preserve peace so that what looks like an inevitable Cold War with China can, like the Cold War with Russia, end without a nuclear or biological catastrophe.

The hope is still that one day such an authoritarian world government can pass into the democratic World State into which both West and East, levelled-down and levelled-up respectively, can pass peacefully, bringing prosperity to all humankind as I set out in three works: *The World Government, World State* and *World Constitution*. Securing peace amid threats of war is the best outcome, and the fall of the West into first an authoritarian world government that can include China, and then turn into a democracy, a democratic World State, is the best outcome for the West. Such a World State will not last for ever but it will last for a while and bring prosperity to the world before history reverts to the law of the rise and fall of civilisations set out in *The Fire and the Stones* and *The Rise and Fall of Civilizations*.

If this cannot be achieved, then the Deagel nightmare may be ahead, in which the West, overborrowed, living off printed money, undergoes the collapse of its financial and banking system and, its countryside laid waste, has to undertake disorderly mass migrations to safer climes, with many millions of deaths.

The West looks like the Roman Empire in a historical atlas whose successive pages show it expanding and then contracting until it is like small puddles rather than a lake. I was in Libya when Gaddafi took Libya out of the West, and North Africa is not now in the West. As I write, Afghanistan is being removed from the West in what many have called a display of Western incompetence and lack of willpower, and Israel will now be the most eastern part of the West. Otherwise the West is confined to Northern America and Europe, with 'blobs' in former colonies such as Australia and New Zealand which perpetuate the Western way of life. Any contraction of the West and its ideals of constitutional government and collective defence is to be regretted.

Choice between two New World Orders
I wrote in *The Syndicate*[8] that there is a choice between two New World Orders and two Universalisms: one (the bad kind) in the Syndicate's revolutionary image of Lucifer, god of worldly wealth and power over flesh, that owes much to Freemasonry, is dominated by the occult and is comfortable with an authoritarian, tyrannical and totalitarian world government; and the other (the good kind) in the spiritual image of Christ which thinks globally about the whole of humankind and of the souls of human beings – each of whom has equally emerged from the One, the metaphysical Fire or Light – and works towards the ideal of a democratic World State and world government.

I asked which will triumph. The answer now is that the bad one, the Syndicate's world government, is winning in the short term and has a chance of coming into being during 'the Great Reset', whereas the good one is farther away and until the medium term is blocked by the conflict between West and East (both of whose funding is controlled by the Syndicate), which can destroy the West.

In the 1980s I led a group calling ourselves 'The Heroes of the West', whose actions defended the interests of the West by exposing threats to the West. Over the years I have taken action against: Mao Zedong (by exposing the Cultural Revolution); Scargill (by exposing Soviet undermining of the British economy during the miners' strike); Philby (by exposing his involvement in the deaths of Hungarians, exposing Soviet undermining of the West and arranging for a Czech scientist with nuclear knowledge to defect to the West); Gaddafi (by exposing his missiles aimed at the West from near Sebha in Libya in 1986 and securing their destruction by going to President Reagan); bin Laden (by examining the evidence of 9/11 and exposing his 69 attempts to obtain nuclear weapons, including nuclear suitcase bombs, details of which I sent to President Obama on 5 April 2011, after which Obama took the decision to kill bin Laden on 2 May 2011); the Syndicate (by exposing Cheney's role in 9/11 and its attempt to weaken the West for its own authoritarian New World Order); and the Brexiteers' splitting of the West (by exposing their illusions and untruths that weakened the West). All these actions are documented in my works: *My Double Life 1: This Dark Wood*, *My Double Life 2: A Rainbow over the Hills*, *The Syndicate*, *The Secret American Dream*, *Fools' Paradise* and *Fools' Gold*. In the course of doing all this I saw the West as embodying the right anti-authoritarian values.

Now what can the Heroes of the West do to prevent the eclipse of the West by China? I began this work, which is guided by evidence and based on truth rather than propaganda, hoping to expose China's attempt to weaken the West by releasing SARS-CoV-2, and although this is still a possibility, I believe this work contributes to exposing the US-Syndicate's weakening of the West by releasing SARS-CoV-2. I am not averse to the West's entering a world government now that communications technology (the internet, digital phones, smart TV, CCTV) has advanced to make this possible, but I want the democratic and human-rights values the West has stood for to be preserved.

I stand for a vaccine-protected democratic, presidential, part-federal world government that can replace the UN, which the post-Covid West is ready to create, a World State with sufficient authority to abolish war, enforce disarmament, combat famine, disease and poverty, and solve the world's financial, environmental and virological problems – the good New World Order, with a universalism that understands local religious, tribal, historical and national differences and why countries want to rule themselves, that can hold the Syndicate in check.

Support the Syndicate's New World Order to avoid biological war and the fall of the West, and bring in a democratic World State at a later date
It pains me to reach the conclusion that we are where we are and that the worst solution would be a Chinese biological attack (or hypersonic nuclear weapons) and the sudden fall of the West without any long-drawn-out Third World War; that we cannot turn the clock back to before the pandemic; and that the only way of preventing the abrupt and sudden fall of the West after a biological (or hypersonic) attack that destroys the West's financial system is to go along with the Syndicate's attempt at a world government and Great-Reset New World Order, bring in international legislation to ban negative, abusive brain control by 5G (see pp.104,126), work with what the Syndicate are doing and then modify their authoritarian world government into a fully democratic World State in the future, perhaps in a generation's time. A democratic World State without negative, abusive technocratic control of brains is the best solution; the Syndicate's New World Order without negative technocratic brain control is Bismarck's "next best" solution.

We are where we are, and the worst solution would be a Chinese biological (or hypersonic) attack and the fall of the West. To preserve the West we need the Syndicate to neutralise China, which seems to be preparing for war, and manoeuvre China into a world government with the West and East together and sharing power, and then, when the time is right and the Chinese people are agitating for freedom within China, turn the world government into a democratic World State.

In *China vs America: A Warning*, Oliver Letwin, the British ex-politician who used to work for Rothschilds and has remained close to 'Rothschildian' and Syndicate thinking, warns that if the power struggle between America and China continues it can only lead to something worse, and quite possibly a nuclear catastrophe; and rather than battle for a global hegemony it cannot win, the US should accept that peaceful rivalry ("peaceful competition through enterprise internationalism") is the only rational option. The title of Letwin's book may be a 'Rothschildian' urging of China to pursue peaceful rivalry with the US after being on the receiving end of a bio-weapon event that has left it seething and hostile, but peaceful rivalry is the first step towards the Syndicate's plan to unite West and East.

I need to make what I have just said very clear. Overtly – in the press and media – there appears to be no problem. But China appears to know there is a problem, hence President Xi's speech on 1 July 2021 saying that China will not be "bullied" by the US, and there is a dangerous situation which could lead to retaliation unless the rivalry between China and the US to be the world's number-one superpower is ended. There is now a new Cold War between the West and China, between the 1 billion in the West and 6.9 billion who look towards China. And so, as a Peace Laureate concerned to keep world peace, I say it is better to go along with the Syndicate's plan for West-East unity to defuse the dangerous situation.

In early September 2021 the Chinese foreign minister Wang Yi said the US had made a "major strategic misjudgement" in thinking climate co-operation could be separated from other issues, and that the US should stop seeing China as a threat and containing China around the world – and that all foreign ships should register their presence with China's maritime authorities when entering its (disputed) territorial waters in the South China Sea, a demand the US Pentagon dismissed. Add this demand to China's routinely sending warplanes to test Taiwanese defences and its military exercises simulating amphibious landings on Taiwan, and a British warship (the frigate HMS *Richmond*) equipped with torpedoes and anti-aircraft missiles navigating the Taiwan Strait, provoking China to accuse the UK of harbouring "evil intentions", and the Cold War is hotting up.

In early October 2021 China sent 56 warplanes into disputed Taiwan airspace, including 38 J-16 fighter jets, on one day, and warned that a Third World War could be triggered "at any time". The State-run newspaper *The Global Times* claimed the Chinese people were ready to back all-out war with the US over Taiwan, which China sees as a breakaway province.

The most urgent need in the present situation of a new Biological Age's having begun is to block future biological attacks and prevent the West from falling. The US is under weak leadership that is leaving Afghanistan to the Taliban and Iraq to Isil and perhaps Iran. How best can the fall of the West be avoided? How best can bio-attacks be avoided? By West and East coming together. And if they can only come together in an authoritarian World State like the regime of Communist China, should the West decline to join and be subjected to further bio-attacks and a massive population reduction? No. The West should join, and then alter what it has joined from within over a generation and get to a democratic, presidential, part-federal World State and world government when the expected uprising against authoritarianism and Communism takes place in China.

Some would say it is so important to avoid living under an authoritarian State that the West should fight, which means risking a nuclear and biological war. And if the West's population is reduced by 50 to 80 per cent as Deagel forecast,[9] that is collateral damage, like the 75 million killed in the Second World War while fighting to stay free from Fascism – 0.5 billion instead of 75 million. No, the price for humankind is too high. Humankind has a right to life, and this outcome of half a billion deaths must be avoided at all costs. Even if the population reduction of 50 to 80 per cent turns out to be for all the Western societies only[10] – the total population of the US, Canada, the UK and EU was around 879 million in 2019 – 50 to 80 per cent of 879 million would be around 439–703 million people, up to ten times the number killed in the Second World War, and the price is still too high.

You may say I am wrong – that, despite the Great Reset focusing on (and perhaps already having used) the biological, there is no bio-warfare threatening the West, only an unexplained natural virus; that there is no new Biological Age, just the existing Nuclear Age; that hypersonic missiles travelling at 3,850 mph can still be spotted in mid-air, giving time for a retaliatory nuclear strike to be triggered; and that the Syndicate should not be supported in the short term as nothing has changed since 2019. But I have intelligence skills and have assembled a jigsaw of evidence. I can look at the picture the evidence provides from an intelligence point of view and see what is probable and state my opinion even if I am the only person in the world to reach that conclusion.

I have a history of being proved right. I was the only non-Chinese who was right in March 1966 in saying that students were forcibly being sent out to work with peasants and that a purge of the bourgeois, later known as the Cultural Revolution, had begun in China, news of which did not break until August 1966. I have already told (on pp.xix–xx and xxiv–xxv) how Frank Tuohy, the novelist and short-story writer with whom I went to China, and I were invited to lunch at the British Legation to brief the British Chargé d'affaires Sir Donald Hopson and all the Legation staff, and Hopson said they had not heard there was a purge in progress, and that we had scooped the entire world. I encountered evasion and lying by Chinese at the University of Peking – I experienced extensive Chinese lying at first hand in 1966, and was on the look-out for it now.

And I was right regarding 9/11 in seeing Cheney standing down the air-defence system to give the planes a clear run at the Twin Towers[11] – regarding the roles of Dick Cheney and Saudi Arabia – and regarding bin Laden's 69 attempts to obtain nuclear weapons (see *The Syndicate, Armageddon* and *The Secret American Dream*).[12] I have told (on pp.21–22, 30 and 172) how I sent details to President Obama on 5 April 2011 and bin Laden was dead under a month later on 2 May 2011.

And I may now be right that we are in a new Biological Age and in a very dangerous situation. It would be easy to say 'There is no proof there was a bio-weapon attack in Wuhan by either side, and so we can live as we did until late 2019' – in the old world when biological warfare seemed inconceivable. It would be easy to say (ignoring the trillions in which they deal) 'The Syndicate have no power, only governments have power, the idea that governments are controlled by Syndicate bankers and commercial corporations is preposterous' and carry on as before.

But I am a realist, and as Otto von Bismarck said (see p.168), "Politics is the art of the possible, the attainable – the art of the next best." I can see how advanced the Syndicate has become in bringing in an authoritarian drawing-together of West and East which is now called the Great Reset. That is why I think that at present the West's best hope is that the Syndicate can involve China in the Great Reset and head off any US-China war and the use of biological weapons that can bring about the sudden fall of the West. From that half-way Bismarckian ("next best") position, at a later date there can be a move to democratise the drawing-together into the democratic World State the world needs. That is my position, and that is what I, the author of *The World Government, World State* and *World Constitution*, now recommend in this warning – in the sense of an alert – to the Western, and Eastern, world.

My poem, 'The Fall of the West' (see p.xx), saw the fall of the West as "a mental attitude". In other words, the fall of the West can be resisted by having a tough positive vision that can see off the threats to the West's traditional predominance. This may still be the case, only the main threat to the West is no longer international terrorism from Afghanistan and the Middle East, but China. And in the short term the Syndicate is an ally in working to neutralise this threat.

So, members of the jury, I say it again, the best way of coping with the new biological threat is to support the Syndicate in the short term to get to a democratic World State in the medium term without a war that reduces the West's population by 50 to 80 per cent as in Deagel's forecast.

Being a realist and a pragmatist, and having acquired the British Empire's realism and pragmatism and alertness to intelligence findings in seeking the best way to realise philosophical and political Universalism, I have concluded that this is the best way of leading the West through a precarious decade into safety by 2050, without seeing it destroyed – seeing the fall of the West as in my 1976 poem 'The Fall of the West', as "a mental attitude". Like Moses considering how to escape destruction at the hands of Ramesses II and reach the Promised Land (see my work *The Promised Land*), I have looked for the way that works best and is safest, and have found it in $+A + -A = 0$, the West + the East = an eventual democratic World State that bypasses a biological war and the otherwise real danger of the abrupt collapse of the West's financial system and the fall of the West – all of which the West can eventually, through a democratic World State, prevent.

*

The verdict
Members of the jury, in these pages we have studied all the bits of evidence linked to the outbreak of SARS-CoV-2, and we have connected them all together like pieces of an incomplete jigsaw, bits of which we are still receiving every day, to give an idea of what the finished picture will be. (It's as if someone said, 'Here are three-quarters of the pieces of a jigsaw, we'll send the rest a piece at a time every day, tell us what the picture is as soon as you can see it.' The bits of evidence are still coming in.)

We have considered whether the Syndicate, the West's "military-industrial complex", has devised a biological way (engineered Covid) of capping the world's population growth at 8 billion, when the world's population is now 7.91 billion. We have considered whether its levelling-down of the West is leading up to an integrated authoritarian

New World Order that includes West and East. We have considered the evidence for the origins of coronavirus and have focused on its engineering in a US lab, and whether there was a deliberate release both in Wuhan – to infect participants at the Military World Games, to disrupt Chinese expansion towards becoming the number-one superpower with a trading empire based on Belt-and-Road infrastructure projects – and in Tehran, to disrupt Iranian expansion in the Middle East; with the overall objective of stopping the world's population from rising above 8 billion in accordance with the aims of the Great Reset.

We have considered whether the West is now living under a new biological threat, and if retaliatory warfare has passed into a new Biological Age. And we have considered whether the best way to cope with the new threat is a democratic World State which includes the US and China, and whether in the short term the West should go along with the Syndicate's authoritarian unity of East and West to prevent the fall of the West. We have suggested that if this does not happen, the fall of the West could be imminent in this new Biological Age.

Analysis draws distinctions and reduces to parts, and smashes an urn into fragments. What Coleridge called "the esemplastic power of the imagination" reverses this process, reassembles the pieces and restores the urn to a whole. It sees unity, just as an archaeologist in a trench and later the curator of a museum sees a reunited urn above its scattered fragments. We have been considering the smashed bits of evidence and have painstakingly restored humanity's urn into a whole.

Members of the jury, who all have a heart, I am now about to rest my case on this very important matter of possible criminal activity: a possible deliberate American-Syndicate release of engineered SARS-CoV-2 in an attempt to prevent the world's population (7.91 billion in 2021) from rising above 8 billion in 2023 and to maintain it at 8 billion thereafter (while setting back China's rise to number-one superpowerdom). It is time for your verdict.[13] Is the picture on this finished 'evidence jigsaw' one that you can accept as the covered-up and hitherto fragmented truth? Has the prosecution established its case, or is there still reasonable doubt? If your verdict is "Not proved beyond all reasonable doubt", there is enough circumstantial evidence to present an extremely worrying picture indeed – the picture on the completed bits of jigsaw evidence, the painting on the restored urn.

The criminal and civil standards of proof differ. A criminal case requires the jury to be satisfied by the evidence beyond all reasonable doubt. A civil case requires that on the balance of probabilities a case has been made. I submit that at the very least on the balance of probabilities the case has been made. I finally rest my case. The verdict is yours.

Timeline

List of dates of key events relating to the origin of SARS-CoV-2 referred to in *The Fall of the West*

29–31 May 1954	First meeting of Bilderberg Group.
19 Mar 1966	Nicholas Hagger interrogates Vice-President of Peking University and is first to discover the Chinese Cultural Revolution.
7 Apr 1968	Club of Rome founded.
Jul 1968	Nelson Rockefeller mentions a "new world order".
1970	Zbigniew Brzezinski's *Between Two Ages: America's Role in the Technetronic Era*.
1972	Club of Rome's *The Limits of Growth*.
Feb 1972	President Nixon visits Beijing.
Aug 1973	David Rockefeller visits China.
10 Dec 1974	*The Kissinger Report, National Security Study Memorandum (NSSM 200)*.
Dec 1978	Deng Xiaoping's Open-Door Policy.
4 Sep 1980	*The Global 2000 Report*.
1981	*The Global 2000 Report to the President – Entering the Twenty-first Century*.
1982	'Rothschilds' take control of the People's Bank of China.
1984	Dr Fauci becomes Director of the National Institute of Allergy and Infectious Diseases (NIAID).
24 Mar 1986	Nicholas Hagger sends news of Gaddafi's missiles near Sebha pointed at London, Paris and Bonn to President Reagan.
14 Apr 1986	Gaddafi's missiles near Sebha eliminated by US air strike.
1992	UN's Agenda 21.
27 Oct 1993	Nicholas Hagger meets Alexander King, co-founder of the Club of Rome.
9 Dec 1998	Nicholas Hagger meets Martin Taylor, Secretary of the Bilderberg Group.
1999–2021	American gain-of-function research funded by NIAID, part of the NIH.
11 Sep 2001	9/11, attack on US Twin Towers and WTC7.
2002	Three engineered features of SARS-CoV-2 patented in the US (ACE-receptor, ACE2 binding domain, S1 spike protein furin cleavage).

Jan–Mar 2004	Nicholas Hagger assembles the *The Syndicate* (2004).
Jul–Nov 2004	Nicholas Hagger assembles *The Secret History of the West* (2005).
2004	Collaboration between Peter Daszak of EcoHealth Alliance and Shi Zhengli of the Wuhan Institute of Virology begins.
2008–2019	73 US patents issued for three main features of SARS-CoV-2 (ACE-receptor, ACE2 binding domain, S1 spike protein furin cleavage).
2009–2010	America's new policy of hostility towards China.
2010	Rockefeller Foundation and Global Business Network present a report, *Scenarios for the Future of Technology and International Development,* including the scenario of Lock Step.
5 Apr 2011	Nicholas Hagger sends *The Secret American Dream* to President Obama with bin Laden's 69 attempts to buy nuclear weapons flagged. Bin Laden dead on 4 May 2011.
2012–2013	China hostile towards the US and expansionist.
2013–2021	China's Belt-and-Road Initiative, infrastructure projects in now 140 countries.
2013	Ralph Baric of the University of North Carolina sends a humanised mouse to aid Shi Zhengli's research at the Wuhan Institute of Virology.
2013–2021	EcoHealth Alliance receives $103 million from US Pentagon and State Department.
2014	President Obama's moratorium on gain-of-function research. NIH funds the Wuhan Institute of Virology via EcoHealth Alliance.
2014–Apr 2021	Deagel.com's forecasts of a drop in world population of 0.5 billion in 2025, and the collapse of the West's financial system.
2015	UN's Agenda 2030 and 17 Sustainable Goals.
19 Dec 2017	President Obama's moratorium lifted.
19 Jun 2019	UN (Guterres) and World Economic Forum (Schwab) sign a deal to accelerate the 17 Sustainable Goals of the UN's Agenda 2030.
6–11 Oct 2019	"Hazardous event" reported in Wuhan, evidence dubious.
7–24 Oct 2019	No traffic and increased cellphone activity reported in Wuhan, evidence dubious.
14–19 Oct 2019	Roadblocks in Wuhan, hospital car parks reported full, evidence dubious.

18 Oct 2019	Event 201, funded by Bill and Melinda Gates Foundation, World Economic Forum and Johns Hopkins Center for Health Security, expects a coming viral infection to end in 2025 and a new virus to infect humankind from 2025 to 2028.
18–27 Oct 2019	CISM (*Conseil International du Sport Militaire*, International Military Sports Council) Military World Games held in Wuhan; some athletes have Covid-like symptoms.
Oct 2019	Birth of a new Biological Age.
12 Dec 2019	NIAID and Moderna present coronavirus vaccine candidates to University of North Carolina (Baric).
31 Dec 2019	China announces a new coronavirus, Covid-19, SARS-CoV-2.
12 Jan 2020	China publicly shares the genetic sequence of SARS-CoV-2.
22 Jan 2020	China announces human-to-human transmission of SARS-CoV-2.
Late Jan 2020	The People's Liberation Army's Major-General Chen Wei reported to have taken over lab at the Wuhan Institute of Virology.
Feb 2020	World Health Organization (WHO) says a lab leak of SARS-CoV-2 is unlikely.
2 Apr 2020	World Bank's Covid-19 Strategic Preparedness and Response Program expects Covid-19 to end in 2025.
24 Apr 2020	NIH withdraws grant from EcoHealth Alliance.
8 Jun 2020	NIH restores grant to EcoHealth Alliance.
Jun 2020	World Economic Forum (Klaus Schwab) introduces the Great Reset and Fourth Industrial Revolution at the 50th annual meeting of the World Economic Forum.
Jul 2020	WHO (Embarek) says a lab leak of SARS-CoV-2 is possible. The Wuhan Center for Disease Control lacked the expertise of the Wuhan Institute of Virology.
15 Aug 2021	Fall of Kabul in Afghanistan, Afghanistan taken over by the Taliban, end of *Pax Americana*.
End of Aug 2021	Report by intelligence community in the US to President Biden says the origin of coronavirus is inconclusive.
Early Sep 2021	Total worldwide cases of Covid 219 million, total worldwide deaths 4.55 million.

Notes, References and Sources

(See p.xx on access to the links to Mercola's interviews of experts – all these can now be accessed at Substack, paid membership $50 per year)

Preface

1. Nicholas Hagger, *The World Government*, p.110, p.278, note 37, http://bushstole04.com/monetarysystem/rothschild_bank.htm. Also see Donald V. Watkins, 'The Rothschilds: Controlling the World's Money Supply for More Than Two Centuries', 27 December 2019, https://www.donaldwatkins.com/post/the/Rothschilds/controlling/the/world-s-money-supply-for-more-than-two-centuries.

2. https://www.worldometers.info/world-population/?content_title=Why+You%27re+Losing+Proposals&content_format=ebook&offer_by_author=Jami+Oetting.

3. See https://www.nicholashagger.co.uk/78-79-80-81-82-83-84-encounter-december-1966-from-a-china-dia.

1. The Story of the Syndicate's New World Order So Far, and Population-Capping

1. Peter Heather, *The Fall of the Roman Empire*, p.227.

2. *The Rise and Decline of the Nation State*, ed. by Michael Mann, essays 2, 3 and 4.

3. Hagger, *The Syndicate*, p.23.

4. Hagger, *The Syndicate*, pp.23–25.

5. Hagger, *The Syndicate*, p.8: "[Nathan Rothschild speculated] on the outcome of the Battle of Waterloo. On June 20, 1815 his selling triggered a mass sale of stock and a price collapse, and his subsequent buying of the market and all government bonds left him owning the country's cash flow and the Bank of England." See George Armstrong, *The Rothschild Money Trust*, p.35 and John Reeves, *The Rothschilds: Financial Rulers of Nations* (1887), p.167, quoted in Armstrong, *op. cit.*, p.27.

6. Hagger, *The World Government*, p.110, p.278, note 37, http://bushstole04.com/monetarysystem/rothschild_bank.htm. Also see Donald V. Watkins, 'The Rothschilds: Controlling the World's Money Supply for More Than Two Centuries', 27 December 2019, https://www.donaldwatkins.com/post/the/Rothschilds/controlling/the/world-s-money-supply-for-more-than-two-centuries.

7. George Armstrong, *The Rothschild Money Trust*, pp.21–22.

8. Hagger, *The Syndicate*, p.9.

9. Emanuel M. Josephson, *Rockefeller "Internationalist"*, p.224. Also Myer Kutz, *Rockefeller Power*, p.87 note.

10. Hagger, *The Syndicate*, p.15.
11. Hagger, *My Double Life 1: This Dark Wood*, p.415.
12. Hagger, *The Syndicate*, p.22.
13. Hagger, *The Secret American Dream*, p.116.
14. John Coleman, *Conspirators' Hierarchy: The Story of the Committee of 300*.
15. Coleman, *op. cit.*, p.179.
16. Ralph Epperson, *The Unseen Hand: An Introduction to the Conspiratorial View of History*.
17. Coleman, *op. cit.*, p.172.
18. Eisenhower, farewell address on radio and TV, 17 January 1961, Public Papers of the Presidents of the United States at https://www. ourdocuments.gov/print_friendly.php?flash=false&page=&doc=90&titl e=President+Dwight+D.+Eisenhowers+Farewell+Address+%281961%29; Coleman, *op. cit.*, p.172.
19. Hagger, *The Syndicate*, pp.34–36.
20. John Daniel, *Scarlet and the Beast: A History of the War between English and French Freemasonry*, p.498.
21. Hagger, *The Syndicate*, p.15.
22. Harvey O'Connor, *The Empire of Oil*, p.38.
23. Hagger, *My Double Life 2: A Rainbow over the Hills*, p.594.
24. Hagger, *The Secret History of the West*, ch.5.
25. Hagger, *The Syndicate*, pp.120 and 41–42; and *The Secret Founding of America*, p.139.
26. Hagger, *The Syndicate*, p.120.
27. Stan Deyo, *The Cosmic Conspiracy*, p.200; Hagger, *The World Government*, p.262.
28. Deyo, *op. cit.*, p.200.
29. Hagger, *My Double Life 2: A Rainbow over the Hills*, pp.472–473.
30. Brian Clowes, 'Exposing the Global Population Control Agenda', https://www.hli.org/resources/exposing-the-global-population-control/?gclid=CjwKCAjwi9-HBhACEiwAPzUhHPmgUQybjq22YSWF7 HY3sAMCjzM2dQFRqIDDOAxBKA_jJfD-I-b3zRoC5a4QAvD_BwE.
31. USAID's website, https://pdf.usaid.gov/pdf_docs/PCAAB500.pdf.
32. 'About us, Rockefeller Brothers Fund', https://www.rbf.org/about/about-us.
33. *Global Future, Time to Act*, p.ii.
34. *Summary of The Global 2000 Report to the President of the US*, pp.1, 3.
35. *Summary of The Global 2000 Report to the President of the US*, p.12.
36. *Summary of The Global 2000 Report*, pp.41–42.
37. *Summary of The Global 2000 Report*, p.1.
38. *Global Future, Time to Act*, p.50; Hagger, *The Syndicate*, pp.271–272.
39. *Global Future, Time to Act*, pp.54–58.

40. *Summary of The Global 2000 Report*, p.7, paragraph 7; p.8, paragraph 4; p.9, paragraph 4.
41. *Global Future, Time to Act*, p.50; also Hagger, *The Syndicate*, pp.271–273.
42. See Hagger, *The Syndicate*, p.433, note 23: Term used by Coleman in *Conspirators' Hierarchy* (pp.4, 22, 26, 65, 164) in quotation marks, taken from the Global Reports. For the prominence of the phrase "useless eaters", see Paula Demers, 'Eliminate the useful eaters', http://www.whale.to/b/demers.html, a response to The Executive Intelligence Review's report *Global 2000, A Blueprint for Global Genocide*.
43. Coleman, *op. cit.*, p.164.
44. Hagger, *The Syndicate*, pp.274–277.

2. The Syndicate's Authoritarian Levelling of the West and the East through Pipelines and Integration

1. Hagger, *The Secret American Dream*, pp.132–136.
2. Hagger, *The Syndicate*, p.139.
3. Hagger, *Armageddon*, pp.582–595; *The Secret American Dream*, pp.242–250.
4. Hagger, *The Secret American Dream*, pp.138–141.
5. Hagger, *The Secret American Dream*, pp.141–144.
6. Hagger, *The Syndicate*, pp.76–77.
7. Josephson, *The "Federal" Reserve Conspiracy and Rockefeller*, p.292.
8. John Cotter, *A Study in Syncretism*, p.105.
9. *Spotlight*, 22 April 1996, pp.4–5.
10. Hagger, *The Secret American Dream*, pp.129–130.
11. Frederic Morton, *The Rothschilds: A Family Portrait*, pp.150–152.
12. Hagger, *The Secret American Dream*, pp.145–148.
13. Taken from *The Secret American Destiny*, pp.204–205; also see Hagger, *The Secret American Destiny*, p.285, http://www.businessinsider.com/the-15-oil-and-gas-pipelines-changing-the-worlds-strategic-map-2010-3?op=1&IR=T.
14. Video of Representative Paul Kanjorski, https://www.c-span.org/video/?281382-5/federal-intervention-financial-markets.
15. Hagger, *The Secret American Dream*, pp.151–152.
16. Hagger, *Peace for our Time*, pp.91–94.
17. Hagger, *The Syndicate*, p.37.
18. Hagger, *Peace for our Time*, p.93.
19. Hagger, *Peace for our Time*, pp.202–206.
20. Patrick Don http://www.whale.to/b/demers.htmlahue, 'Putin Promotes Trade Zone from "Lisbon to Vladivostok"', *Bloomberg*, 25 November 2010.
21. Louise Armitstead, 'Putin: Russia will join the euro one day', *The Daily Telegraph*, 28 April 2011.
22. Hagger, *The Secret American Dream*, p.143.

23. The Rockefeller Foundation, *Scenarios for the Future of Technology and International Development*, produced by the Rockefeller Foundation and Global Business Network, May 2010, https://www.nommeraadio.ee/meedia/pdf/RRS/Rockefeller%20Foundation.pdf.

24. Robert F. Kennedy, Jr, 'Press in His Pocket: Bill Gates Buys Media to Control the Messaging', article in *Columbia Journalism Review*, https://childrenshealthdefense.org/news/press-in-his-pocket-bill-gates-buys-media-to-control-the-messaging/. Also Tim Schwab, 'Journalism's Gates Keepers', https://www.cjr.org/criticism/gates-foundation-journalism-funding.php.

25. The World Bank, 'Covid-19 Strategic Preparedness and Response Program (SPRP)', https://projects.worldbank.org/en/projects-operations/project-detail/P173789.

26. Dr Joseph Mercola, 'NIAID, Moderna Had Covid Vaccine Candidate in December 2019', https://www.organicconsumers.org/news/niaid-moderna-had-covid-vaccine-candidate-december-2019.

3. The Syndicate, China, Wuhan Institute of Virology and Evidence for the Origins of Covid-19

1. See dug88, 'China, the Rothschilds and the Global Rise of Communism', https://www.abovetopsecret.com/forum/thread1282378/pg1.

2. https://quotepark.com/quotes/1869552-mikhail-bakunin-this-whole-jewish-world-comprising-a-single-explo/

3. 'Bill Gates and Population', https://populationmatters.org/search/node/bill%20gates.

4. *The Daily Mail*, 3 July 2021, p.48, https://www.mailplus.co.uk/edition/news/world/81809/china-builds-145-nuclear-missile-silos-in-desert.

5. https://www.scientificamerican.com/article/how-chinas-bat-woman-hunted-down-viruses-from-sars-to-the-new-coronavirus1/.

6. See https://www.frontiersin.org/articles/10.3389/fpubh.2020.581569/full; https://www.sciencemag.org/news/2014/03/new-killer-virus-china; https://www.ncbi.nlm.nih.gov/pmc/articles/PMC7606707/; and https://www.wionews.com/opinions-blogs/did-the-covid-19-virus-cause-the-chinese-miners-deaths-in-2012-322617; also Sarah Knapton, 'Did Covid come from Chinese miner in 2012?', *The Sunday Telegraph*, 10 October 2021, p.7, https://www.telegraph.co.uk/news/2021/10/09/new-theory-claims-covid-19-may-have-evolved-chinese-mineworker/.

7. Isabel Vincent, 'COVID-19 first appeared in a group of Chinese miners in 2012, scientists say', 15 August 2020, https://nypost.com/2020/08/15/covid-19-first-appeared-in-chinese-miners-in-2012-scientists/.

8. See MACE E-PAI, 'Covid-19 analysis', https://www.documentcloud.org/documents/6884792-MACE-E-PAI-COVID-19-ANALYSIS-Redacted.html;

and Keoni Everington, 'US investigating "hazardous event" in Wuhan lab in October', https://www.taiwannews.com.tw/en/news/3934444.

9. Sara Reardon, 'US government lifts ban on risky pathogen research', https://www.nature.com/articles/d41586-017-08837-7.

10. USA Today Fact Check, https://eu.usatoday.com/story/news/factcheck/2020/05/04/fact-check-obama-administration-did-not-send-3-7-m-wuhan-lab/3061490001/.

11. Reuters staff, 'Fact check: The COVID-19 pandemic was not orchestrated by pharmaceutical companies, investment groups and philanthropists', https://www.reuters.com/article/UK-factcheck-pharmaceuticals-philantrop-idUSKBN29Z0TM.

12. *British Medical Journal*, 12 August 2015.

13. Reardon, 'US government lifts ban on risky pathogen research', https://www.nature.com/articles/d41586-017-08837-7.

14. *The Times*, 4 September 2021, excerpt from Sharri Markson, *What Really Happened in Wuhan: The Cover-Ups, the Conspiracies and the Classified Research*.

15. Knapton, 'Wuhan's coronavirus plan to infect humans', *The Daily Telegraph*, 22 September 2021, p.15; also Knapton, 'Wuhan and US scientists planned to make "new" virus', *The Daily Telegraph*, 6 October 2021, pp.1, 2.

16. Letter from NIH's Michael S. Lauer to Drs Chmura and Daszak, 8 July 2020, http://downloads.vanityfair.com/lab-leak-theory/Daszak_7_8_20_Reactivation_and_Suspension.pdf.

17. Mercola, 'New cache of documents exposes lies to Congress'.

18. In Mercola, 'Will Fauci be held accountable for lying to Congress?', https://media.mercola.com/ImageServer/Public/2021/September/PDF/fauci-lied-to-congress-pdf.pdf.

19. Jo Nova, 'China lied about the bats in the lab, and WHO helped cover it up', https://joannenova.com.au/2021/06/china-lied-about-the-bats-in-the-lab-and-who-helped-cover-it-up/.

20. Ian Birrell, 'Leading US scientist: I was told about the Wuhan outbreak two weeks before Beijing warned the world', *The Mail on Sunday*, 5 September 2021, p.16, https://www.mailplus.co.uk/edition/news/coronavirus/102113/leading-us-scientist-i-was-told-about-the-wuhan-outbreak-two-weeks-before-beijing-warned-the-world.

21. Birrell, 'Leading US scientist: I was told about the Wuhan outbreak two weeks before Beijing warned the world', *The Mail on Sunday*, 5 September 2021, p.16, https://www.mailplus.co.uk/edition/news/coronavirus/102113/leading-us-scientist-i-was-told-about-the-wuhan-outbreak-two-weeks-before-beijing-warned-the-world.

22. https://www.livescience.com/coronavirus-origins-letter-science.html.

23. Rowan Jacobsen, 'Inside the risky bat-virus engineering that links

America to Wuhan', 29 June 2021, https://www.technologyreview. com/2021/06/29/1027290/gain-of-function-risky-bat-virus-engineering-links-america-to-wuhan/.

24. Hagger, *My Double Life 2: A Rainbow over the Hills*, pp.228–229.
25. Mercola, 'The bombshell outbreak in the Wuhan lab', https://media. mercola.com/ImageServer/Public/2021/September/PDF/covid-19-lab-leak-report-pdf.pdf.
26. Mercola, 'Expert scientists testify on virus origin', https://www. organicconsumers.org/news/expert-scientists-testify-virus-origin.
27. Ian Birrell, 'The Batwoman dossier', *The Mail on Sunday*, 15 August 2021, pp.46–47.
28. Mercola, 'Analysis proves SARS-CoV-2 lab origin', https://www. organicconsumers.org/news/analysis-proves-sars-cov-2-lab-origins.
29. Knapton, 'Scientists "covered up" links to Wuhan lab', *The Daily Telegraph*, 11 September 2021, p.10.

4. A Syndicate Bio-weapon: The Pentagon, Patents, The Rise of China and Wuhan's Military World Games

1. David Nikel, 'Controversial coronavirus lab origin claims dismissed by experts', https://www.forbes.com/sites/davidnikel/2020/06/07/controversial-coronavirus-lab-origin-claims-dismissed-by-experts/?sh=2182502468f6.
2. Milton Leitenberg, 'Did the SARS-CoV-2 virus arise from a bat coronavirus research program in a Chinese laboratory? Very possibly', 4 June 2020, https://thebulletin.org/2020/06/did-the-sars-cov-2-virus-arise-from-a-bat-coronavirus-research-program-in-a-chinese-laboratory-very-possibly/.
3. 'China Deliberately Spread the Coronavirus: What Are the Strategic Consequences?', *Strategika*, issue 69, https://www.hoover.org/research/china-deliberately-spread-coronavirus-what-are-strategic-consequences.
4. Minnie Chan and William Zheng, 'Meet the major general on China's coronavirus scientific front line', 3 March 2020, https://www.scmp. com/news/china/military/article/3064677/meet-major-general-chinas-coronavirus-scientific-front-line.
5. European Parliament, www.europarl.europa.eu/doceo/document/E-9-2020-005724_EN.html; www.europarl.europa.eu/doceo/document/E-9-2020-005963_EN.html;
6. European Parliament, www.europarl.europa.eu/doceo/document/E-9-2021-003287_EN.html.
7. William H. Schneider, 'The origin of the medical research grant in the United States: the Rockefeller Foundation and the NIH Extramural Funding Program', https://pubmed.ncbi.nlm.nih.gov/25862750/.
8. Sam Husseini, 'Peter Daszak's EcoHealth Alliance has hidden almost

$40 million in Pentagon funding and militarized pandemic science', 16 December 2020, https://www.independentsciencenews.org/news/peter-daszaks-ecohealth-alliance-has-hidden-almost-40-million-in-pentagon-funding/.

9. Mercola, 'The real reason we locked down the healthy', 19 June 2021, https://www.organicconsumers.org/news/real-reason-we-locked-down-healthy.

10. Mercola, 'Blistering backstory behind Covid-19', 28 June 2021.

11. Jonathan Calvert and George Arbuthnott, 'China's plot to take over the World Health Organization', *The Sunday Times*, 15 August 2021, pp.6–8.

12. Professor Amitai Etzioni, 'Who Authorized Preparations for War with China?', *Yale Journal of International Affairs*, vol. 8, issue 2, p.37.

13. See Mike Whitney and Ron Unz, 'The Covid BioWeapon: Made in the USA, Aimed at China', https://www.unz.com/mwhitney/the-covid-bioweapon-made-in-the-usa-aimed-at-china/.

14. Whitney and Unz, 'The Covid BioWeapon: Made in the USA, Aimed at China', https://www.unz.com/mwhitney/the-covid-bioweapon-made-in-the-usa-aimed-at-china/.

15. Gallagher told *Fox & Friends*, "284 Americans, athletes and staff that participated. There were a total of 9,000 athletes from 100 countries that came to Wuhan in October so this would have been two months before the Chinese government recognized that they had an outbreak", https://www.foxnews.com/media/wuhan-military-games-china-athletes-covid-sick-gallagher.

16. Roger Frutos, Laurent Gavotte and Christian A. Devaux, 'Understanding the origin of COVID-19 requires to change the paradigm on zoonotic emergence from the spillover to the circulation model', *Infection, Genetics and Evolution* (2021), https://doi.org/10.1016/j.meegid.2021.104812; https://www.sciencedirect.com/science/article/abs/pii/S156713482100109X?via%3Dihub.

17. The Saker, 'A Bristling Array of Implausibility: Reflections on the Unz Bio-Warfare Attack Hypothesis', https://thesaker.is/a-bristling-array-of-implausibility-reflections-on-the-unz-bio-warfare-attack-hypothesis/, for which the author reviewed over a hundred scientific papers of the 1,200 recent papers on SARS-CoV-2, including the paper by R. Frutos and others.

18. 'China's rulers see the coronavirus as a chance to tighten their grip', *The Economist*, 8 February 2020; and Steven Lee Myers, 'China spins tale that the US army started the coronavirus epidemic', *The New York Times*, 13 March 2020.

19. Huang *et al* 2020, 'Clinical features of patients infected with 2019 novel coronavirus in Wuhan, China', https://www.thelancet.com/journals/lancet/article/PIIS0140-6736(20)30183-5/fulltext.

20. Reported in The Saker, see note 17.
21. Mercola, 'Patents prove SARS-CoV-2 is a manufactured virus', https://www.organicconsumers.org/news/patents-prove-sars-cov-2-manufactured-virus.
22. Hong Zhou *et al*, 'A novel bat coronavirus reveals natural insertions at the S1/S2 cleavage site of the spike protein and a possible recombinant origin of HCoV-19', https://www.biorxiv.org/content/10.1101/2020.03.02.97413 9v2; and Kristian G. Andersen *et al*, 'The proximal origin of SARS-CoV-2', https://www.nature.com/articles/s41591-020-0820-9.
23. See https://patentimages.storage.googleapis.com/a8/c0/6a/0584dd67435ef 2/US7279327.pdf.
24. See the American Bar Association's website, https://www.americanbar. org/groups/intellectual_property_law/publications/landslide/2018-19/ march-april/english-origins-judicial-exceptions-35-usc-section-101/.
25. See https://english.pravda.ru/world/144467-covid_usa_patent; and http s://covid-unmasked.net/agenda-21-year-2021-depopulation-sustainable-development-humans-this-could-form-a-website-in-itself-ed/.
26. See https://www.reuters.com/article/uk-factcheck-patent-idUSKBN27C 34O.
27. See https://patentimages.storage.googleapis.com/61/a3/0d/3d91325d9093 86/US20200279585A1.pdf.
28. See https://www.pirbright.ac.uk/news/2020/01/pirbright%E2%80%99s-livestock-coronavirus-research-%20-%20-your-questions%20answered.
29. See https://www.reuters.com/article/uk-factcheck-pirbright-patent-cov-id-19-idUSKCN2521X4; and https://eu.usatoday.com/story/news/factch-eck/2020/03/27/covid-19-fact-check-bill-melinda-gates-foundation-did-not-patent-coronavirus/2919503001/.
30. See https://www.biorxiv.org/content/10.1101/2020.03.02.974139v2.
31. Merck, one of Big Pharma's biggest pharmaceutical companies and chains of research laboratories, reveals its Covid-19 vaccine and therapy plans, https://www.sciencemag.org/news/2020/05/merck-one-big-pharma-s-biggest-players-reveals-its-covid-19-vaccine-and-therapy-plans.
32. Ian Birrell, 'So what are they hiding?', *The Daily Mail*, 3 October 2021, pp.26–27, https://www.dailymail.co.uk/news/article-10052689Governme nt-condemned-refusing-release-details-key-email-conversations-Covid-origins.html.

5. China's Preparations for War, the Syndicate's Great Reset and the Collapse of the West's Financial System
1. Chris Jewers and William Cole, 'China threatens its enemies with "broken heads and bloodshed" in thinly veiled swipe at US as President Xi boasts of Communist Party bringing "order" to Hong Kong on party's

100th anniversary', *Mail Online* and *Wires*, https://www.dailymail.co.uk/news/article-9743653/Chinas-celebrates-centenary-Communist-Party-anniversary-British-handover-Hong-Kong.html.

2. Patrick Knox, 'War footing: WW3 fears as Chinese state media reveals "three-stage battle plan" to invade Taiwan as US stages war games in Pacific', *The Sun*, 2 July 2021, https://www.thesun.co.uk/news/15465131/ww3-fears-chinese-state-media-three-stage-battle-plan/.

3. Knox, *The Sun*, 2 July 2021, https://www.the-sun.com/news/3203525/ww3-fears-chinese-state-media-three-stage-battle-plan/.

4. Jewers for *Mail Online*, 'Satellite images show China is building more than 100 "nuclear missile silos" in the desert', https://www.dailymail.co.uk/news/article-9748801/Satellite-images-China-building-100-nuclear-missile-silos-desert.html.12FF.

5. Wendy Tang and Alistair Dawber, 'Virus did escape from lab in Wuhan, claim Republicans', *The Times*; and Nick Allen, 'Covid leaked from Wuhan lab, claim Republican', *The Daily Telegraph*, 3 August 2021.

6. Edward Curtin, 'Second Stage Terror Wars', https://off-guardian.org/2021/05/16/second-stage-terror-wars/.

7. Mercola and Cummins, *The Truth about Covid-19*, p.31; and Mercola, 'Meet the World Economic Forum', paper online, https://media.mercola.com/ImageServer/Public/2021/July/PDF/klaus-schwab-world-economic-forum-pdf.pdf.

8. Schwab and Malleret, *COVID-19: The Great Reset*, p.173.

9. Mercola, 'Meet the World Economic Forum', paper online, https://media.mercola.com/ImageServer/Public/2021/July/PDF/klaus-schwab-world-economic-forum-pdf.pdf.

10. Johnny Vedmore, 'Schwab Family Values', *Unlimited Hangout* report, https://unlimitedhangout.com/2021/02/investigative-reports/schwab-family-values/.

11. Sandi Adams, 'The Real Meaning and Origins of the Great Reset', 8 March 2021, https://sandiadams.net/the-real-meaning-and-origins-of-the-great-reset/.

12. Interview: Klaus Schwab of the World Economic Forum, *Newsweek*, 1 January 1998, https://www.pranaygupte.com/article.php?index=24.

13. Mercola, 'The Great Reset is accelerating into global tyranny'.

14. Danielle Sheridan, 'Johnson and Sunak in "lockstep" despite demotion joke', *The Daily Telegraph*, 9 August 2021.

6. **The Tottering West: The End of American Supremacy, Deagel's Forecasts, China's Belt-and-Road Initiative and a New Biological Threat**

1. Hagger, *World State*, pp.296–297, 302–310.

2. 'Deagel organization predicts massive global depopulation of 50 to 80% by 2025', https://www.astediscovery.com/COVID/DEPOPULATION.htm.
3. https://www.youtube.com/watch?v=jY4Wahyo5n0&t=2s.
4. https://greatgameindia.com/deagel-intelligence-depopulation-covid-19/.
5. https://covid-unmasked.net/agenda-21-year-2021-depopulation-sustainable-development-humans-this-could-form-a-website-in-itself-ed/.
6. https://covid-unmasked.net/agenda-21-year-2021-depopulation-sustainable-development-humans-this-could-form-a-website-in-itself-ed/.
7. www.yidaiylu.gov.cn.
8. https://green-bri.org/countries-of-the-belt-and-road-initiative-bri/.
9. https://green-bri.org/countries-of-the-belt-and-road-initiative-bri/.
10. Hagger, *The Syndicate*, pp.32–33.
11. Council on Foreign Relations, 'Countries in China's Belt and Road Initiative: Who's in and who's out', https://www.cfr.org/blog/countries-chinas-belt-and-road-initiative-whos-and-whos-out. (Sources: Green Belt and Road Initiative Center; Belt and Road Portal.)
12. https://www.green-bri.org/countries-of-the-belt-and-road-initiative-bri/ (Source: IIGF Green BRI Center, 2021); https://www.cfr.org/blog/countries-chinas-belt-and-road-initiative-whos-and-whos-out. (Sources: Green Belt and Road Initiative Center; Belt and Road Portal.)
13. Hagger, *The Syndicate*, p.33.
14. Nigel Perkins, Chair, European Rail Campaign (UK), 'Boris Johnson's "Hard Brexit" cut the UK off from Europe's green rail plans', https://www.theneweuropean.co.uk/this-green-governmentsrail-policy-is-a-train-wreck/.
15. Andra Maciuca, 'Ministers pass permanent emergency powers to handle Brexit lorry queues', https://www.thelondoneconomic.com/news/emergency-powers-lorry-brexit-285458/.
16. Victoria Allen, 'Danger of China's addiction to coal', *The Daily Mail*, 11 August 2021, p.19; *Mail Online*, https://www.dailymail.co.uk/news/article-9881957/Danger-Chinas-addiction-coal.html.

7. America's Withdrawal from Afghanistan, and the Syndicate's Planned Decline and Reset World Government

1. Quoted in Ronnie Cummins, 'Murder most foul: the perps [perpetrators] behind Covid-19', 29 April 2020, https://regenerationinternational.org/2020/04/30/murder-most-foul-the-perps-behind-covid-19/.
2. Claire Ellicott, 'Humanity's 5–1 down at half time and facing collapse like the Romans', *The Daily Mail*, 30 October 2021, p.9.
3. Hagger, *The Secret American Dream*, p.132.

4. F. William Engdahl, 'The Afghanistan debacle, Zalmay Khalilzad and The Great Reset', online magazine *New Eastern Outlook*, 19 August 2021, https://journal-neo.org/2021/08/19/the-afghanistan-debacle-zalmay-khalilzad-and-the-great-reset/.

5. Karen DeYoung, in 'Bin Laden Took Part in 1986 Arms Deal, Book Says', https://www.washingtonpost.com/wp-dyn/content/story/2008/03/31/ST2008033102952.html, states that Osama bin Laden flew to London in 1986 to help negotiate the purchase of Russian-made surface-to-air missiles to be used by Arab fighters battling the Soviet military in Afghanistan, according to Steve Coll's *The Bin Ladens: An Arabian Family in the American Century*, Penguin Press, 2008. The deal for Russian SA-7 missiles was arranged via contacts with the German arms manufacturer Heckler & Koch through an associate of Salem bin Laden. Osama bin Laden and his half-brother Salem bin Laden met the contacts several times at the Dorchester Hotel, London. According to 'Context of (Early-Mid 1986): Salem Bin Laden Asks Pentagon to Supply Missiles to Arab Afghans, Receives No Reply', sub-heading 'Mid-1986: Osama and Salem Bin Laden Purchase Anti-Aircraft Missiles in London', the bin Ladens were in London in mid-1986 buying anti-aircraft missiles, and in late 1986 Osama bin Laden was establishing the first training camp in Afghanistan for Arabs fighting in the Soviet-Afghan war. They apparently flew from London to America. They may have stopped in London in early November during their return to Afghanistan.

6. Paul Nuki and Sarah Newey, 'Why the Chinese believe Covid was leaked from an American lab', *The Daily Telegraph*, 26 August 2021, https://www.telegraph.co.uk/global-health/science-and-disease/china-wants-world-believe-covid-leaked-american-lab/.

7. James Crisp, 'Covid "more likely lab leak than weapon", US spies find', *The Sunday Telegraph*, 31 October 2021, p.9.

8. Mercola, 'Chinese defector reveals Covid origin'.

9. Mercola, 'New cache of documents exposes lies to Congress'.

8. The Fall of the West: The Syndicate's Totalitarian New World Order and a Future Democratic World State

1. Hagger, *The Syndicate*, p.323.

2. Hagger, *The Syndicate*, p.265.

3. Hagger, *The Syndicate*, p.316.

4. Hagger, *The Syndicate*, p.322.

5. US military deployments: https://www.politico.com/magazine/story/2015/06/us-military-bases-around-the-world-119321/ and https://www.trtworld.com/magazine/explained-the-us-military-s-global-footprint-45029.

6. See map in Hagger, *The Secret American Dream*, pp.254–255.
7. Hagger, *The Secret American Dream*, pp.132–135.
8. Hagger, *The Syndicate*, p.203.
9. 'Deagel organization predicts massive global depopulation of 50 to 80% by 2025', https://astediscovery.com/COVID/DEPOPULATION.htm.
10. https://greatgameindia.com/deagel-intelligence-depopulation-covid-19/.
11. Hagger, *The Secret American Dream*, pp.36–38, 132–138.
12. Hagger, *The Secret American Dream*, pp.242–250.
13. Compare Hagger, *The Syndicate*, pp.276–277.

Bibliography

Armstrong, George, *The Rothschild Money Trust*, Omni Publications, California, 1940.

Coleman, Dr John, *Conspirators' Hierarchy: The Story of the Committee of 300*, America West Publishers, 1992.

Cotter, John, *A Study in Syncretism*, Canadian Intelligence Publications, 1979.

Daniel, John, *Scarlet and the Beast: A History of the War between English and French Freemasonry*, Volume I, Jon Kregel, USA, 1995.

Deyo, Stan, *The Cosmic Conspiracy*, West Australian Texas Trading, 1982.

Epperson, A. Ralph, *The Unseen Hand: An Introduction to the Conspiratorial View of History*, Publius Press, 1985.

Fukuyama, Francis, *The End of History and the Last Man*, Penguin, 2006.

Global 2000 Report, The, Gerald O. Barney, Study Director, Pergamon Press, New York, 1980; Penguin, London, 1982.

Global 2000 Report to the President – Entering the Twenty-first Century, reprint from the University of Michigan Library, Penguin, 1981.

Global Future, Time to Act, reprint from the University of Michigan Library, 1981.

Hagger, Nicholas, *Armageddon*, O Books, 2010.

Hagger, Nicholas, *Collected Poems*, O Books, 2006.

Hagger, Nicholas, *My Double Life 1: This Dark Wood*, O Books, 2015.

Hagger, Nicholas, *My Double Life 2: A Rainbow over the Hills*, O Books, 2015.

Hagger, Nicholas, *Peace for our Time*, O Books, 2018.

Hagger, Nicholas, *The Fire and the Stones*, Element, 1991.

Hagger, Nicholas, *The Promised Land*, O Books, 2022.

Hagger, Nicholas, *The Rise and Fall of Civilizations*, O Books, 2008.

Hagger, Nicholas, *The Secret American Dream*, Watkins Publishing, London, 2011.

Hagger, Nicholas, *The Secret Founding of America*, Watkins Publishing, London, 2007, 2016.

Hagger, Nicholas, *The Secret History of the West*, O Books, 2005.

Hagger, Nicholas, *The Syndicate*, O Books, 2004.

Hagger, Nicholas, *The World Government*, O Books, 2010.

Hagger, Nicholas, *World Constitution*, O Books, 2018.

Hagger, Nicholas, *World State*, O Books, 2018.

Heather, Peter, *The Fall of the Roman Empire*, Macmillan, 2005.

Josephson, Emanuel M., *Rockefeller "Internationalist": The Man Who Misrules the World*, Chedney Press, New York, 1952.

Josephson, Emanuel M., *The "Federal" Reserve Conspiracy and Rockefeller*, Chedney Press, New York, 1968.

2

Kutz, Myer, *Rockefeller Power*, Pinnacle Books, New York, 1974.

Letwin, Oliver, *China vs America: A Warning*, Biteback, 2021.

Markson, Sharri, *What Really Happened in Wuhan: The Cover-Ups, the Conspiracies and the Classified Research*, HarperCollins, 2021.

Mercola, Joseph and Ronnie Cummins, *The Truth about Covid-19: Exposing the Great Reset, Lockdowns, Vaccine Passports and the New Normal*, Chelsea Green Publishing, Vermont, 2021.

Morton, Frederic, *The Rothschilds: A Family Portrait*, Atheneum, New York, 1962.

O'Connor, Harvey, *The Empire of Oil*, Monthly Review Press, New York, 1955.

PNAC, *Rebuilding America's Defenses: Strategies, Forces and Resources for a New Century*, 2000.

Rachman, Gideon, *Easternisation: War and Peace in the Asian Century*, Bodley Head, 2016.

Scenarios for the Future of Technology and International Development, The Rockefeller Foundation and Global Business Network, https://www.academia.edu/44400416/Scenarios_for_the_Future_of_Technology_and_International_Development, May 2021.

Schultz, Kenneth, *The Decline and Imminent Fall of the West: How the West Can Be Saved*, 2017.

Schwab, Klaus and Thierry Malleret, *COVID-19: The Great Reset*, World Economic Forum, Geneva, 2020.

Smith, Craig and Tom Miers, *Democracy and the Fall of the West*, Societas, 2011.

The Rise and Decline of the Nation State, ed. by Michael Mann, Basil Blackwell, 1990.

The Rockefeller Foundation, Annual Report 2010, https://www.rockefellerfoundation.org/wp-content/uploads/Annual-Report-2010-1.pdf.

Index

BOOKS

O-BOOKS

O is a symbol of the world, of oneness and unity; this eye represents knowledge and insight.